THE EMPEROR
OF
PEACE RIVER

Eugenie Louise Myles

Western Producer Prairie Books
Saskatoon, Saskatchewan

Western Producer Prairie Books wishes to acknowledge the contribution of William Clarence Richards, who as president of the Institute of Applied Art Ltd. (Edmonton) made the creation of this book possible through his personal desire to have the history of Western Canada recorded while the people who made that history were still alive.

First published in hardcover and softcover by the Institute of Applied Art, Ltd., in 1965
This SPECTRA Series edition by Western Producer Prairie Books in 1978

Text illustrations by Michael J. Lee

Printed and bound in Canada
by
Modern Press

Saskatoon, Saskatchewan

Western Producer Prairie Books publications are produced and manufactured in the middle of Western Canada by a unique publishing venture owned by a group of prairie farmers who are members of Saskatchewan Wheat Pool. Our first book in 1954 was a reprint of a serial originally carried in *The Western Producer*, a weekly newspaper providing news and information to western farm families since 1923. We continue the tradition of providing enjoyable and informative reading for all Canadians.

CANADIAN SHARED CATALOGUING IN PUBLICATION DATA

Myles, Eugenie Louise.
The emperor of Peace River

First published in 1965 by the Institute
of Applied Art, Edmonton.
ISBN 0-919306-52-7 pa.

1. Frontier and pioneer life — Alberta — Peace River District.
2. Lawrence, Sheridan, 1870-1952.   3. Lawrence, Julia Scott, 1879-1974.
I. Title.
FC3693.3.L38M9   971.23'1'02
F1079.P3M9

To the pioneers, the missionaries,
and the priests, who laid the beginnings
in the land of the mighty Peace.

ACKNOWLEDGMENTS

For assistance in assembling the material for this book I wish to thank the following:

The members of the Lawrence family and especially Mrs. Sheridan Lawrence, Mrs. Velma McLeod, Mr. Malcolm Lawrence, Mrs. J. H. Mjolsness; also Mrs. Doris Leedham Hobbs; Miss Lillian Gibbons; Miss Verena Garrioch; Bishop B, J. Pierce; Rev. T. S. B. Boon; Dr. Morden Long; Dr. Lewis B. Thomas; Mrs. Ward Rivard; Mrs. Robert Holmes; Mrs. Robert Little; Mr. Frank Jackson; Rev. Richard Cawley; Miss Shirley Hogue; Mr. Eckart Ehlers; Mr. J. L. Grasswick.

I wish to acknowledge also the helpfulness of *The Beaver, The History of Manitoba* by W. L. Morton, and *The Land of Twelve-Foot Davis* by J. G. MacGregor.

For permission to quote from their pages I thank *The Winnipeg Tribune; The Edmonton Journal; The Family Herald* and Mrs. J. S. Cram; *The Country Guide; The Peace River Record; The Atlantic Monthly;* and publications of the Ryerson Press, *A Hatchet Mark in Duplicate* by Rev. A. C. Garrioch, and *The Anglican Church from the Bay to the Rockies* by Rev. T. C. B. Boon.

PART I

*"The whole earth is the Lord's,
and where, as in His sight, you
lead good and useful lives, there
is your home."*
      The Swiss Family Robinson.

The small girl followed her red-bearded father out of the telegraph shed and into a radiant world. The pelting rain shower had ended and now the sun burst from under the sombre masses of cloud. It lighted like green diamonds the wet leaves that were newly-unfolding on the aspens and the balm of Gilead growing thick on either side of the trail. Across the eastern sky arched a gigantic rainbow.

At once the wide blue eyes of the girl, Juey Scott, were attracted to the goings-on where the trail led to a river-bank and a broad-bottomed ferry. Several men were attempting to direct the wheels of a bulky steam engine with big upright boiler down the muddy slope and onto the heavy planks of the ferry. The huge metal beast nudged against it, disdainfully shoved it out of the way, and then plunged itself into the river water.

There followed a conference among the men. Obviously the engine was too cumbersome and heavy to load onto the ferry.

"Sheridan!" called a tall man who seemed to be supervising the operation. "Bring the oxen!"

Obediently a lanky lad came forward driving a yoked team of red and white oxen. As Juey watched, the youth whipped the animals down the greasy bank and into the flowing water. Following close behind, he waded into the stream. For some minutes, working under water, he bent to the task of hitching the yoked pair to the low axle between the front wheels of the engine.

"Quite a chore, getting that monster across," murmured Juey's father, the Rev. Malcolm Scott, in a tone of sympathy. "That water must be ice-cold."

With the oxen at last hitched to the axle, the youth turned the team down stream. Dragging the engine through the shallow water edging the bank, they reached a spot pointed out by the ferry operator. Here was evidently a fording place that was relatively free of big rock boulders. The boy guided the beasts in their struggle across the river, and the metal monster bumped and splashed behind them. Finally he succeeded in coaxing them to haul it out of the water again and part of the way up the slippery opposite bank.

Suddenly Juey heard a great thud and saw a spray of roiled water splash high. The chain had given way and the reluctant engine dropped back down into the river. Helping hands hustled to get another chain and a second yoke of oxen. Eventually, hitched from the top of the bank by chains and ropes to the team below, the second team with its added pull brought success. The balky brute was dragged out of the water and raised right to the top of the opposite bank.

Presently all of the rest of the outfit to whom the engine belonged and which seemed to include a large family as well as a great assortment of freight and animals, was transported over the river via the ferry. Now it was the turn of the wagon train in which Juey's family travelled to be shifted across. Anna, the girl's brown-eyed mother, took her by one hand and her young brother, Osborne, by the other, and together they walked down the bank and onto the ferry. Behind them followed her father, the Rev. Malcolm, who was joined by his assistant, Burton. The two men were keeping an eye to the wagon loaded high with the family's possessions as it took its place in the string of horse-drawn vehicles.

Once safely across, the driver pulled this wagon over to a tiny clearing in the bush, for it was time to make evening camp. While Anna started preparations for supper, her husband and Burton got a bright fire blazing that radiated a cozy friendliness that seemed to shelter them a little from the unknown that surrounded them. Back of the small clearing sprawled, fold on fold, a blanketing wilderness of berry bush and trembling aspen; a few feet in front of

4

it the river they had just crossed thrust itself singingly forward over a mosaic of silt and stones; above them, lighting dark bands of cloud hanging in the north-east, a trace of the rainbow still glowed.

For a few minutes, Juey helped her mother fetch and carry as a big girl almost seven was expected to do. Then she turned to the sport that felt so good after long hours of sitting in the bumping wagon. Round and round the fire she chased her five-year-old brother Osborne.

"Hello!" a voice called. Flaxen-haired Juey looked shyly up, to see the lad who had struggled with the oxen in the river now stepping toward their fire. Shivering, he held his hands above the vermilion flames. Juey was cosily clad in a full-skirted frock of navy blue serge and sturdy high-button shoes. The tall visitor may have been covered well enough for comfort in the cool of a northern spring evening, but he had just finished helping with an onerous task that meant wading deep in the cold water to coax the oxen and the big engine across the river.

"Come away, Sheridan!" called a gruff voice from the large party that had crossed ahead of Juey and her family and that was now making camp a short distance away. "If you want to dry yourself, build your own fire."

"You're welcome to our fire," quickly smiled Anna in her soft English voice.

"No, thank you." Reluctantly the lad called Sheridan began to move away. "My uncle's called me. I must go."

Juey's eyes followed his retreating figure and she thought, "I'm glad I don't have a cranky old uncle like that."

She looked down the length of log where her father sat a little apart. His long red beard was motionless now and his blue eyes were intent, for already he was absorbed in a book — Juey's most vivid recollection of her missionary father was always this, of his constant engrossment in studies, in his Bible and his books. He, too, was strict, but when he wasn't reading he was full of teasing fun. A missionary, he repeated often to his family, should be happy because he is so rich, because he knows and enjoys the love of God.

"Vermilion is red, scarlet is red," Juey began to chant

5

to Osborne. This was the lesson her father had taught her so that she would remember their destination at the end of this long, long journey. There were many other things for a girl to learn and to remember. It was now the month of May of the year 1886 and a fortnight earlier they had left their home near Winnipeg in the middle of this country which some people called Canada, but which her father always insisted was British North America. Already, over a brand-new railway line, they had travelled eight hundred miles or more west across the wide prairie until they had reached a tiny village called Calgary. There they had gazed at the shining Rocky Mountains until their eyes seemed to smart and then they had climbed onto a heaped-up wagon pulled by a two-horse team and began to drive north over more prairie. So far, they had jogged a hundred miles behind the team of bays and now they had experienced their first ride on a ferry.

"This is the Waskesoo or Red Deer river," explained her father as he pored over a map to point out their present bearings to his family. "Like the Bow river which we crossed at Calgary, its water is cold because it rises in the Rocky Mountains."

"Do we have to go much farther?" asked impatient Juey. "When do we get to Fort Vermilion?" It seemed as if they had been travelling for ever and for ever.

"Fort Vermilion. Mm. Well, we'll have to travel, I calculate, at least another eight hundred miles. By trail and by boat. It would certainly be much shorter if you could fly on the wings of that crow."

Juey flung out her arms and pretended to fly. "Vermilion red, Red Deer, Red river," she shouted as she circled round and round the camp-fire. They were going to Fort Vermilion, which meant red. This was the Red Deer river; her home on the outskirts of Winnipeg had been perched above the Red river. Red, red, red, that was the color everywhere she went.

Presently the Rev. Malcolm stepped through the shrubbery that was a wild tangle of dwarf saskatoon and hazel nut and dogwood, to pay a neighborly call on the large group camped near by and to whose party the lad Sheridan belonged. Judging by the smoke, they now had a warm enough

6

fire to dry him out thoroughly; judging by the shouts of merriment, they were enjoying to the full the evening's relaxation.

"What a happy coincidence," exclaimed Juey's father when he returned. "That is the Lawrence family. And they also are on their way to our mission at Fort Vermilion."

"Hooray," smiled Juey. "I'll have some one to play with." Among the swarm of children at the other camp-fire, she had spied two girls.

"Sheridan's father, Henry Lawrence, is already working as farm instructor at the mission. He went in last year. The family waited behind because of the Rebellion."

With deep feeling in his voice, the Rev. Malcolm went on to talk about how Henry Lawrence's brother, Erastus, had begun to set up the mission school seven years before and about the things they hoped to accomplish in their work among the Indians. The big engine that this Lawrence family was taking in and that was giving them so much trouble was, he said, intended to make the mission school and farm really up to date, for the new equipment also included a stone mill and a small saw mill for which the engine would provide power.

More and more shouting and laughter echoed from the camp-fire of their neighbors. Enviously Juey listened and looked. How wonderful to have so many to play with! From time to time she caught glimpses of the big boy called Sheridan. But at this point she was more interested in his young brothers and sisters. Bounding to her feet, she began to chase Osborne in and out among the bushes.

Next morning she glanced longingly across to where all the young Lawrences were busy with chores similar to those going on about their own camp, the business of packing up after breakfast and reloading things in the wagon. The shouts and the laughter still echoed across the lonely bush.

"You'll see all those Lawrences at Fort Vermilion, never fear," commented her father after he had conducted morning prayers for his own small group. "Remember, though, they're travelling behind oxen. They'll be a long time on the trail."

Soon the driver brought the team of bay horses and proceeded to hitch them to the loaded wagon. The Rev. Malcolm checked to make sure that all the Scott possessions were once more stowed aboard. Anna, too, looked anxiously about, for each small possession became the more precious the farther they journeyed from their former home. In making ready for the new life in the northern Anglican mission, preparations had posed a serious dilemma for her. Because they would be living nearly a thousand miles from a railroad, they had to bring every thing with them that they might need. Yet because of the high cost of freighting and of the limited space that would be available to them on river boats and wagon trains and cart portages, Anna had to leave behind all the comfortable furnishings of her home. Only two luxuries were permitted to her, the organ and the green carpet that had been shipped to her as a wedding present from England; these, with two new Carron stoves that her husband Malcolm had procured, were to form the nucleus of the equipment in the new manse.

Into the wagon containing as well as the trunks and boxes crammed with clothing and bedding and books, Burton shoved two crates, one containing a dozen Rhode Island Red hens and a rooster, and the other a pair of young pigs. Juey handed up a small basket containing two tiny kittens, and the family clambered aboard. Once more the driver took his place in the chain of freighting vehicles that headed northward along the winding trail.

Perched high on the load on either side of their small mother, Juey and Osborne found this rattling behind horses in a wagon even more tedious than banging along in the great train that had brought them to Caglary. The smiling May sun burned their fair skins and the dust from the dry stretches of trail choked their parched throats. With a deafening clatter and with a jolting that rattled their teeth, the wagon shuddered its way up onto hard ridges and down into deep ruts and mushy mud-holes.

At last came a heavenly respite. "Whoa!" shouted the driver to his team. Ahead extended a steep bank, down which the trail led to a creek to be forded. With their parents and Burton, the handyman, the bored young passengers dismounted. The men hurried to lend the driver a hand with the chains involved in the tedious business of wheel-blocking, a process of wrapping chains about the spokes and rims of the wheels and securing them in such a way that the wheels would be "braked," that is, they would slide and not revolve down the bank.

With lady-like dignity Anna lifted her skirts a little and proceeded to descend the hill on foot while the children scampered ahead. At first, on the trip north from Calgary, Juey had been petrified with fear at the sight of a steep hill. Only a couple of months before, she and her mother and Osborne had been involved in a near-accident on the bank of the Red river near her home. A stable boy had been driving them out from Winnipeg to the old family house at St. Andrew's on the outskirts and he had permitted the cutter to edge too closely to the ice-shod bank. All at once it had careened down the slope, pitching the occupants out onto the river ice. Osborne was tossed close to an open water hole. With a lightning gesture his mother Anna had thrown the robe out and around him, rescuing him from possible death by drowning.

Now, after the tedium of the wagon, the delightful chance to skid on foot down a steep trail made Juey forget her fear. Presently, at the creek's edge, she was permitted to remove her shoes and stockings. While her father carried Osborne, she clung to the safety of his hand and waded through the ice-cold and refreshing water. In a few minutes the children were shouting and panting their way up the opposite bank, and having as much fun as those Lawrence children at that camp back by the Red Deer river.

For Sheridan, eldest of the family trudging afoot on their way northward, the journey was not enjoyable at all. In fact, during the long days since they had left Calgary, he had come to have a secret reason for being most unhappy about it.

Chapter 2

SHERIDAN

If only, Sheridan sighed to himself as he wheedled the shuffling oxen onward, if only he were back again on the little clearing in the Ontario sugar bush. There he had known exactly what was expected of him and exactly what to do about it.

His mother Maggie was kindness itself; perhaps she sensed his predicament. Back east she had looked to him and Jim, who was after all more than a year and a half younger than he, to manage things for her and to carry on the work of the homestead. This had been the way of things for a long time; in fact he could hardly remember when she hadn't turned to him. Each winter during the long months when his father Henry had been absent in the logging camps, and during the past year when he had been gone to Fort Vermilion in the distant north-west, it had become his responsibility to help her in every possible way.

When she had at last received a letter from his father directing the family to join him in this year of 1886, he felt sure that he and Jim could somehow have contrived to see to everything. With his mother Maggie in charge, they could have managed the transfer of their freight and their six brothers and sisters even though it meant travelling by train and ox team and boat and raft some three thousand miles from their homestead grant in the maple woods.

His father had decreed otherwise. He had written to his brother Isaac Lawrence, Sheridan's uncle, who lived near the old Lawrenceville home in the Eastern Townships of Quebec, and he had invited him to take charge. Of course there was now all this extra cargo that had been bought in

Winnipeg for the mission school and farm, dry goods and animals and machinery, grist mill and saw mill and the great engine for which a Mrs. Wright away in England had donated the purchase money; all these things his Uncle Isaac was supposed to look after.

Already, at Calgary, Sheridan sensed that his uncle did not understand that a youth of sixteen who towered to a height of six feet two, and who was accustomed to almost sole responsibility, expected to be treated more as man than boy. He did not know that his mother Maggie had already foreseen the conflict that was going to arise and that this was partly responsible for her objections to his uncle's arrangements for them all.

"It's three hundred miles from Calgary to Athabasca Landing," Isaac told his mother. "You and the smaller children should take the stage as far as Edmonton." There was now a regular horse-drawn stagecoach service between the tiny settlement on the Bow and Fort Edmonton, two hundred miles to the north.

Isaac explained that he and Mr. W. J. Melrose, who had also been hired by the Church of England Missionary society for work in the far north, would see to the outfit. They would need Sheridan and Jim to spell them off in the driving of the three ox-teams and the herding of the other animals along the way.

With spirit Maggie demurred. For one thing, she reminded Isaac, riding by stage would mean a twenty-five dollar fare for her plus extra charges for several of the children. "If I take the stage, that will mean a long wait, too, at an Edmonton stopping house." This, with her large brood, would incur much more expense as well as the tedium of waiting for the slow-footed oxen.

But the trail between Calgary and Edmonton, argued Isaac, could be crowded with unknown problems and dangers. Everywhere lurked Indians whose friendliness toward the white man had been called into question only the previous year.

Maggie did not need to be reminded of this. It was the shocking news of the Saskatchewan rebellion that had interfered so cruelly with their plans the previous year. She and her husband Henry had accepted with alacrity the offer

11

of a position at Fort Vermilion. Clearing the great trees from their grant near Plevna in Ontario was a slow, painful process and the only cash they could count on came from his earnings in the logging camps and the annual sale of the three hundred pounds of maple sugar that represented their only saleable crop. By comparison, a salary of three hundred dollars per year managing a farm and teaching agricultural methods to the Indians suggested a gold mine. They had begun to sell off their possessions and to make ready to travel all together as a family when word of rebellion in the North West Territories brought dilemma. What were they to do? The offer had reached them by way of Henry's school-teacher brother Erastus and the glowing picture which he had painted of the possibilities of the land of the Peace suggested that he had found the paradise which once had been denied to man. The Indians among whom he lived and worked, he assured them, were a friendly people who looked to the white man for help. But if those along the way were intent on driving out the white invaders or even on killing them off, should they, Henry and Maggie, dare to journey into the north-west with their children?

Finally, Henry had gone on alone. Months later, Maggie received a single letter from him. Now that the Rebellion was a thing of the past, she was to bring the family and join him. With the help of Sheridan and Jim she undertook the move, travelling by wagon to the nearest rail line, thence to Kingston and on to Montreal and from that city by rail and boat to Winnipeg. From Winnipeg, she knew, Erastus and his wife Lydia and their three young children had, seven years before, been obliged to continue their journey by Red river cart to Prince Albert, thence by boat and portage over lake and stream to the Clearwater and Athabasca rivers until eventually they had reached Fort Chipewyan, from which post they had shipped up the the Peace to Fort Vermilion. Now that a transcontinental rail line was almost complete, Maggie and her family faced a less devious route. Service to the end of steel at Calgary was still sketchy; after a week's wait at Winnipeg, they were able to entrain for the foothills settlement.

Here Maggie stood firm. Having contrived with the assistance of her big boys to get this far, she opposed the plans of her double brother-in-law Isaac, who was not only her husband's brother but the husband of her sister Lennie. Something told her that she must stay with her sons, that a clash of wills was sure to rise. She thought of another point to help convince Isaac that they must all keep together.

"I'll be on hand to do the cooking for you men," she pointed out to him.

Isaac yielded, perhaps, Maggie wrote in her diary, because he knew that she, like his own wife Lennie, had a reputation as a good cook.

For the time being there was peace, and the high spirits that prevailed seemed to match the dazzling sunshine and the expansive stretches of wide-open prairie. Compared with the heavily-wooded eastern region that the children had always known, the uncluttered expanses of empty space stretching northward from Calgary were unbelievable.

Just outside the Calgary settlement, Sheridan had his first taste of the kind of conflict that was to become almost lifetime fare. The spring flood from melting mountain snows had washed downstream the bridge on the Bow river. The Lawrence party hitched their three teams of oxen to it and assisted in dragging it back against the current to its place in conjunction with the Edmonton trail.

In the friendly sunshine, gleefully his young brothers and sisters accepted the delay. While their mother Maggie hustled to wash clothing and to spread it to dry on the dwarf willow bushes, they fanned out over the sage-spiced prairie trying to catch the tawny gophers that frisked everywhere about them. Everything was so different in this western land; instead of leaping from tree to tree to escape danger, these lively squirrels flicked their tails at you as they disappeared down deep holes burrowed in the earth.

At the family's first overnight stop, Sheridan understood a little better why his father had decreed that they postpone their journey until this year. Beside them was bivouacked a company of soldiers that was still being retained in the west to keep an eye to the restless Métis and the often-hungry Indians. The sight seemed to justify his Uncle Isaac's uneasiness. He understood that in the far north where his Uncle Erastus and Aunt Lydia and his own father were living, the Indians there too often faced starvation. It was precisely

13

to help cope with this problem that his father had been hired by the Church Missionary society; by teaching the natives to grow crops, periods of famine when game was scarce might be curtailed.

Next morning the fine weather still prevailed. With all their worries forgotten, in high spirits the family resumed the twisting northward trail. While Sheridan and Jim urged onward the lethargic animals, their mother, their sisters Grace, thirteen, and Minnie, eleven, and their four younger brothers, Harry, Arthur, Isaac and Jack, aged respectively nine, seven, six and four, covered much of the distance on foot.

"This was the greatest lark of our lives," so Maggie afterward described the snail's-pace journey from Calgary to Fort Edmonton. "Fifteen miles a day was our average speed. The youngsters and I usually kept ahead of the wagons."

When the small boys found their legs failing them, they clambered up to a snug resting-place amidst the freight. Maggie remembered how "each day was filled with new adventures and new discoveries for the children. It was always a tired but happy family that slept at night under the clear prairie sky."

In Calgary they had been able to buy some bread but no potatoes at all. Rapidly the ravenous group exhausted this supply and Mr. Melrose demonstrated his skill in turning out a big batch of bannocks. Then Maggie contrived a bread-baking routine similar to that followed by Juey Scott's mother Anna. From their sugar-bush homestead back at Plevna, Maggie had brought twenty maple-sap buckets. Each morning in one of these she set a big batch of dough, bundling it into the wagon for the daily travelling. At night she shaped it into loaves, baking it Dutch-oven fashion in smouldering coals of western poplar.

By the time they reached the Waskesoo or Red Deer river, where under the great arch of a rainbow the Scott family overtook them, clouds and rain had somewhat dimmed the delights of the trail. Now for Sheridan, not even the magic of the rainbow nor the friendly smiles at the Scott campfire could dispel the antagonism he felt toward this stranger uncle whose manner toward him was becoming so dictatorial. Like his mother and his brothers and sisters, he too wanted to see the wondrous northland of which his father and his uncle Erastus had written with such enthusiasm. But there were moments when he felt that he must turn and run, back to the woods at home in the east where he could find work and be at peace again.

From this Red Deer river crossing, so Mr. Melrose said, it was still another hundred miles to Fort Edmonton and a further hundred miles of trail through the bush to Athabasca Landing. Here, as his father had directed, they would have to hire a passage on the river boats. Since they did not travel at all on Sundays and not too far on rainy days, and since the fording of creeks and rivers and the navigating of steep hills with the big "boiler" and all their equipment, including a saw-mill and farm machinery as well as the livestock, was a slow and tedious business, this meant that he might be in for several months of being ordered about by Uncle Isaac.

Alone, Sheridan wrestled with his problem. There was his mother who needed him. There was little Jack, not much more than a baby, who looked to him as to a father because their father was absent so much. When the child had been born, their mother had been all alone and he, Sheridan, had made his way through the woods in a winter snowstorm to get help for her.

For the sake of his mother and the family, he must try to stay with them and stick it out. That missionary with the long red beard, the Rev. Malcolm Scott, and his family were the lucky ones. They were travelling behind a freighter's horses instead of oxen. They would probably be crossing the next big river, the North Saskatchewan, within four or five days.

CHAPTER 3

JUEY AGAIN

Juey held her breath in fear. Suddenly the trail ahead, framed on either side with dense woods of spruce and aspen, shot down a steep declivity.

"Whoa!" shouted the driver and the wagon creaked to a stop. With thankful heart Juey allowed herself, along with her mother and Osborne, to be helped onto the hard earth.

"We've reached the south bank of the North Saskatchewan river," her father, the Rev. Malcolm, announced formally because it was an important milestone along the way. He beckoned northward over the forest. "Edmonton lies just beyond on the north bank."

Squealing with delight, the children raced down the sharp slope leading to the river's brink and their mother followed at a more sedate pace. The men proceeded to the blocking and braking of the wheels, soothing the nervous horses as they worked. Next they concentrated on the dangerous business of guiding the string of top-heavy wagons down the treacherous bank.

At last that wagon which was loaded with the Scott possessions, with trunks and cases and boxes and sewing machine and organ and green carpet, with a crate of Rhode Island Reds and the pair of pigs, reached the safety of the south flat by the river's edge. Across the muddy water of the swirling Saskatchewan rested the ferry, tied up at the north bank. In vain the men shouted and whistled. No ferryman could they rouse.

"I'll go get it," offered Burton, Malcolm's helpful assistant.

He slipped into the dogwood brush, undressed, tied his clothes on his head, and plunged into the ugly water up-stream from the waiting wagons. As Juey watched him strike out for the opposite shore, she dipped her fingers into the water. It was icy to the touch.

"It's so cold," she puzzled.

This river is like the Red Deer and the Bow, her father explained to her; it rises near the feet of the snow-capped Rocky Mountains. "So do the Athabasca and the Peace, which we are presently going to travel on," he added. "All are swift and swollen now with the spring run-off of melting snows in the western foothills."

Finally Burton mastered the sucking currents and scrambled ashore. In a twinkling he had pulled on his clothes, released the ferry and begun to bring it across the water for the use of the waiting travellers.

"When are we getting to Edmonton?" persisted impatient Juey after the long boring business of crawling to the top of the north bank.

"This is Edmonton," smiled her mother.

The child frowned with disappointment as she looked about. She had envisioned a city like the Winnipeg she had left behind. "It's nothing but a mud-hole."

Aware that the most difficult part of the journey still lay ahead, Malcolm hastened to secure accommodation with a wagon train freighting over the one-hundred-mile trail that led north to the Athabasca river. Their way now led them out of the pleasant parkland that was streaked with brush and prairie and dotted with small sloughs, and into what seemed to Anna to be an everlasting ocean of forest. As a result of the building of the Canadian Pacific railway to Calgary, this Athabasca trail had been hewed through the bush in 1883, only three years before, by the medium of the Hudson's Bay company. It was so incredibly rough, Anna found, that while the wheels on one side of the wagon tilted crazily above rotted stumps, those on the other side slushed deep in ruts formed by stagnant muskeg water. Even more terrifying than the sucking muskeg were the boulder-bedded creeks and the rivers to be forded and the steeper and steeper

17

hills to be ascended and descended. Sometimes a wagon had to be partially unloaded; sometimes extra teams had to be hitched on to help horses struggling up to their bellies in what seemed to be bottomless bog.

Juey soon wearied of this slow progress through bush and muskeg, and she turned to her favorite sport of teasing younger Osborne. During one quarrel with his irritating big sister, the lad gave her an extra-hard shove. Down she shot from the wagon right in front of a wheel. Like a lightning bolt, Malcolm hurled himself down after her, in time to pull her to safety.

Swarms of mosquitoes and flies, much blacker and more vicious than anything they had ever known, added to their troubles. But even the hordes of insects could not take away from the delight of the evening camp, with the welcome smoke driving away some of the pests and the sweet fragrance of their mother's bread a-baking in the glowing coals and the exquisite liberty to explore the resin-scented woods.

In the late-evening sunlight, small Osborne wandered downstream along a creek by which they camped. He ran back, shouting for his father, and his brown eyes were bursting with excitement. His small boy's mind was staggered by a strange find.

"I don't know, Father, if it's an elephant. Or maybe only a snail."

To satisfy his son and his own curiosity, Malcolm followed the lad down the creek. There, with its bleached rib-cage looking giant-like in its nakedness and its immobility, lay the whitening skeleton of a full-grown horse.

"Ah," murmured Malcolm. "It's a poor horse that has found this trail too difficult."

Such was, for Juey and Osborne, this third leg of the excursion into the never-never land beyond — a composite of boredom and excitement, of fear and mystery and magic.

To Juey at the end of this one-hundred-mile Athabasca trail came enchantment such as she had never before known. A great wood of balsam fir shaded the south bank of the river at Athabasca Landing. Here under these fragrant evergreens the family camped and here Malcolm and Anna were forced to resign themselves to a long wait.

Alas, the boats on which they were to hire passage for themselves and their possessions were only in the process of being built.

At this Athabasca Landing stood one building only, a powder house sheltering the precious gunpowder which the Hudson's Bay company distributed to its trading posts in the North West Territories. Near by camped the crew of "Bay" men busy building the boats known as "sturgeon heads," which were to take passengers and freight up the Athabasca. So, while Malcolm and Burton lent a hand where they could, thereby mastering new points of frontier lore, Anna enjoyed the utter peace of the surroundings and busied herself with household chores and with caring for the chickens and the pigs. For the children there was the ecstasy of play by the singing river and in the roomy arena under the magnificent balsams.

"It's my cathedral," pretended Juey, a little girl with a passionate love for the out-of-doors. None of Winnipeg's dwarfish trees could match this vast fragrant world of spire-topped firs.

"Mm. If only we had trees like this back at St. Andrew's," commented her father as he girdled one with his arms and discovered that its circumference measured more than five feet.

Juey looked up at the wide-spreading branches that were dark shining green above and silvery-white below. With her finger nail she scraped the thin blisters on the bark and watched the pungent oily resin, that gives this fir its name of balsam, ooze from underneath. She sniffed the delicious piney odor and she sucked the resin from her finger tip.

"I smell smoke," an Indian exclaimed one evening. The tall native had come to pay a visit to their camp-fire and he stood about drinking the tea which Anna hospitably offered him.

Juey pricked up her ears. "It's from this fire," some one scoffed, shrugging off the Indian's worried notion.

The native shook his head. "Not this fire," he insisted.

To allay any fears of a forest fire, a couple of men climbed a near-by steep height of land and there one of them scrambled up a tree. The pair returned on the run.

19

The Indian, they reported breathlessly, was quite right. Not far away, billows of smoke were swirling above the up-river woods and with the prevailing direction of the wind, the fire would be upon them within minutes.

Malcolm and Burton hustled to pull up the tent that was so cosily situated under the fragrant balsams. Already every one was moving on the double quick. The boat-builders shoved all their perishable freight, their supplies and their equipment down to the edge of the water. Then they rushed to the aid of the missionary's family.

Juey and Osborne lugged what they could, for now down the bank and right to the river's brink had to go tent and trunks, and boxes and crates, and hens and pigs and the pair of kittens. To keep showers of sparks from setting them afire, the men stretched all available tarpaulins over them and began dousing the tarpaulins with water.

With unbelievable rapidity, the fire was upon them.

"Into the water, children," commanded Anna.

As Juey splashed her bare toes in the cold water, she listened to the mighty roar of sheets of flame that swept crazily over the beautiful balsams. She wanted to shut her eyes and stop her ears, but something made her gaze in fascination and in horror at the blazing crashing boughs.

Waves of heat from the fiery furnace flushed the faces of the anxious adult watchers. They were imprisoned at the edge of an endless wilderness of forest, their only avenue of escape perhaps an Indian's canoe on the river. What should they do?

"God will take care of us." It was Malcolm's deep assured voice answering for all.

Even as Malcolm prayed, the flames, still leaping with mad speed from one tree-top to the next, began to race away. As quickly as it had hurled itself upon them, the fire pelted scornfully away again, leaving behind the choking smoke that was still afloat with flakes of grey ash, leaving behind the incredibly ugly skeletons of the flame-blasted trees.

Next morning the men hurried on with the construction of the sturgeon-heads, the boats which they so named because of the flattened shape of the bow. Building their bodies some forty feet long and eight wide, they fashioned them so as to contend with river waters of varying depths.

Eventually they completed this consignment of vessels and now, in the lavishly-leafed month of June, the Scott family began the next phase of their travel. For the first few hours aboard one of the boats, Juey and her brother found this new method of locomotion to be vastly exciting. A crew of dark-skinned Métis manned the snub-nosed sturgeon-head in which they snuggled beside Anna, and the men's method of compelling the long narrow craft up-stream alternated between poling and tracking.

This Athabasca river abounded in vagaries. Sometimes its main channel was narrow and deep; sometimes it wandered over a wide apron of boulders and then amused itself by dancing above sand and gravel bars in a thousand eddies and rapids; sometimes its waters skirted close against banks tangled deep with undergrowth; sometimes they edged long ribbons of rough gravel.

For fifty up-stream miles these vagaries meant for the children a kind of endless entertainment that was being performed for them by the sturdy crew, whose powers of endurance amazed Malcolm and Anna. Sometimes with long poles the men reached out into the turbulent water and with rythmic pushing propelled the long boat forward. Presently the family were to see a picturesque variation of this "poling" on loaded freight scows; these latter were provided with running boards sunk a foot down along the inside of the scow, and as the crew pushed with all their might to make the scow shoot forward, on quick moccasined feet they tripped backward on the running board with the pole. Then, swift as a bird, they regained their place at the prow to repeat the process.

Sometimes in their sturgeon-head the muscular Métis crew changed from poling to tracking. Four men hitched a heavy harness of duck over their shoulders or foreheads and "tracked" the craft against the swift current. Lightfootedly they skimmed over a path trampled in the brushy bank or over beds of gravel, or they waded through the slime of shallows or the mouths of creeks, all the while tugging the thick rope attached to the vessel and forcing it to breast the powerful current.

Occasionally a channel led into a shallow where neither poling nor tracking moved the heavy boat. Then, to the great delight of the watching children, the Métis, laughing and calling to each other like so many wild geese, leapt into the water and bent their agile backs under the sides of the craft. Walking edgewise as they lifted, bodily they transported the boat into deeper water.

After some fifty miles of working up-stream on the broad Athabasca, they entered the Lesser Slave river, which between steep, heavily-wooded banks carries the waters of Lesser Slave lake to the Athabasca. Here they encountered swift rapids, which meant for the children a delightful interval ashore while the men portaged the bulky freight.

Finally, upstream forty miles or more from the point where it empties into the Athabasca, the zigzagging Lesser Slave led them into its wide mother water, the lake bearing the same name. Here by turns the crew rowed and rested if a favorable wind billowed the sail which they erected, and here again was tedious boredom for young Juey and Osborne. For nearly ninety miles the brigade of sturgeon-heads pushed its way westward, crossing the huge lonely lake while the now-friendly-seeming yet endless forest sometimes retreated far from them with the retreating shoreline.

At the western extremity of this Lesser Slave lake, the men coaxed their craft into Buffalo bay. Here, on a site which Malcolm knew was to be designated for the new Anglican St. Peter's mission, the family thankfully set up camp ashore. Immediately ahead, he discovered, extended the toughest obstacle so far obstructing their further progress toward their own mission field. This was the ninety-mile portage northwestward through the woods to Peace River Crossing.

On this portage a rough trail had been hewed over what was said to have been an old Indian war-path. It was a trail so narrow and rugged that only the puny Red River carts, hired by the "Bay" to transport supplies and furs to and from the trading posts of the far north-west, could manoeuvre their way from Lesser Slave lake to the Peace river.

So far this present season of 1886 had been so very wet that the whole portage was one continuous bog.

"Freighter Anderson is your man," Malcolm was told. "If any one can make it through, he's the one who'll do it."

Freighter Anderson looked dubiously over all the Scott possessions, the boxes and the crates and the trunks, that were to be moved over the primitive trail through the sopping bush. Juey remembered that his conversation with her mother went something like this:

"I'm sorry, ma'am. We can't possibly take all this stuff."

"Oh, but I'll need it. I'll need it all." Already she had had to leave so much behind. And these precious possessions she had already seen buffeted about over rail and wagon and portage. She couldn't possibly abandon them in this tiny oasis between the great forest and the vast lake.

Anderson relented a little. "You can take one trunk, ma'am. This one, I think, we could somehow squeeze in."

When would the balance get through? He didn't know. Maybe later this summer. Maybe next. "Depends on the weather," he told her.

Faced with such a Hobson's choice, Anna scurried to rearrange her packing. Deep in this strange silent wilderness, some of the items she had brought seemed ridiculously out of place. Into the designated trunk she transferred winter clothing for the children, just in case. And bed linen and other articles of greatest necessity.

Now began a nightmarish journey in the caravan of Red River carts. At the head of his single-file brigade, Anderson placed the carts drawn by oxen, that would set the pace. Next came those pulled by horses, and lastly, bringing up the rear, followed a cart dragged by a big red ox. In this Anna and the children rode. Malcolm and Burton walked alongside, it being Burton's special duty to hang onto the rope round the great beast's head and to guide his footsteps over the most passable terrain.

Again the pattern of travel became one creaking wheel high on stump or log, the other deep in rut or bog. The encroaching forest reached out jagged branches to slap at the travellers; beneath them corduroy thrown down to make a bottom for carts ahead up-ended jagged pieces that threatened to tear the stomach from the ox and the floor from the cart. Sometimes the cart mired so deeply that all the muscular power of the husky ox could not pull it through.

To add to Anna's anxieties, both children contracted whooping cough. She had noticed a suspicious cough among the little ones at their first stopping-place not far from Edmonton. For a few days now, Osborne was a very sick boy. Caring for the pair in the persistent rain within the narrow confines of the bumping cart or during camp at night in the dripping woods provided a fresh test for Anna's durability. Repeatedly she was startled by her daughter's leaping from the cart to relieve her sick stomach.

"Mother wondered how it was that I didn't break a leg," the wiry youngster remembered of that experience.

One day Anna herself found what it was like to catapult unexpectedly to the ground. Leaving Burton in charge of the ox and cart, Malcolm had walked on to speak to a man near the head of the caravan.

Presently the Englishman became absorbed in his hobby of birch-bark writing. "He was always stopping to cut strips from the birch trees. He'd write notes on these, recording bits of diary which he was going to send back to England."

Finding himself free to please himself, the big ox dragging the cart suddenly became obsessed with loneliness. He wanted not to tail any longer behind a string of horses but to join his own kind at the head of the brigade. He shook his massive shoulders and in a minute Juey and Osborne and their mother were having a terrifying ride.

Staging a small stampede of his very own, with tail in the air and big feet crashing through the underbrush the ox began to run. Over logs, over stumps, against trees the cart crashed. Men shouted to each other to halt the beast. At last the cart tilted crazily, and down and out into the tangled bush tumbled the occupants. Finally a driver ahead was able to grab and hang onto the restraining halter rope. Then the woods rang with the tongue-lashing with which Anderson flailed the unfortunate Burton.

Fortunately, no one was more than shaken and bruised. From then on, Malcolm himself held tight to the guiding rope.

When Juey recovered from both the shaking-up and the whooping cough, with her normal high spirits and her avid interest in the out-of-doors, she joined with her mother in spying out the beautiful wild flowers that skirted the feet of aspen and birch, of balm of Gilead and spruce and occasional tamarack and pine. The procession forded the Hart river and finally burst upon a sight that took the breath away.

Primordial folds of land shaped into giant hills sloped down to an enormous river. Here and there these gigantic hills were ridged with woods or blotched with low brush; otherwise, in spite of their covering of dwarf vegetation, they appeared stark and naked. Mountain-sized they seemed; yet they swept backward and outward, as if they too were in awe of the dancing river that curved about their feet.

Spell-bound the little family gazed and Malcolm pointed out that here, within the immediate range of their vision, this wide river, the celebrated Peace, formed a composite of three streams. Right at hand the small friendly Hart flowed into it and in the near distance spread the wide island-studded junction of the Peace and the Smoky.

Afoot the family plunged down the sheer hill-side that dropped eight hundred feet to flats beside the river. This reaching of the waters of the Peace was epochal; now they were at home yet not at home. Their mission was on its shore but it was still far-distant; to reach it they were dependent now upon their own resources and upon the pleasure and might of this river.

By a pleasant creek which a few rods away emptied into it, they chose a camp-site. Here they were going to have to spend some time while Malcolm and Burton constructed a raft sturdy enough to meet the challenge of three hundred twisting miles on the breast of the mighty current of the Peace.

For the children it might have been magic that had produced hills so enormous and a river so wide. Now magic produced another surprise. Up from a journey on the Peace came their old friend and neighbor and the new bishop of this diocese, the Right Rev. Richard Young. Joyfully they all welcomed him and they joined with him in awesome admiration of the majesty of the panorama that nature spread before them.

"Switzerland has nothing to surpass this," exclaimed the tall athletic bishop.

All at once Anna's pleasure in the scenery was spoiled by a heart-breaking discovery. Anderson's men were now delivering their possessions to them. These included a small supply of provisions, including five hundred pounds of flour, a little sugar, the black and white pigs, the crate of Rhode Island Reds, the kittens and one trunk.

"Malcolm," she said quietly, "they've brought the wrong trunk."

"Perhaps they'll get the stuff through in the autumn when the portage dries out," consoled her red-bearded husband.

Anna lost no time bewailing. After the fearful ordeal of the portage, this Peace Crossing was a heavenly if lonely spot. Only a solitary log building, a tiny trading post used seasonally by the "Bay" and now deserted and forlorn, suggested human habitation. Quickly Anna set to work to make her tent campsite as comfortable as possible. After the children had tended their kittens, she sent them scouring about for discarded cans in which to plant her bulbs and her cuttings. While the men fed the fire and the "livestock," she set about preparing supper.

"I never guessed how useful this would be," smiled the genial bishop as with his bishop's "apron" he lifted a burning-hot pot from the fire. Anna had noted with admiration his correct bishop's dress that was complete with apron and gaiters.

With twinkling eyes he added, "These gaiters, too, are so useful. They're a wonderful defence against mosquitoes."

Shortly, upon discovering the arrival of Anderson's caravan, Indians appeared with semi-starving dogs. Viciously these beasts tried to set upon Anna's imprisoned crate of chickens. Aware that her fowl might be preyed upon by hawks and coyotes, she had deliberately selected the Rhode Island Red breed. "Their color will help to protect them," she told Malcolm. She hadn't anticipated the threat of Indian dogs. In spite of every one's watchfulness and of much stick-brandishing, several heads poking through the slats were snapped off by the ravenous dogs and next day the family unwillingly dined upon chicken.

Juey and Osborne were enjoined to keep a sharp look-out upon the pigs, which Burton set free to feast upon the lush wild growth. During the evening the young black boar came grunting to the Rev. Malcolm. "Oingh! Oingh!" he repeated insistently. Then he turned back toward the creek. In a few minutes he was on hand again, still excited and still seeming to be asking for help.

"Why don't you follow him?" suggested Anna. "Perhaps there's something the matter."

Below the bushes edging the creek's bank, down on the gravel by the water squealed the little white sow.

Malcolm gathered her in his arms and hefted her up the small but steep bank. The care and coddling she had received thus far on the trip north had robbed her of initiative.

He grinned as he rejoined the family gathered around the fire. "She's just plain lazy. She could have walked down the creek a few yards and found a place herself where she could have climbed back up."

After that, the pair became known as Jack and Jill.

Presently it was Jack who was in disgrace. Juey caught him in the act of nipping off the precious flower bud from her mother's arum lily. This was especially precious to Anna because she had brought the bulb, tucked in the toe of a shoe, all the way from England. Apparently the bud was peppery hot and for a few minutes Jack danced about with his mouth open, emitting tiny squeals of distress.

"I know just how he feels," Juey commented gravely.

"What do you mean?" her mother asked.

"Once when I was little," her daughter confessed, "I picked that yellow thing out of your lily and chewed it up. Ooh! how it burned my tongue."

"Rest assured your sins will find you out," moralized her mother. "I often wondered what happened to my lily bud."

Early next morning the men paddled up-stream to build the raft and for nearly a week Anna was left alone in camp with the children, the remaining chickens, the kittens and the pigs. Now she rejoiced that she had, after all, permitted the youngsters to bring the frolicking kittens. Days before they had quitted Winnipeg, a mother cat had fortuitously presented Mrs. Grisdale, wife of the dean of St. John's cathedral, with several bundles of soft fur.

"Mother," Juey had begged, "may we take some kittens? Mrs. Grisdale says we may have two."

"Oh no!" Anna had protested in horror. "They're much too small to leave their mother." In the end she had relented a little. "Well, perhaps. If their eyes are open before we leave. Remember, you may have to do without milk for your porridge and give it to the kittens."

"That's all right," the child had answered. "I'll eat it with butter."

At departure time, the children had produced two adorable kittens, the gift of Mrs. Grisdale. Of the pair of mewing balls, one was snow white, the other a soft grey. Their small slanted eyes were barely opened enough to get even a glimmer of awareness of the great world.

"All right," Anna had agreed. Her brown eyes twinkled. "I declare you children must have pulled their eyes open!"

Here in this immensity of loneliness by the Peace she found that the endless antics of the kittens helped to relieve the tedium of waiting, for herself as well as for the young ones.

To guide them in this first raft-building, Malcolm had hired an old Indian named Mooneyass, and in his canoe they had gone seeking the island where, he assured them, they would find the necessary logs. Mooneyass was a Cree term for greenhorn and the Indian, it seemed, had earned the sobriquet through some quarrel with the far-away government authorities at Ottawa. According to his vague conception, that government could have been as distant and shadow-etched as the moon. But he firmly believed that it owed him treaty-money and to all and sundry he told his tale of injustice. Whether it was fancied or real, no one seemed to know.

In native skills, however, Mooneyass was neither vague nor confused but completely capable. On the island to which he directed the mission men was a large stand of spruce trees that had been girdled by his people. That is, the trees had been stripped of their bark for the making of summer teepees. These, now semi-dry, the men chopped down, cut into matching lengths and rolled into the snye or shallow channel between the bank of the Peace and the island. When they had floating there, in neat side-by-side rows, a sufficient number to form the base of a sizeable raft, they bound them together with a pair of sturdy logs laid across the ends. With an inch auger they bored holes through every other log, alternating the holes at either end. Through these holes they drove long wooden pins, thus securing them to the cross logs.

From poplars also growing on the island the men prepared, in one corner of the raft, a yard-square cooking platform for Anna's use. They topped it with a quantity of earth and beside it piled a neat store of kindling and firewood.

Over more small poles at the other end of the raft they piled spruce boughs and above, for shelter, they stretched a tarpaulin. From pieces of spruce pole they fashioned rowlocks and for sweeps they cut eight-foot-long poles with one end shaped like a paddle. All round the "deck" of their craft they ran a railing and low on each side they lashed giant spruce trees with all the branches still intact. These latter would help keep the raft drifting in the main current.

Thanks to the splendid skill of Mooneyass, who could anticipate all the needs and the problems of an uninitiated white family trusting themselves to an immense river, at last everything was shipshape. The men guided the raft downstream to a makeshift mooring by the mouth of the creek where the family was encamped.

"Well," smiled Malcolm with obvious pride, "how do you like our new ship?"

Exclaiming with delight, the children jumped aboard. They skipped all about its log floor, no doubt giving their mother, Juey afterward realized, many shivers of fear lest they disappear in the swift water below. If fragile Anna was secretly terrified of having to entrust her family to this clumsy creation, she smiled in spite of fear and duly admired it.

It was the evening of July the sixth, 1886, and Osborne's fifth birthday.

"So we'll name it the Osborne raft," announced Malcolm.

Delightedly the child danced up and down to claim his "ship," which early next morning would take them on their way to the new home.

"We thank God for his gifts," Malcolm prayed that night as usual. "And we put our trust in Him . . . "

Before turning in, Handyman Burton decided to enjoy a last dip in this area of the Peace. The family and Bishop Young lingered about the camp-fire, chatting and resting.

Plunging back through the trees, Burton came on the run.

"Get your gun," he shouted breathlessly. "There's a bear out here."

"How do you know it's a bear?" The bishop's tone was skeptical.

"It is a bear. Swimming in the river," panted the green Englishman. "I can still hear its tail splashing in the water."

Every one raced from the camp-fire to have a look. Nothing moving or living could they see. Malcolm smiled with reassurance at the concerned children. "I guess Mr. Beaver is lurking somewhere along the bank. He's having a good look at us and he's laughing a little."

The talk turned to anecdotes of this little-known land. Already the tall bishop, who back in England in his college days rowed in a championship team, had journeyed many hundreds of miles by river in his new diocese of Athabasca. His territory covered more than three hundred thousand square miles, an area larger than all of the old province of Ontario, an area in which one could lose the whole of the British Isles. Already he had spent time at Fort Vermilion, the important trading post far down the Peace which was the headquarters of his diocese.

With anxious heart Anna listened to his report of the work going forward in her new home-to-be. Already the bishop was looking forward to his own wife and family joining him there.

"Next summer, God willing, we'll have a house under way, and Julia and the children will be with us again."

Young Juey pricked up her ears. "Aunt" Julia, the bishop's wife, their nearest neighbor back home in Manitoba, was the godmother for whom she was named and whose birthday she shared.

Meantime the bishop went on to mention some of the problems confronting Erastus and Lydia and Henry Lawrence at Fort Vermilion, and now by the dimming fire the thoughts of Malcolm and Anna drifted back to the big Lawrence family with all the equipment, that was following them in snail-pace fashion. Compared with their own difficulties, those that the Lawrence party was going to confront in such areas as the portage and the mountain-like hillside above the Peace might prove insuperable.

Isaac Lawrence, who was in charge of the "expedition", had told Malcolm Scott that he planned to reach Fort Vermilion and return "outside" to the railway before the autumn frosts imprisoned the northern waters. Could he make such a journey, in all a matter of some eighteen hundred miles or more, before navigation closed for the season?

The congenial little group circled about the campfire, wise with the accumulation of their own experiences that had enriched them thus far, pondered with sympathy over what the Lawrence party must yet face. They did not guess that even then a crisis had occurred that threatened this latter expedition's ever reaching their common destination on the Peace.

CHAPTER 4

SHERIDAN ENCOUNTERS THE PEACE

Perhaps it was the dragging pace of the oxen that allowed hostilities to feed and fester. At the end of this first week of July, Sheridan and his family at last sighted the freshly-burned blotch of woods by the Athabasca, where fire had struck terror to the hearts of the Scott family.

All the way from the Red Deer crossing the youth had helped to push the creeping beasts onward. By day innumerable flies and mosquitoes began to torment both animals and travellers; by nightfall billowing smudges of smoke brought respite. Sometimes then the distant cry of yapping coyotes replaced the incessant whir of insect wings and Sheridan's mother, Maggie, listened anxiously while her children slept undisturbed.

With experience gained at numerous lesser hills, the little party chained fast the wheels of engine and wagons and negotiated successfully the steep south bank of the North Saskatchewan river at Edmonton. This time the ferry man was right on hand and soon they were all clambering up the long north bank. They headed northward along the Athabasca trail and now found to their dismay that, in this area of bush and muskeg and swamp, whole armies of flies and mosquitoes were ambushed in wait for them.

Finally they emerged on a point overlooking, beyond fire-blackened trees, a broad band of water. This, Mr. Melrose informed them, was the Athabasca river.

"It looked like a mighty stream to us," Maggie noted. "And there was no way at all of crossing it."

Actually there was no need for all of the party to cross the river. What they needed, for Maggie and the children and the bulky freight, the engine and the chickens and the pigs, was transportation on it that would carry them upstream to the Lesser Slave river and thence to Lesser Slave Lake. Alas, for them as for the Scott family, there were no immediate means available.

Under the charge of a foreman, near by a camp of Métis was still busy building more boats for the Hudson's Bay company. The newcomers would have to wait, he told them, until several craft were completed or until others arrived back from freighting either up or down stream. It might be a matter of several weeks before they could go on.

For the first few days, while they waited, the mounting tension between Sheridan and his uncle slackened. Assisted by his brother Jim, Sheridan set to work to build a poplar-pole living room for his mother, while Isaac Lawrence and Mr. Melrose supervised the children's herding of the animals or lent a hand to the boat-builders to hustle the work along. The family's camp-site was a short distance from that strip of forest that had, just weeks before, been ravaged by fire and from which the Scott family had fled in such haste. As Sheridan moved amidst the jungle-like growth that had escaped the fury of the flames, he selected slim aspens that grew not far from magnificent firs comparable with the splendid trees they had left behind in eastern Canada. Soon he and Jim had a sturdy shelter erected, the roof of which the younger children covered with branches. Now on fine days, especially at meal-time, they found refuge within it from the scalding sun, which here in the north-west beamed upon them a heat that was truly unbelievable.

While the younger boys continued to share in the dull chore of herding the cattle and the pigs, the girls, Grace and Minnie, searched for wild berries. They found delicious strawberries, which their mother served with cream from one of the cows, raspberries and saskatoons, which she baked in pies sunk in an earthen pit in the same manner as she "buried" for baking the daily ration of bread.

Gradually the exasperation of waiting for transportation played on sensitive nerves that had already suffered many an irritation on the trail, and one evening the simmering friction between Sheridan and his uncle flamed into open warfare. Isaac, moved to fury by his rebellious nephew, swung his bull-whip across the lad's shoulders. Maggie rushed from the tent to intervene and Sheridan slipped behind it out of reach of the long whip.

He would endure no more of his uncle's bossy ways, he decided then and there. In the morning he would ask his mother for what bread she could spare. With that and with his gun, he would manage to keep alive. He would work his way back over the trail and eventually he would reach his home in Ontario. There, somehow, he would get employment.

In burning bitterness he nursed his smarting shoulders and his resolve to get away as fast as he could. From the other side of the tent, he heard his mother's voice.

"You undertook to look after the equipment," Maggie snapped at her brother-in-law. "You were to see to delivering it safely and to driving the cattle. You weren't to drive my sons."

Sheridan listened and his anger cooled a little. At that moment he still hated his uncle with every shred of his being. But there were his mother and his seven brothers and sisters, with Jim still fourteen and Jack such a little fellow, a little fellow that he'd been looking out for since before he was born. He thought of the winter night when his father had as usual been absent at a logging camp and his mother Maggie had begun to suffer the birth pains and he'd made his way through the woods in a snowstorm to fetch a neighbor to help her. Now they were all camped here in the midst of this north-west forest that was so big you could drop all of Ontario inside it and his father still expected him to look after them.

He reconsidered. Maybe he had better stay with them and help them through to their destination.

Maggie, sensing her son's desperation and longing to keep him, the crutch she had learned to lean upon, safe by her side, continued to do her best to act as mediator. Fortunately, within days after the fracas, a brigade of narrow-bodied York boats belonging to the "Bay" appeared. In charge of one of these craft was a Capt. Daniel, and he agreed to accept the family as passengers on the upstream voyage to Lesser Slave lake.

Maggie held council with Isaac and Mr. Melrose; she

34

breathed easier when arrangements were completed. The boat brigade would undertake to transport all of the freight except the cattle; these Mr. Melrose and Sheridan and Jim were to drive overland. Fortunately, Isaac Lawrence had been able to hire an Indian guide who had served in that capacity for Bishop Bompas, the enterprising former head of the diocese who had shaped the beginnings of the mission at Fort Vermilion. This Ned would guide the little party of drovers through woods that might seem impassable.

Squeezed into the heavily-laden York boat, the family marvelled to see how human muscle now propelled them forward on their journey.

"Our boat," so Maggie described it, "had to be towed from along the shore by men who were attached to each other by straps that braced their shoulders. They worked in shifts and like galley slaves as we journeyed up the Athabasca and Lesser Slave rivers. Large beads of perspiration dripped from their foreheads and their bodies lathered under the strenuous labor."

Meanwhile the cattle drivers succeeded in persuading the small herd, which comprised the six oxen, two young pure-bred bulls and two cows, to swim across the Athabasca. They headed them north-west, wherever possible keeping close to the river bank. Through woods and swamp they pushed them forward, fighting flies and mosquitoes, following Indian paths wherever they were to be found, breaking their way through bush when there was no path to follow.

From time to time either Sheridan or Jim would cut across to the boat brigade to re-stock with provisions, particularly with their mother's celebrated bannocks that formed the mainstay of their diet. Once, as the little party of drivers stopped to camp, Ned distributed to them the last of the bannocks on hand. Although Jim had known only the rugged life of the eastern Canadian backwoods, he had a squeamish stomach unsuited to the wilderness. He reached to pick up his bannock. Quickly he dropped it again. Over it a fat "greyback," a husky louse, was crawling.

That night Jim rolled supperless into his blanket.

Finally overland party and boats reached a rendezvous where the Lesser Slave river hurls itself from the huge inland bulk of Lesser Slave lake. All gazed upon an unforgettable scene of grandeur and of gloom. A fierce wind was whipping the wide waters of the lake that were now lighted by the setting sun and shadowed by the creaking woods that were densely massed along the shore.

Some five hundred miles of journeying still lay before them. For Sheridan and Jim, the next leg of the trail would not be too different from that which they had just completed. They, with Mr. Melrose and Ned, were to continue driving the cattle through the bush to the north-western tip of the lake. For Maggie and her family in the York boat, the next hours were among the most terrifying of their lives.

Time meant money to Capt. Daniel; so also did a favorable wind. On reaching Lesser Slave lake, he decided to push on at once. His crew put up a sail but presently they took to oars alone, and many and exciting were the stories which the children afterwards told their big brothers of the night's experience.

Finally, because the high waves were endangering the cargo, Capt. Daniel was obliged to order his men to the shelter of an island.

"All that night," said Maggie, "the roar of the wind and the waves was in our ears."

There was worse to come. About noon the next day, Capt. Daniel decided he could wait no longer in the lee of the island, and the craft proceeded on its way.

"We were out of sight of land, and the waves tossed our boat around. It called for all the courage that our hearts could muster."

Maggie's young daughters, Grace and Minnie, nicknamed the boat Daniel's Den. Its captain tried to reassure them all. "She's weathered worse storms."

"It was a consoling thought to me," wrote Maggie, "that by nightfall Daniel's Den would rest on land. Never have I had since, nor do I want to have, such a rocking and splashing as we received that afternoon."

At last they set up camp near the Hudson's Bay post at the western extremity of the lake. Here they had to wait for the overland party with the cattle.

"Near us Indians were camped in their tepees. But Isaac was with us, so we felt quite safe."

The overlanders arrived and with a will Sheridan helped his uncle and Mr. Melrose in preparations for the portage to the Peace. One article of freight was a large wagon which Isaac had shaped out of timbers hewn on the old family homestead at Lawrenceville in Quebec. This they reassembled and into it stowed a considerable portion of their freight. Oxen were hitched to it and to the big "boiler." Luckily for them, dryer weather now prevailed and they were not faced with the dilemma that had confronted Anna Scott as to what to leave behind. Fortified by their months of hard-won experience, within a week they had traversed the portage and emerged above Sagitawa, or Peace River Crossing.

Around and below them extended the landscape that Bishop Young had contrasted with Switzerland. Here, "above the mighty Peace was a panoramic grandeur," so Maggie commented, "that could not be appreciated in one glance," a grandeur surpassing anything they had ever seen.

Here was, they realized, the impressive gateway to their new world. But here, too, was at the same time an immense barrier or obstruction that could prevent their entering it. The equipment they were bringing, mills, machinery and the bulky engine, was to bring modern ways and comforts into the land that beckoned ahead. Could they possibly manouevre it all down this great hillside?

They had come too far now to turn back. Co-operating to the utmost of his youthful strength and skill, Sheridan joined with his uncle and Mr. Melrose in the challenging task of shuffling their freight down into the valley far below. Rough-locking the wheels of the engine, they hitched one team of oxen to the front to set the monster in motion and the other teams they hitched to the rear to keep it from moving too fast. Again with experience earned on such hills as those of the North Saskatchewan, they inched it foot by foot downward. Hours later it rested eight hundred feet below and in the valley of the river whose pleasure it might be to carry them all the balance of the journey and to the very doorstep of the new home.

In after years, Sheridan agreed that the difficulty of entering the Peace River country was part of its charm.

It was now the first week of August and time pressed. At dawn the next morning Sheridan and Jim accompanied the men up-stream to the island where, more than a month before, the Rev. Malcolm Scott had engaged in building a raft.

With all the force of which his young arms were capable, Sheridan swung his axe so that it bit eagerly into the girdled spruces. Close by moved a power that might prove to be friend or foe, a possible adversary whose might made human bickering fade into insignificance. Though its name was Peace, this adversary could challenge to the utmost the skills of those embarking on its waters.

CHAPTER 5

JUEY
DISCOVERS
AN
EDEN

Surely the native wisdom of Mooneyass, so Malcolm Scott assured himself on the morning of July 7, 1886, as he supervised the loading of his raft, would see his family safely down the flood of the twisting stream to which he was now entrusting them.

Besides, he himself was something of a river man. All his life so far had been spent beside Manitoba's Red river, a sluggish stream not to be compared with this Peace but still a force to be reckoned with.

Thus, in the bright sunshine of the summer morning, Malcolm found reassurance in his thoughts and he hustled with the family to stow aboard all the possessions that had accompanied them on the portage. Back and forth Juey and Osborne scurried, loading their arms with camping equipment. With the help of Mooneyass, Malcolm caught and crated the pigs, Jack and Jill, and he added their wooden home to that of the hens and to the store of boxes and packages and the one trunk he had already ranged on the raft. Finally the children brought their kittens and Anna her potted plants. They said good-bye to Bishop Young, who with Burton was proceeding to visit Anglican missions upstream and who, in the autumn, would come to make his home with them at the centre of his diocese. Then Malcolm and Mooneyass poled the craft out into the swirling current.

At first, as the Indian guided it toward the central channel, the raft turned and twisted in a way that was terrifying to Anna and the children. Swollen by the June rains and by the melting snows in the Rocky Mountains, the river was at peak level. Here in this area after it had received the waters of the small Hart and of the long and sinuous Smoky, its channel expanded to a full quarter of a mile in width and the raft seemed tiny and helpless in the push of its powerful current.

Downstream it hurtled, past small islands, following a path that twisted and turned as the river twisted and turned in innumerable bends and curves. With every slight change of direction, before the devout eyes of Malcolm and Anna there unfolded on a giant scale amazing new vistas of God's untouched universe. Though she continued to keep an eagle eye to the children, Anna found herself beginning to relax in the face of such ordered immensity.

Soon the raft bounced onto a series of rapids and Malcolm and Mooneyass worked with their poles to steady it. Anna hid her fears; the children laughed with delight as their "ship" spun about in the boiling water. In spite of the tearing force of the river, it held together and soon reached a region of less turbulence.

For a while Juey gazed in fascination at the water beneath them. It was like a grey monster, with more eyes than Argus, not still staring eyes like those in a peacock's tail but moving eyes that would form and peer at her. Then those eyes would dance away and always others would replace them.

Ahead now, so Bishop Young advised her father, lay no more rapids of consequence. But between Peace River Crossing and Fort Vermilion lay other obstructions, in all twenty-eight islands against any one of which, without constant watchfulness, they might become enmoored. Malcolm peered forward as they approached one of these hazards and he puzzled to know through which channel, between island and shore, to pole the raft. Then it was that Mooneyass proved his worth. With a grunt and a wave, the wrinkled Indian designated the proper turn, and within minutes they swept safely again into a central unimpeded current.

Other than these islands and occasional sand and gravel bars, this Peace, so the bishop assured them, was completely navigable over the near-three-hundred-mile length that would bring them to Fort Vermilion and he forecast a day when steamers would ply its waters all the way from up-stream

Hudson Hope to their destination. Some fifty miles beyond Fort Vermilion, he told them, the river became exceedingly treacherous. Here it whirled into a sea of rapids that presently boiled down the celebrated Vermilion Chutes.

Because their craft was approaching the fifty-eighth parallel where at this time of the year there was no true night but only a short sunless period of deep grey, Malcolm planned a non-stop journey. So, during the day, while the raft spun forward with the racing river, Anna prepared meals in her kitchen corner. In the evening Malcolm asked Mooneyass, the expert native, to take the next watch. Then, relaxed and unworried, he flung himself down and, like the children, sank into deep sleep.

By his side Anna lay wide awake. She listened to the gurgling of the water beneath them, the creaking of the raft, the occasional strange voices of birds or animal calling from the forest-clad banks; she worried about the unpredictable might of the temperamental river; she dare not sleep while her children lay at the mercy of such a monster.

At last the sounds changed. Surely there was something wrong. Or did she imagine it only? Perhaps something had been wrong for a long time. She knew that Malcolm was exhausted from all the labor of the past few days. But she could no longer keep her fears to herself.

"Wake up, Malcolm," she prodded her husband. "There's something wrong. I don't think we're moving at all."

Malcolm crawled from the tarp's shelter and went to reconnoitre. Near the other end of the raft snored the watchman Mooneyass.

Peering into the grey pre-dawn, Malcolm saw that their "ship" was caught at the end of a small island. Soon the incessant pounding of the current against its sides might do irreparable harm. Rousing the guide, Malcolm began to prod and push, and presently the combined efforts of the pair of them freed the raft from its prison.

Malcolm said little about the near mishap, for fear, Anna guessed, of alarming her further. With relief she noted that, for the remainder of the journey, he himself kept watch all the time.

Next morning at four o'clock, in the soft warmth of a bright summer dawn, they rounded still another goose-neck

41

in the twisting river that now for the past hundred miles had been flowing north-easterly rather than north. After this last sharp double curve, with a brief gesture Mooneyass signalled the direction in which to pole past a pair of approaching islands. He waved ahead to indicate that they were nearing their homeland.

There followed still another jog in the river and more islands. Then in the distance, on the right bank, loomed a string of small white-washed buildings. Their home-to-be was in sight.

With fresh interest their eyes swept the horizon. Here the imperious river had swelled its might so that it stretched a mile wide from shore to shore. Across from the dwarf settlement extended another island majestically spired with tall spruce. Back from the water, the river's banks that at Peace River Crossing had been mountainous and almost sheer, became in this region a series of forested steps or ridges pushed back from wooded flatlands.

Only in the northern distance did a gigantic string of blue-lighted hills break the horizon's monotonous pattern of never-ending forest.

Mooneyass had noticed Anna's glance. "Caribou mountains," he informed her.

Her anxious eyes strained forward to try to glimpse the building that was to be their dwelling place. "It's nearly a mile down river from the fort," he told her from the store of information supplied to him by Bishop Young.

He identified several buildings perched back from the shallow bank which they were now passing, a Roman Catholic mission and structures comprising the trading post that had been erected on the site where, back in 1803, men of the Hudson's Bay Company had chosen to build its very first "fort" on the Peace not far from the spot where, fifteen years earlier, Alexander Mackenzie's man Boyer had raised a post.

Lastly, they descried ahead those buildings which, Anna knew, represented the fruits of the combined toil of the Rev. A. C. Garrioch and Erastus Lawrence and their helpers. These were first the mission-house and the tiny church, and then the school and the outbuildings of the Unjaga mission, which Mr. Garrioch had so named in deference to the Unchaga, the Beaver Indian name for the Peace, and which Bishop Young had re-named the Irene*, also in honor of the Peace. With a full heart and with a little prayer that his own work might prove acceptable in the sight of God, Malcolm took careful note of each building.

Poling the raft out of the main current, with his guide's help he made it fast against a log pier immediately below the mission-house. It was July the ninth, 1886; in less than forty-eight hours this home-made contraption had carried them all intact down three hundred miles of racing river and to the very doorstep of their first dwelling in the north.

Malcolm climbed the ten-foot earthen bank and went to reconnoitre. He hurried back, shaking his head.

"We'd better have breakfast on the raft." From the few words he spoke Anna surmised that the house was unfit for occupancy. She knew that she must not expect too much, for Mr. Garrioch, she knew, had gone out the previous summer, journeying to London, England, to get translations printed in the Beaver and the Cree tongues and to rouse help for the mission work. After all, he had been gone a whole year.

Beside the depressing dwelling a patch of potatoes struggled for survival amidst smothering weeds. As Malcolm walked downstream toward the school to notify the E. J. Lawrences of their arrival and to beg some fresh milk, the sight of a barley-field lush with half-grown crop and an indication of the amazing possibilities of growth in this latitude, lifted his spirits.

Aboard the raft, Juey played wth the kittens and watched for her father's return. Suddenly her pets lost all interest in frolicking. Mewing frantically, they tried to find a way to scramble from the raft to meet Malcolm.

"Look, mother," shouted the little girl. All at once she was as excited as the kittens. "They smell milk."

The fresh milk that embellished breakfast for all of them seemed like a symbol. Before going ashore, the little family knelt in a prayer of thankfulness and hope. Juey listened to the rich deep tones of her father's voice, ringing out assuredly as it had done the previous day on the raft

---

* Peace Gr.

and on all the days of the long, long journey behind them. She listened and she remembered the fervor of his voice while he thanked God for bringing them in safety to their new home.

Before them now for the children lay a kind of Eden, a whole new world of excitement and of wonderment to explore in the summer sunshine. For Anna disappointment was banished and her heart emboldened by the confidence and zeal in her husband's tone and manner; here was an enormous field, a field of limitless possibilities, in which they could labor for Christ and for the betterment of their fellow-beings.

At the mission school, Malcolm met the new farm supervisor, Henry Lawrence, and he was able to report to him about the accidental meeting with his family back at the Red Deer river crossing. With luck, he predicted, they should by this time have reached Athabasca Landing, where they would probably have to await some kind of river transport. There was much conjecturing and calculating between the two tall Lawrence brothers; finally it was agreed that Erastus, or E. J. as he preferred to be called, should presently, because of his greater experience on the river, go to their assistance.

With his home-made canoe and with an Indian to help him, he was going to pole and paddle his way upstream over the tortuous water path that the Scott family had followed.

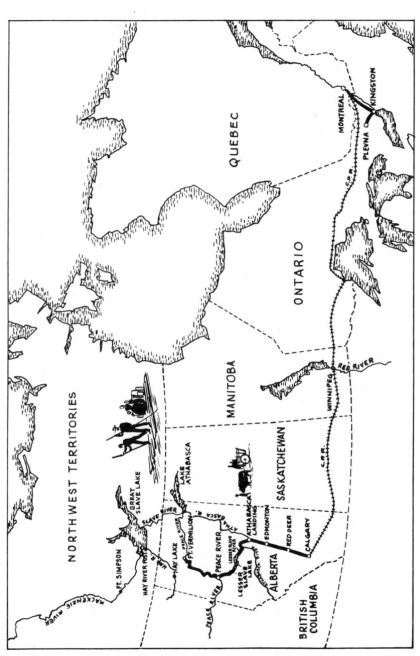

Route taken by the Scott and Lawrence families.

CHAPTER 6

SHERIDAN OVERTAKES
HER THERE

"Hallooo!" boomed a voice from the river.

Already Sheridan and Jim were upstream helping with the building of a giant raft. The younger Lawrence children shouted from their play by the big tent to warn their mother and raced through the bush toward the river.

A bronzed bearded figure emerged from the edging brush. The children looked and felt disappointment; it was not their daddy. At once Maggie recognized the tall hook-nosed man who was grinning a welcome to them all. It was her brother-in-law, Erastus, whose venturing with his spirited wife Lydia seven summers earlier had been the original lure now enticing them also into this awesome land.

In a moment she was tearing open a letter he brought her from Henry. Since the latter had quitted their homestead in the sugar bush at Plevna in that previous disturbed spring-time of 1885, she had but that one letter of news and instruction from him.

His scrawled words now, written from their final destination at Fort Vermilion and buoyant with promise for the future, made up for the long silence.

"My dear Maggie," she read. "The goose hangs high. We have been using new potatoes for the past month. The grain promises immense returns . . ."

Maggie smiled. Her Henry had always been an optimist. Several years before, with grand plans for their future he had moved them to the Ontario bush; in the log home there he had erected a fireplace that was large enough for a palace and that consumed wood like a starving whale.

But his mention of new potatoes made her mouth water;

only once, in the weeks on the trail, had they tasted potatoes; passing through Edmonton, they had been able to buy a few there. Now to Maggie they seemed like a symbol of hope and of better days ahead.

Henry's optimism was contagious; the children, too, chattered happily of the day when they would be re-united with him; after all, he was only three hundred miles away. Now the brooding immensity of the timeless hills above them seemed more friendly and the broad waters of the Peace seemed to invite them to hasten on their way. The lonely flat by the junction of the creek and the river where before them the Scott family had camped and where now a herd of wild horses was the only sign of life, buzzed with the sounds of young voices making fresh plans.

At once E. J. proceeded to join the raft-builders, and Sheridan harkened to his words of experience with an always-ready ear. If the raft were to convey their whole load and all of themselves safely down the Peace, he realized that extra-special care must go into the assembling of it.

While E. J. worked beside his brother and his nephews, he described the raft on which Mr. Garrioch had floated a herd of cattle downstream to Fort Vermilion six years before. Driving them all the way from Edmonton to the Peace as Mr. Melrose and the lads had herded their animals, the missionary also had constructed a raft here. His floating zoo, which comprised nineteen head of cattle, one horse and one crate of hens and a rooster, "created a sensation" when it reached Fort Vermilion. It was part of this herd and the increase from it which Henry Lawrence as farm manager had taken charge of during the previous winter.

Soon a sturdy raft thirty feet wide and sixty feet long was completed to the satisfaction of E. J.

"They wore proud faces," Maggie remembered, "when they stole alongside our shore."

With their monster craft heaped with all the modern equipment and the hefty twelve-horse-power "boiler," they, too, were going to create a sensation at Fort Vermilion. "Loading the engine was an undertaking in itself; so much care was necessary to keep the raft from upsetting and the log gang-planks from splitting under the weight."

Next came the saw-mill, the stone mill with its Watrous

bolt sixteen feet long, the heavy hardwood wagon, and all the accumulation of other freight. The men built a sturdy fence around the outside of the raft "to prevent the animals from pushing each other into the river," wrote Maggie further, and finally drove them aboard. Maggie and her eight children, her two tall brothers-in-law and Mr. Melrose all clambered on deck. Sheridan took his place at one of the long sweeps and helped to pole the craft out into the current.

At once E. J. assumed command, selecting channels whenever they approached obstructing islands. It was August 13th, and now the high waters of June had subsided. This much heavier raft did not move with as much speed as that which had hurled the Scott family on its way ahead of them. At the same time the "crew" had to be extra watchful that their bulky craft did not run aground. Yet after they had passed the region of rapids, they could relax a little. Following the long ordeal of the trail and the hectic stint of raft building and loading, it was a delight to feel the energetic current beneath them now bearing the brunt of the toil and propelling them forward to their final destination. While the children watched along the shores for wild animals and squealed with pleasure whenever they caught sight of black bear cubs, the men who had been spelled off from duty with the sweeps tinkered with the bulky engine.

Early in their sixth morning on the Peace, Sheridan and Jim built a roaring wood blaze in the fire-box of the big engine. They were, so E. J. told them, almost at their destination and the engine must announce its and their arrival in fitting fashion.

The raft swerved with the current as it curved into the sharp goose-neck turn and now began moving more east than north. E. J. directed it along a snye lying between the wood-fringed shore and two narrow islands. All eyes gazed where he pointed toward a long hay-meadow that skirted the river shore beyond the edging woods. Maggie caught a glimpse of a tiny pole shack and grazing cattle surrounded by a straggling stake fence.

These were mission animals, E. J. told them, under the care of their husband and father Henry, and here the latter spent part of his time while he built fences and saw to the needs of the herd. The site of the mission itself was a further fifteen miles down stream.

To get steam up in readiness, the boys heaped more wood into the fire-box. Presently their uncle gave the word. Every one gaped at the huffing engine and Sheridan pulled the wire to release its compressed power. Shrill and loud the whistle sounded. Seemingly shocked by this first man-made defiling of their ancient silence, loud and shrill the woods echoed the sound.

If any human within earshot heard, during a whole hour there was no sign. Anxiously the family glued their eyes downstream and at last their watching was rewarded. A small canoe hove into sight.

From time to time as the man in the tiny craft fought the current, wildly he waved his paddle.

"Mother," the children shrieked. "It's Daddy!"

It was indeed their father, Henry Lawrence. With him was a young girl whom they guessed at once to be their cousin Susie, their uncle E. J.'s fifteen-year-old daughter.

Henry boarded the raft and took Maggie in his arms. He hugged his children each in turn and marvelled at how they had grown in the sixteen-month period since he had seen them. He shook hands with his grown son, Sheridan, and he realized that this six-foot-two lad towering above him physically could have more than filled his own shoes.

Drawn by the strange whistle of the steam engine calling to them like some fresh manifestation out of the spirit world, near the little pier down the bank from the Irene Training Mission, a crowd of Indians lined the shore to watch the amazing arrival.

Today was the 18th of August, 1886. More than four months had elapsed since Maggie and her family had quitted their Ontario homestead, four months of journeying that had brought them at last to Henry's side. To Maggie this moment that culminated "the greatest lark of our lives" was a joyous one that transformed their new homeland into a setting of glorious beauty and she remembered always that her first impression of "the clear water, the clearer sky, with the birch, poplar and spruce-clad shoreline made a romantic sight."

She stepped ashore, to be embraced by her brown-eyed

sister-in-law, Lydia Lawrence. Shyly an old and sienna-skinned Indian woman stepped forward. Into Maggie's hand she thrust a ball of spruce gum which she had chewed to a fine malleable state.

Maggie, the mother of Sheridan, the man who came to be known as "Ooki-Mauw," and "Friend of the Indian," smiled as she afterward recollected the mute gesture. "This was tendered to me as a welcome and a symbol of good will."

With a zest matching the bracing air Sheridan turned to the business of helping to move everything ashore. There were, he found, so many things to be learned here; every hour by this Peace brought the stimulation of fresh challenge.

Among those welcoming the new arrivals were the members of the Scott family. By forty days the fair-haired girl Juey who had smiled shyly up at him as he shivered before their fire at the Red Deer river, had preceded him here. Afterwards, teasingly he protested that he never did catch up with her knowledge of the new homeland.

"Ask Juey," he told those enquiring about their "early days" on the Peace. "She's been here longer than I."

It was true that Juey could usually supply an answer. Her period of probation here imprinted upon her memory unusual experiences that were varied and unforgettable.

CHAPTER 7

On a bench outside the kitchen door stood a steaming bowl. Juey, rushing in from play, caught a whiff of its fragrance.

"Oh-h, meat!" she screamed in ecstasy to younger brother Osborne who raced after her.

Hungrily the pair dipped their fingers into the bowl and began stuffing the meat into their mouths.

"Children, children!" excaimed Anna. "Don't touch that!" She shook her head in horror. "That's horse-meat, part of old Charlie. I cooked it for the hens."

"It's good, Mother," the children protested, continuing to dip and chew.

Sternly their mother forbade them to touch any more.

Charlie was an ancient and dying work-horse which their father, casting about in desperation for ways to eke out the food supply, had bought from the "Bay" trading post. During their first months ashore at Fort Vermilion, this problem of finding food for human beings and for animals soon became acute, not only for the Rev. Malcolm Scott but for the Lawrences and for Trading-Post Manager Trail, for upon all of them also devolved the humane task of trying to help the hundreds of starving Indians in the near-by woods.

Within hours after he had set foot on land on that pleasant dawn of July the 9th, Malcolm had seen that, in this his first mission posting, reality was far short of his dreams. With cheerfulness and zeal and almost-round-the-

51

clock toil, he threw himself into the gigantic demands that awaited him.

For some time, he saw, sheer physical need, that was presently to become desperate, must take precedence over intellectual and spiritual requirements. All of his life he had known pioneering and this conflict he had learned to accept. As a boy of twelve, so his mother recalled, he had kept a book beside him while he mixed the mortar for his father's new stone house and studied while he stirred. In the gigantic tasks that now confronted him, he had the example and the benefit deriving from the work of others who had previously dedicated themselves to the task of bettering the lot of the Indian peoples.

From his own area, the Red River colony in Manitoba, Archdeacon Hunter of the Anglican faith had journeyed by boat brigade into this north-west in 1858. The Rev. William Kirkby had followed him, and his expense money for his mission trip had been furnished by Malcolm's own congregation at St. Andrew's outside of Winnipeg.

Then, in 1868, Rev. W. C. Bompas made a first trip upstream on the Peace and he noted the desirability of Fort Vermilion as the site for a mission. He also reported to his church the existence of problems among the Indians, particularly among the Beavers, who "were very pitiable and fast dying off." During his second journey on the Peace, he found the native peoples further decimated by small pox and during the course of the summer he vaccinated some five hundred of them.

"Starvation, sometimes attended by cannibalism," he recorded, also afflicted them. There was urgent need "to minister not only to the souls but to the bodies and minds of these peoples."

In the summer of 1876, just ten years before Malcolm's arrival, another Manitoban, the Rev. A. C. Garrioch, became the first resident Anglican missionary here on the Peace. First of all he erected the log mission-dwelling which Malcolm and Anna found to be still basically sturdy and serviceable in spite of its state of sad disrepair. Back in Portage la Prairie where the young Garrioch had grown to manhood, so he wrote in his diary, "any young fellow who could not build his own log house would have been called a kipooch, a useless fellow."

Mr. Garrioch's dedication to the cause of trying to help the Indians arose perhaps in part from a love of this new land instilled in him by his antecedents. His grandfather, Colin Campbell, had been chief factor upstream on the Peace at Fort Dunvegan when it had re-opened in 1826; Colin had married a daughter of John McGillivray, a factor in this region of the North-West company in the earlier years of the century. The young clergyman's mother had been born at Fort Dunvegan, in what was largely Beaver Indian territory.

"She brought us up," he recalled, "on tales of bears and beavers and Beaver Indians."

Thus his choice of the Beaver name Unjaga for the new mission at Fort Vermilion. Since his great grandfather's and his grandfather's days, this tribe had been shockingly decimated by disease, particularly by scrofula, which among old-timers of the Peace to this day is known as "Beaver disease."

Sorrowfully Bishop Bompas had been forced to conclude that "no human power can save the Beavers."

At least, added Mr. Garrioch in his diary, "may we not redeem the dying remnant of this tribe as some fitting amends for what we have taken from them?"

So, "to ameliorate their hard lot," as well as to reach out on both sides of the Peace to neighboring tribes of Crees and Slaveys and Chipewyans, the young man builded and planned. With the blessing of Bishop Bompas, presently he had gone outside to try to raise further funds for the work, and in Montreal he had hired Erastus or E. J. Lawrence to set up a school. While the latter's wife, Lydia, who was also a schoolteacher, attended to the first pupils, E. J. worked at the erecting of a combined school and residence for his family and his students and in what time Mr. Garrioch could spare from mission duties, he turned to the building of a small church.

With delight the Rev. Malcolm Scott now examined the edifice that was the product of his predecessor's ingenious toil. From E. J. and Lydia Lawrence he learned the story

53

of its slow piece-by-piece creation. A single native helper had assisted in getting suitable logs from the near-by forest. Then the young missionary had contrived to produce boards by means of the arduous process of whip-sawing. With only the simplest tools available to him, he had raised the four walls, roofed them over, erected a belfry and topped the building at either end and over the chancel with Grecian crosses.

Inside the building Malcolm admired the painstaking and loving care with which the missionary had produced pews, pulpit, communion table and chancel rail. He had decorated the whole interior with white and blue paint and mahogany stain and with his jack-knife he had carved figures on the front panel of each.

In addition to residents of the tiny white community, members of the Rev. Malcolm's congregation included neighboring and transient Indians drawn largely from the Beaver and the Cree tribes. Years before, after incessant warring, these two tribes had come to terms on the banks of the Unchaga or Peace, the former agreeing to dwell in the land to the left of the river and the latter in that to the right.

Admiringly members of the Beaver band shared Malcolm's pleasure in the tiny church.

"Oochu meotati," they exclaimed with him. Beautiful.

Cree neighbors who also visited the mission were equally delighted with Mr. Garrioch's labor of love, the building in which all were to worship together in peace.

"Miyon-a-koosie," they admired. Beautiful.

While the ornamented interior of the church had weathered well during the year since its builder had departed, the five-room mission house told quite another story. Within, it was a den of mould and mice, a challenge to daunt the stout hearts of Malcolm and Anna. Stains everywhere on the walls and floors indicated that the water had poured through the roof of rough poles that was surfaced with hand-made "shakes." Against one wall of the living-room squatted a crumbling fireplace of mud and in the kitchen stood a small rusted stove.

After so many weeks of travel, the prospect of a fixed though leaky roof over her head delighted Anna. Lydia

Lawrence urged them to shelter in the mission school with her family and the Indian pupils. But Anna insisted that they could manage nicely in the mouldering mission house.

"All right," agreed her husband. "We'll put the tent up in the living room."

To Juey and Osborne this prospect of "camping" inside a house offered untold possibilities for frolic and fun. Gleefully they introduced their now milk-contented kittens to the "double" home within a home beside the Peace.

Anna built fires in both the rust-eaten stove and the mud fireplace to drive out the smell of dank mould. For a moment only she thought of the pair of sturdy Carron stoves that, like most of their freight, probably still waited at the far end of the portage. Years before, as a girl in England, she had yearned to be a missionary; true missionary spirit, she knew, makes do with what is at hand.

Soon Malcolm found time to come to her aid in the chore of cleaning up the small house. With a ready knack he organized boxes and crates into makeshift cupboards and benches. All day and into each night he hustled, re-shingling the roof so that the tent could be removed from the living-room and in his spare time fashioning simple pieces of furniture, beds, tables, cupboards and stools, to add to the comfort of the home.

Though now they were "settled," soon Anna found the preparation of the meals more of a challenge here than on the long road in. They had been permitted to bring five hundred pounds of flour over the portage, but Post Manager Trail came with a request that they could not refuse. Since the freight of the "Bay" had also been held up by the impassable roads, could he borrow for immediate trading use four hundred pounds of their flour?

"I'll return it just as soon as the freight gets through," promised the factor.

Among the first of the myriad tasks that Malcolm tackled was the hoeing of the weed-infested patch of potatoes that had been planted beside the mission-house. Here, as Henry Lawrence had promised in his glowing letter to Maggie, Anna found to her delight that, despite the weeds, small potatoes had formed. These she began to serve as a main staple of diet.

In the flats and the nearby woods grew wild fruits that challenged her housewifely ingenuity; soon she devised methods of preserving part of this lavish crop which she and the children picked, methods which circumvented the lack of sugar and of glass jars and sealing rings. A portion of the raspberries and the saskatoons she dried; the balance of these and as well black currants and mooseberries she boiled to a mush.

Meantime, in the tall grasses near the post Juey and Osborne gleaned empty cans that had been discarded after "trading" days. These their mother scrubbed with sand, scalded, coated with tallow or fat and into them she packed her cold berry jam, pouring over it yet another layer of melted fat. This sugarless jam she stored in the cool cellar under the house; here it kept quite as well as any of its sweeter counterparts.

Presently it became apparent that the freight, including the trading post's supplies with the expected flour, and all of the remainder of the Scott family's possessions and particularly that specially-packed trunk, was not going to arrive in this year of 1886. So Anna began to conserve the precious balance of her one and only sack of flour; in an enamel saucer she baked only one tiny loaf of bread each week.

"It was just like a large bun," pictured Juey, in whose memory was etched for a lifetime the griping hunger of that first fall and winter.

Fortunately, Anna's Rhode Island Reds laid a few eggs and for added protein there was the balance of some sowbelly they had brought on the raft. Thanks to Mr Garrioch's initiative and pluck in bringing that original herd into the land, and to the farming success of E. J. Lawrence, there was on hand a herd of some forty cattle belonging to the mission that was now being cared for by his brother Henry. Of these a white milk-cow was assigned to the use of the Scott family.

Precious breeding stock could not be eaten; some grain and some potatoes must be saved for seed. When the snow began to fall, the hens and the two porkers, Jack and Jill, could no longer rustle in meadow and brush. Thus it was that the resourceful Malcolm, stretching his wits to help furnish nourishment for all, saw in Charlie, the retired "Bay" work-horse, many meals for Anna's chickens.

For Maggie Lawrence also, leading her children up the path from the raft that August morning forty days after the Scotts had arrived, the moment of beauty and wonder was quickly and rudely dissipated. Her eyes searched in vain for the waiting home that had been promised to her and her family. To her dismay she found a choice of two "dwellings." They could crowd into the already-filled school-house that was reigned over by her sister-in-law Lydia, that also sheltered E. J., the three children who had accompanied them into this country, Susie, Fred and Fenwick, and a fourth, the toddler Clara who had been born since. It also provided as well a home away from teepee or tent for varying numbers of Indian pupils.

Or Maggie could set up housekeeping in one end of a granary-storehouse behind the main dwelling. Again, Lydia urged the newcomers to take shelter with her family. On the trail Maggie had seen how too much family "togetherness" resulted in bitter clash; she chose now to establish her big brood in the storehouse.

In spite of all the difficulties previous animosities were forgotten and the reunion among these members of the Lawrence clan who had strayed so far from Lawrenceville in the Eastern Townships was exceedingly joyous.

"They gave us a real western welcome," said Maggie. And Sheridan remembered of this grand reunion that "We were a big happy family of relatives."

His optimistic father, Henry, for whom the geese always honked high, "had a wonderful way of jollying" his mother Maggie, and banishing all her dark forebodings. True to the rosy forecast contained in that letter, both the potatoes and the barley promised ample food for the winter. With a will Sheridan's brothers and sisters turned presently to the dull chore of potato digging and picking. Back on the Ontario homestead the youth's long arms had already acquired skill with the scythe; now when the fifteen acres of barley which his father had planted reached a golden maturity, he wielded the same scythe to cut the grain. Then he and Jim, using withes of straw, bound it into sheaves, stooked it, and when it had dried sufficiently they built the sheaves into a compact stack close by the school. As need or time dictated, by hand they flailed out the precious kernels of grain.

Meanwhile the magnificent engine that was to initiate modern ways began to prove itself an incomparable treasure. The men set up the mill's twenty-inch grinding stones in the big school kitchen and here they ground the barley with power supplied by the engine, repeating the process twice when the grist was to be used for porridge and bannocks and bread. The thunderous huffing of the twelve-horse-power engine echoed splendidly along the quiet river flat, and gradually Métis neighbors on near-by holdings came to depend on the mill for succour against starvation.

Upstream at the manse or mission-house, the Rev. Malcolm and Anna Scott determined to take complete charge of their own family needs. The E. J. Lawrences, they saw, had many helping hands but many mouths to feed; Lydia taught "school" and religion five hours per day for her own children and the Indian pupils, thus releasing her husband to other duties. On hand also were her brother Mr. Kneeland and Mr. Melrose, who were undertaking to build a home for Bishop Young and his family. Like the Scotts, the Henry Lawrence family had also arrived without any furnishings at all; for their comfort benches, tables, beds and cupboards must be shaped whenever time permitted. Enormous quantities of wood had to be cut and piled ready to provide warmth for all during the long winter; adequate food and shelter had to be in readiness for the needs of all the precious livestock.

Since the Lawrences had more than enough to do to see to the school and their own needs, Malcolm and Anna determined to provide for themselves on their very own. Out of the butt end of a broad balm of Gilead trunk, Malcolm shaped a pounder. He hollowed this butt, which stood about three feet high, down to a depth of twelve inches and around its circumference he stretched lengths of wet rawhide. Into this pounder each morning Anna poured barley grains that she had first soaked in boiling water.

Now it was time for young Juey to begin her share of

the day's work. Wielding a mallet which her father fashioned for her, she pounded at the grain to crack off the outside hulls.

Her mother next washed the battered mass and dried it in the oven, and Juey rubbed it in her hands to loosen more husks. If the day were fine and windy, she spread it on a sheet on the grass to allow the breezes to winnow away the hulls. Otherwise, since husks in their porridge were anathema to young throats, she and Osborne blew long and hard to rid the mass of the shells.

From the pearly kernels that remained, Anna prepared porridge and puddings. These foods, together with potatoes from the neglected patch which Malcolm had soon coaxed into more robust growth, and with milk from the cow allotted to the manse, provided the family with a nourishing if monotonous daily diet.

By the end of September ice forming along the limpid shallows edging the now-placid Peace spelled the warning message of impending winter to the small settlement. It also told Isaac Lawrence that it was time to begin to re-trace his steps back to his home in the Eastern Townships.

His shepherding of the weighty engine all the way from Winnipeg meant the beginning of a new era in an oasis of the forest-shrouded northland. Alas, his departure brought to it a tragic sequel.

Mooneyass, the Indian guide, agreed to transport him in his dug-out as far as Sagitawa, the native name for Peace River Crossing. With the wisdom of a life-time along the river and with the lanky white man as a willing pupil-assistant, he poled and paddled him over the three hundred miles of turns and twists against the current. Then, after he had wished him goodbye at the head of the portage, he spent a few days resting and visiting among his nomadic people.

Presently he returned to Fort Vermilion with dire news. A terrible scourge was spreading among his people in the Lesser Slave lake area. Many, he reported, were already dying from it.

Soon Malcolm and Anna and the Lawrences were able to identify the sickness. Within days of his return, the elderly guide fell ill with measles. Quickly the epidemic spread through the settlement and into the near-by Indian camps. As well as nursing his own family, Malcolm toiled to give what succour he could to the helpless natives. Only one infant died immediately, but the fever left weakened bodies that succumbed during the winter to respiratory ailments and the dread scrofula.

By this time Malcolm's bishop and former neighbor, the Right Reverend Richard Young, had arrived. Because Fort Vermilion was the centre of his diocese, he was to make the manse his winter headquarters. Upstairs Anna had prepared a small room for his use; there was no stove available to heat it, so Malcolm fashioned through it a kind of chimney leading up from the kitchen.

During the freeze-up season, when visiting of outlying Indian camps was almost impossible, the jovial and zealous bishop lent Malcolm a hand with the building of an addition to the home. This extra room, sixteen by twenty feet in dimensions, they added next to the kitchen so that it would serve handily as an Indian hall. Complete with crude fireplace and benches, it soon became a haven of refuge and of happiness especially for the more unfortunate of the forest-dwellers.

As a winter of record severity brought privation, more and more sought the help of the mission. Because the freight had not come through, the "Bay" post had little to trade; extra-deep snow made the hunting of the winter staple, moose-meat, increasingly difficult. So the ill and the starving lingered in the new Indian hall, where they were nourished by Anna's food and nursing and comforted by the heart-warming words of Malcolm. In exemplary fashion, like Chaucer's parson he taught "Christes loore and hise Apostles twelve but first he folwed it hymselve."

Repeatedly their parents cautioned the children, because of the risk of pesky lice and of the contagion of scrofula, not to move too close to those who sheltered there. At the same time they reminded them,

"If we white people had as little, we might be much worse than they."

One night a great hubbub arose in the hall. Above the

sound of wailing and of angry voices the deep tones of her father's words, calm and confident, soothed Juey's fears.

"Anna," he called presently. "Will you come here?"

Bursting with curiosity, the children wanted to follow her. "No, no," he chided them. "You stay back."

When the ruckus subsided and the listening Juey and Osborne heard departing steps, they ventured to peer into the hall. There a crouching young woman, with black dishevelled hair streaming over her face, sobbed alone.

When she saw the staring children, she held out her hand.

"Ah-na," she murmured.

Mindful of their parents' teaching, they shook the outstretched hand. Later Juey learned why the girl sobbed so broken-heartedly.

A group of angry Crees had discovered her alone, starving and freezing in the bush. They had brought her to the Rev. Malcolm for punishment.

"She is a weentigo," they told him in their own tongue. This, they explained, is a witch whose heart has turned to stone. When this transformation takes place, the weentigo becomes a cannibal. Because they now loathed and feared this girl, they thought it well to consult Teeny-Muttiga-Mututully, the red-bearded praying-man, who had shown himself so anxious to help solve their problems.

"Leave her with me," Malcolm had persuaded them. Perhaps, so he explained to them in the Cree tongue, with the help of God and of Jesus Christ he might be able to change the girl's heart of stone.

Already the hard-working missionary had made himself proficient in both the Cree and the Beaver tongues. The sobbing girl knew no English at all. But in Cree, said Juey, "Father talked to the girl by the hour and piece by piece he got from her the story of the awful tragedy that had befallen her."

During this harsh winter the girl's family, who lived about one hundred and fifty miles from the trading post, had one by one succumbed to starvation. The survivors including this girl, to whom Malcolm gave the name Louisa, and her sister, began to work their way through deep snow toward the post. At last only Louisa and her sister remained alive.

"She was watching me," the girl sobbed in Cree to Malcolm. "I was watching her. I knew she wanted to kill me. Night and day were both alike and everywhere was snow. We'd make a fire and fell asleep. I don't know how it happened," the crazed girl cried in her awful agony of spirit.

"I am here," she moaned on. "And she is dead. I must have killed and eaten of her. Or I would not be here."

Recalling Bishop Bompas' experiences of cannibalism among the starving, with compassionate talk and with prayer Malcolm and Anna succeeded in calming the unhappy Louisa. By day she learned from Anna how to do useful chores about the happy white man's home. By night she rested fitfully in the Indian hall, by turns sleeping and sobbing and crying out. Piecing together the fearful story of suffering, in the dark of night Juey listened to the sounds of her grief. Shivering, the white girl burrowed deeper into her own straw tick. In wide-eyed horror she had gazed at the long-bladed knife which the girl kept at night under her bit of pillow.

"She's still afraid of the evil spirits that torment her," Anna explained. "She keeps the knife ready to kill them."

Fastening on snow-shoes and pulling a small loaded hand-sleigh, from time to time Malcolm set off through the woods to carry spiritual and physical food to the needy. Willingly young Juey hurried to lay the table for his return but less willingly she prepared the starch with which her mother concocted a special pudding to sweeten his arrival.

Using a home-made grater, which was only a strip of perforated tin tacked to a stick of wood, the girl rubbed well-washed potatoes to pulpy mass. After allowing this to settle, her mother skimmed off the upper layer of pulp, and with the under layer, which dried fine and white, she made a pudding which was a family treat.

"But oh, that tedious grating," frowned Juey. "How I loathed it." And all her life long after that, Juey swore that she disliked potatoes.

As the winter's cold intensified, the hauling and sawing

of wood became a chief preoccupation of the men. The river, imprisoned and silent now, was still friend rather than foe, providing easy access to the wooded island across from the mission buildings. Here, with oxen borrowed from the Lawrences, Malcolm and Burton cut and dragged out dry spruces which the Indians had girdled. Like a fire-eating dragon, the mud fire-place in the living room of the manse gobbled down wood without giving off more than a small portion of a dragon's burning heat. There being no heat at all in the children's upstairs room, eventually each night their father arranged their straw ticks on the floor before this fireplace. He and Anna slept in the small study and Burton in the kitchen. Fearing that the chickens, too, would freeze to death, at night Malcolm brought them in to share the kitchen with Burton.

By mid-winter, the sight of meat was becoming almost as rare as manna from heaven. For their mothers' tables the Lawrence youths gunned occasional partridges or snared fool hens and bush rabbits. But the men at the manse felt that they must not spend the time for self-gratification when so much else waited to be done and so many were threatened with starvation. Which meant that Juey and Osborne were thrown upon their own resources in the matter of finding the meat which they craved.

Beyond the small St. Luke's church, which now with the bishop in residence was raised to the status of pro-cathedral, stood a stack of barley apportioned to the use of the Rev. Malcolm and his household. At the base of this stack he had dug a deep ditch to try to protect the precious grain from the invading armies of field mice. In the bottom of this ditch, his children discovered, were numbers of the small entrapped creatures.

Caught, skinned, cleaned and roasted in Anna's oven, the mice made tasty morsels to feast upon.

"How disgusting!" Their red-bearded father shook his head when he discovered what the children were eating.

"They're delicious," smiled his young ones.

Perhaps the blackbird pie of the nursery rhyme inspired their next venture into the culinary field. Whitish flocks of dainty snow buntings sometimes fluttered close to the buildings, seeking the weed seeds dark above the snow. From the Indian children the pair learned how to make snares of horse-hair. When with these they developed sufficient skill to snare snow birds, these like the mice they dressed and roasted and devoured.

"Ughh!" commented their mother, shaking her head.

"They're good," Juey insisted.

Unworried by all the problems that harassed the grown-ups, Juey passed that first winter of privation happily enough. All the tedious chores, pounding the grain, grating the potatoes, feeding the hens, carrying the wood, these made the hours of freedom and play all the sweeter.

One exciting household enterprise there was in which she loved to share, the preparing of the sacks of food for her father's winter trips. Happily she stirred salt, soda and fat with a little water or milk into the barley meal to shape into bannocks; with all her energy she worked fat and salt into mashed potato which she then formed into numerous small cakes. All these bannocks and cakes Anna froze solid before she packed them into rogans or sacks ready for the trail.

Sometimes Malcolm struck out westward, pausing first at the historic camping ground of the Beavers where the pack trail to Hay river crossed the Paddle river. Visiting all the winter lodges along the way, he tramped northwestward more than a hundred miles to where, on the Hay Lakes or along the Hay river, Slaveys and Chipewyans also trapped and cast through the ice for fish. Or he set forth eastward along the Peace until he reached the mouth of its tributary the Loon; this latter he followed a hundred and fifty miles in a southerly direction. Here again, in the land of the Crees, he taught by word and by example the message of Christ's love.

Returning from a long tramp in below-zero temperatures, he stepped into the manse kitchen like a figure of King Winter out of a Norse tale and his children welcomed the gaiety that filled their home again. To Juey the most dramatic moment of this return was the de-frosting of his long thick beard. This splendid forest on his chin was the one small vanity which he still permitted to himself, perhaps partly because it served as such a distinctive mark of identity among all those of his huge "parish."

So, as water began to drip from his rimmed eyebrows and eylashes and moustache and from the icicles that festooned his beard, with a happy grin Teeny-Muttiga-Mututully, "the red-bearded praying man," accepted warmed water from Anna. In fascination Juey watched while he soaked the frozen beard in basin after basin of water and cautiously broke away the translucent icicles.

"It does help to keep me warm," he smiled as he dried and combed it to its former full and gay resplendence.

"Now, Juey how about filling the water-bucket with more lovely clean snow?" Anna spoke to her daughter with a happy facility for wording requests. "It will save your father having to lug water up from the river."

Warmed by the infectious good humor inspired by her father's presence, willingly Juey stepped out to perform yet another of the never-ending chores.

One day an errand took her down the trail nearly a quarter of a mile to the school-house. Again and again she knocked at the back door of the building, waiting to give a message to Lydia Lawrence. No one heeded her. From within rang the sounds of hammering and building.

A couple of native lads, playing near by, edged close to tease the young blonde miss. They taunted her in their strange tongue, they poked at her and they tried to grab at her pig-tails and her scarf.

From round the building came Sheridan, the willowy youth whom she had first watched under the rainbow's arch in the waters of the Red Deer river.

"Don't tease the little lady," he scolded, cuffing the Indian lads away. "Pick on some one your own size."

The incident helped to fix him more romantically in the eyes of the young girl. "He was always there, in the background," she smiled blissfully afterwards in recollection. "He was always my beau ideal."

CHAPTER 8

For Sheridan a dramatic decision by his parents heralded possibilities for a different kind of romance.

In the small school-room of the log dwelling presided over by Lydia Lawrence, an informal evening entertainment was in progress. The chief feature of the program was a debate, "Resolved that wheat can be successfully grown at Fort Vermilion."

This kind of formal "debate" furnished the social core of the tiny settlement during that whole first winter. These entertainments were attended by every one living near at hand, Bishop Young if he were in the community, the Scotts, the Lawrence families and those of Factor Trail, the dozen or more resident Indian children, as well as any Métis neighbors.

Sheridan's father Henry, tall, blue-eyed and brimming with confidence in the country, led the affirmative of the debate. He was eloquent in his assurances of the possibility of growing good wheat near latitude north fifty-eight.

Opposing him as the head of the negative side was his impressive and Roman-nosed school-master brother, E. J. Each year since 1880, when E. J. and Mr. Garrioch had drawn up   formal agreement as to how they would share their harvest, they had planted a patch of wheat. Each year it had proved a disappointment.

Henry Lawrence, the greatest optimist in the country and the man who helped to instil a similar optimism in his eldest son Sheridan, won the evening's honors. His proposed methods and his persuasive confidence carried the field and

66

Maggie recorded that "Henry scored a decisive victory over his brother."

"Why not put your words to the test?" she began presently to coax. "Why don't we begin farming here on our own?"

Maggie had good reason to make this proposal. With its various attempts to bring help and hope to Indians over a continent-sized area, the Church Missionary Society was being hard pressed to fulfil its many obligations. As yet there was no prospect of the home that had been promised to Henry and the large family still had to "make do" with the temporary storage shed.

"My dream is a home to call my own," Maggie reminded her husband. "No matter how humble it may be."

Both parents could see also that with two Lawrence families, each with grown or near-grown sons, all working on the same project, that of the Indian training school and farm, there would be too much overlapping of duties and too little scope for their own boys, especially the two eldest, Sheridan and Jim.

Whereas fifteen miles upstream, on the long meadow flanking the Peace, was that pole shack which she had glimpsed from the raft and which Henry used for shelter when he supervised the feeding of the cattle being wintered there. Repeatedly Maggie urged, "Why not move our family there and begin farming for ourselves?"

Optimistic Henry agreed to consult with his brother and with the bishop. He and Maggie paid a visit together to the little shack and pasture and together they envisioned the garden and the fields that could be planted on the hay meadows skirting the river. Surrounding these were thickets and woods that could be cleared so much more easily than Ontario's tremendous forests.

Though secretly they may have thought it madness, all concerned gave their consent to the move. Once more the family packed up their oft-shunted possessions and behind oxen trekked along the ice-coated Peace to the new home. Here where, except for his father and his uncle, perhaps no other white man had ever set foot, Sheridan helped to settle them on the ranch that presently he was to make famous.

It was February of 1887, in the depth of one of the bitterest winters within Indian memory. Yet this stout-hearted mother looked happily over the long river flat and her piercing blue eyes expressed her joy as she envisioned the snug ranch-house that they would erect. Afterward she remembered wth a smile the amazement and disbelief of those who thought that only by fur trading could one survive.

"They painted ghastly pictures of the horrors of the starvation that we would face. No one, they predicted, could possibly make a success of farming so very far north."

As from a sowing of Cadmus' teeth, in record time log house, and then outbuildings, sprang up. For the remainder of the winter still their staple diet, like that of the Scott family, centred about potatoes and crushed barley. Soon the incredibly long hours of spring sunshine melted the snows and dried the river flats, and Henry and Sheridan, ploughing with an ox and two cows, cultivated a thirty-acre stretch which they hand-sowed to barley, a tiny plot on which they tested some precious wheat seed given to them by the bishop, and a sizeable plot set aside for kitchen garden and potatoes.

On a warm slope that basked in the slanting rays of the sun Maggie planted corn and cucumber, and vegetable marrow and pumpkin. The speed with which she produced early radishes and lettuce for the table began to convince the scoffers that at least vegetables might flourish in this land.

Down at the mission-house, too, young Juey shared with her mother in the delights of planting and of watching seedlings spring up with the speed of Jack's beanstalk. To supply her garden with seeds, Anna had a special bonanza, a hermetically sealed box containing a great variety both of vegetables and of flowers that Sutton's big seed-house in Britain furnished free, a gesture which they repeated to missions all over the world. From the box she selected radishes and lettuce and onions, tomatoes and cabbage and cauliflower, carrots and beets and parsnips, green and yellow beans and peas, as well as an interesting range of flowers.

When, by the month of June, twenty hours of sunlight blanketed in warmth the fertile alluvial soil, the plants in their eagerness seemed to leap toward the sky.

"Mother, I can see the garden grow," Juey assured Anna, and the latter could not but believe her.

With the vigor of young creatures making a very first display of their strength and capability, all of the new gardens throve. Surely, so it seemed to the newcomers, the dire predictions of those who shook their heads at the madness of white people attempting to live off this far northern land must be utterly wrong.

There was one severe drawback. This land of bush and of water, of forest and of lake, of gurgling creek pouring into the tributaries of the Peace or into the Peace itself, suddenly became alive with myriads of mosquitoes and black flies. Human beings sought protection with smudges and mosquito bars; Juey learned even to stuff paper inside her stockings; Sheridan and the others working outdoors draped their necks with handkerchief and netting over their caps. In spite of the smudges, the animals were sometimes driven near to madness; hovering close to the smoke, they dared not leave to search for food. Finally the Rev. Malcolm shut his black cow in the barn to protect her from the mosquitoes which settled upon her in clouds and he set the children to pulling fresh grass for her.

At midsummer in this year of 1887 came a second damper to the enthusiasm of the newcomers. Following several days of cold wind and driving rain, which brought blessed respite from the plague of insects, came clearing skies and dropping temperatures. One night the mercury sank below the freezing point; next morning the barley seemed unharmed but the tender garden crops and all the potatoes were blackened by frost. Most of the plants recovered; yet the potatoes yielded only a few tiny tubers. From Henry Lawrence's extra-large plot the family filled two small sacks, the largest no bigger than a hen's egg.

"We tasted none ourselves," said Maggie. "All of these we had to save for seed."

For Anna Scott the damage done to her garden was cancelled by the joy of at last receiving the family freight. By a trader's raft down the Peace came her trunks stuffed with bedding and books and clothing, the two splendid Carron stoves one of which would take the place of the mud fireplace, and her organ and the green carpet. There were groceries too, some water damaged but still usable; as she drank from moulded tea leaves she tried to show the children an unperturbed expression that would reflect the proper missionary spirit.

Presently, for Anna, there was also the joy of renewing her acquaintance with her first friend in Canada, Julia Young, the wife of the bishop, with whom she had made her home when she had arrived as a missionary helper from England some years before. There was the pleasure too of reversing roles, for now she could introduce Mrs. Young, her daughter's godmother, to all the varied delights of this new land.

A few yards east of the mission-house Lydia Lawrence's brother Mr. Kneeland, assisted by Sheridan, had been hurrying to erect a home for the bishop and his family. When the attractive newcomer and her two youngest children, Walter and Irene—a toddler also named for the Peace—disembarked from the down-river raft, the men had completed the lower storey only. Happily she took possession of these quarters and she agreed with Anna Scott that here seemed to unfold before their eyes a kind of paradise. Surely this magnificent setting with the shimmering waters of the wide-breasted Peace reflecting the delphinium clarity of the sky, suggested a gentle Eden that could never conspire against the humans who sought it out for a homeland.

"Wait till you see the sun setting over the water," added Anna. "I've never known anything more beautiful."

As the bustling summer passed, the radiant colors of the sunset dancing on the limpid waters began to be rivalled by the splendor of the autumn coloring of the foliage. Then, to Julia Young and all, this land of the Peace seemed indeed a paradise of never-ending and golden richness, a kind of dream-world lifted both in actuality and in spirit far from the commonplace pulse of mankind.

Presently there came, with dropping leaves, swiftly dropping temperatures, and more and more frost but no snow. Gradually the smiling river grew silent, hushed and compressed under a steadily thickening weight of ice. At last came snow and more snow, snow which lingered late into the following April.

Suddenly, early in May of 1888, there came an amazing rise in temperature. The melting snow rapidly turned tiny creeks and tributaries into raging streams. Torrents of water boiled into the gigantic basin of the Peace, flooding above the still-solidly entrenched and extra-deep ice pan.

Finally there rose the din of grinding and of crashing ice. All across the broad channel of the river, enormous chunks of ice began to rise through the surface water. Still the mercury continued to soar and still more water continued to race into the swelling basin of the Peace.

Anxiously the Rev. Malcolm Scott looked over the mile-wide spate of still-rising water and he thought of Noah's predicament. In his ears sounded an ominous crackling and growling as more and more ice pans became freed from their winter moorings. Was the friendly Peace becoming a foe that was arming to drive them from the land?

It was Saturday evening, and with the other men he stepped to the river's brink for still another check.

"If this keeps up much longer," he remarked to Bishop Young, "we'll have a flood for sure. The ice must be jamming somewhere downstream. If it doesn't give way, there won't be many out for service tomorrow."

Next morning, the water was still rising and the Indians reported a huge jam twenty-five miles downstream at Big Island. "Let's hope it breaks this morning," remarked Malcolm as his family assembled as usual for prayers and for breakfast.

Anna turned to her daughter. "Juey, would you please get me a pail of water."

The girl followed the narrow foot-path northwest a hundred feet. Here she usually clambered fifteen feet down the bush-edged bank and walked over the gravel to the river's edge to dip her pail. Today this wasn't necessary.

"I just stood on the top of the bank," she shouted breathlessly as she stepped indoors again. "And I filled my pail. I got my feet wet, too."

Even as she exclaimed, she could hear water beginning to pour into the cellar beneath them. She could also hear the terrified mewing of the white cat imprisoned there. She ran, lifted the cellar door, and let the frantic animal escape. Her father hurried down the cellar steps to rescue precious potatoes saved for seed, as well as other perishables. He hoisted what he could to the upstairs rooms and then the rushed over to the bishop's house.

"The water's still rising," he reported to Bishop Young. "Shall we hold service as usual?"

The bishop appeared unruffled. "Yes, I think we should."

Malcolm looked over toward the rampaging river that was quite definitely now not friend but armed enemy. The whole basin was become like an ocean, an ocean afloat with the menace of bobbing icebergs. Already on the long island before the mission only the upper halves of the tall trees were visible. The river had become a great battlefield studded with battering rams of ice that, with a spray of dust that furled upward like smoke, was toppling tree after tree into the water.

With worry in his heart Malcolm took stock of the situation. Water was already lapping about the feet of the shrubs edging the bank and the roadway that paralleled the river. He glanced downstream toward the Irene Training School where signs of preparation to meet the flood were in evidence.

"I see E. J.'s already moving his cows back from the river," he reported to the bishop.

It was drawing close to the eleven o'clock hour for morning service. "We must pray to the Almighty to help us," insisted the tall bishop.

The Rev. Malcolm's faith in the Lord was great. But his years of pioneering in the Red River Colony in Manitoba dictated caution.

"All right, Bishop. You pray, and I'll watch."

A small knot of people had gathered, Anna and the children among them. Dutifully they turned their eyes from the menacing waters and followed their bishop into the tiny church. With dignity, in the deep mellow voice that Juey loved, the bishop began to read the lines of the morning service. "Dearly beloved brethren, we are gathered in sundry places . . . ."

He had just begun to recite the stately lines of the Te Deum when his red-bearded priest stepped forward.

"Excuse me, Bishop. It's coming fast. We'd better put the books up on the pulpit."

There was a scramble to save what could be saved. Malcolm and the bishop lifted the precious organ and placed it across two of the pews that Mr. Garrioch had fashioned.

Then Malcolm and Burton rushed back to the house to rescue precious possessions there. Anna was beginning to suffer from rheumatism that made moving about difficult for her. Now she hobbled slowly to help where she could.

Bishop Young's home was a few yards further removed from the river's brink and it was fronted by a small grove of balm of Gilead which might help to protect it from the flood.

"You'd better come to our house," Julia Young called to Anna as every one dispersed to look to their belongings.

In spite of her rheumatism Anna insisted that she could manage. "If we must move," she protested to Malcolm, "let's camp out, by ourselves."

So Malcolm and Burton loaded up a wagon with bedding and clothing and the tent and provisions and cooking utensils. Juey slushed through the water, fetching and carrying, and she could see the E. J. Lawrence family down at the Training school similarly scrambling to load a wagon. Hitching up a team of oxen, her father drove his family to the safety of a low hill about a half mile back from the river.

Here the children recalled with pleasure the camping routine of two years before and eagerly they shared in the fun of setting up the lovely outdoors playhouse, the veteran tent in which once again they were going to enjoy a night's sleep.

After a noon meal in the May sunshine, Malcolm and Burton drove back, to find the water beginning to wash at the doorstep of the home. Everything small enough they hoisted up into the second storey, and Anna's organ they lifted onto the home-made table. Sacks of barley, more precious than Midas' gold, they hefted into the loft of the little log barn. They caught the squawking Rhode Island Reds and shoved them into the same prison.

Then, whipping the oxen to encourage speed, the men fled the watery desolation. The Young family, so the cheerful bishop assured Malcolm, would be quite safe. If the water rose above the ground-floor level of their home, they planned to take refuge above in the unfinished attic. On the hill-top his own family seemed equally unworried; Anna sat resting and reading, and the children, delighted to find themselves again in the midst of relaxed camp life where Mother's strict rules were less rigidly enforced, frisked gaily round about the tent playing hide-and-seek.

Next morning they awoke to find sunshine streaming onto their tent and streaking below them onto a land awash with a vast ice-dotted ocean of swirling water.

Today was the ninth of May, 1888. In a fortnight and a day they would be celebrating the birthday of the renowned queen, Victoria.

English-born Anna reminded her family of this fact. "So let us call our camping spot Victoria Hill," she proposed.

Delightedly the children agreed that this was a well-chosen name.

After prayers and breakfast, the men paddled by dugout back to the buildings. Dodging round about the grey-white ice cakes, they found themselves poling the canoe right over the tops of fences that surrounded house and barn. Apparently the buildings were still intact on their footings. Wading into the barn, they climbed to the loft and fed some barley to the imprisoned hens. Of the two pigs Jack and Jill they could find no trace.

By afternoon, a sudden heightening and deepening of the sounds of moving water, of crashing ice and jamming debris told Malcolm that the mammoth blockade down stream had at last given way. With a roar the imprisoned waters began to recede, to resume their pelting way toward Lake Athabasca and onward through the channels of the Slave and the Mackenzie rivers to join their mother waters in the Arctic ocean.

Back at his home, Malcolm hurried to salvage what he could. Water had poured into the house to a height of about four feet, floating the table on which they had placed Anna's organ and toppling it into the water. By bucket brigade he and Burton dipped barrels of water from the cellar; then down there they set up a small stove to assist in the drying-out process.

One of the worst features of the flood was that it had carried away all of the huge pile of firewood, a whole winter's accumulation of sawing and chopping. From higher ground they gleaned dry kindling and they chopped up floating fence rails to provide fuel. Rolling up their sleeves, from the floors they scrubbed away the inch or more of muddy silt that the water had left behind as it retreated. Next, while Burton went to fetch the family home, Malcolm whipped up fresh biscuits for the evening meal.

"Father, where's our cat? Where's Snowy?" This was Juey's first concern as with Osborne she raced back indoors. They had worried a great deal about the fate of their pet, the sole survivor of the pair of tiny kittens that they had cuddled and cared for all the way from Winnipeg.

"Look upstairs," suggested Malcolm.

Asleep on the bed they found him, a ball of contented white wool.

"Put him down cellar, Juey," commanded her father. "Until after supper. And both of you get busy and help me."

Immediately supper was over, they rushed to the trap door to release the cat from the cellar.

"Look at him," shrieked the boy. "He's all purple."

"Listen," Juey shouted almost at the same moment as she stood at the open cellar doorway. "It's the water again."

Malcolm looked and listened. Both children's statements were true. The white cat was purple, smeared with black currant jam. He got scant attention, however, for from the opened trap door rose again the ominous sound of rushing water. Again it was rising fast and, in his feverish scramble to escape, the cat had jumped onto a large keg of Anna's jam. The flood water had floated from it the protective covering of tallow.

This time the water streamed in faster than before. Obviously the ice downstream had jammed again. Even while the family once more took time to grab up bedding and clothing, again it was already swirling at the doorstep.

Now Malcolm decided to accept the Youngs' offer of hospitality. During the previous night the bishop's family had taken refuge in the unfinished upper storey of their home, which had remained firm on its foundations, and there was space there for all of them to share these quarters.

Like some primeval monster, the flood was advancing upon them and threatening once again to suck them all up into its great mouth. While each moment was becoming precious, help arrived in the persons of Mr. Melrose and Mr. Kneeland.

"You see to your things," they told Malcolm. "We'll look after your family."

While their father and Burton hustled movables back upstairs, the children thrust clothing into a valise and Anna hobbled about to rescue what she could.

"Come on, Mrs. Scott," urged the men. "You'd better leave."

They formed a chair of their crossed hands and on it they carried Anna out of the house and through the water.

"Take off your shoes and stockings and carry them," she directed Juey and Osborne.

The two children obeyed. To this point for them the flood had been a kind of game. Sobbing now in terror, they slushed behind the men. Underneath the floating field were prickly stubble points and hummocks of slimy mud. And dotted as it was with gigantic ice chunks, the water was cold, achingly cold.

Up an outside ladder they climbed next, to enter through a small window opening onto the upper floor of the bishop's home. Here between rafters sawdust had been filled to serve as insulation; over this their hospitable hostess spread blankets to take the place of flooring.

Looking anxious for once above his cheery red beard, their father arrived and the men consulted together. Judging by the speed of its onslaught, this second attack by the enemy threatened to be more destructive than the first.

Would this home, like Noah's ark, withstand the tremendous pressure of the rising water? Even though it had withstood the previous night's onslaught, if a mightier battering ram of combined water and ice flung themselves against it, what would become of them? If it were swept from its footings out into the great central tide of water, they might all be trapped and drowned. Should they, like the E. J. Lawrence family, have taken to the hills behind?"

"We must put our trust in God," insisted the bishop.

"Amen," echoed Malcolm. They decided to remain within the comparative comfort of their eyrie.

In the warm sunlight of the May evening, the setting rays seemed to jeer at the human beings as they twinkled upon the churning wilderness of water and the drunken cakes of ice that menaced the puny dwellings of the settlement. From time to time Juey squeezed near the small look-out window and her eyes sought out the forlorn animals below.

Against a ridge of higher ground an assortment of firewood and fence rails had been swept into a kind of rough platform. To this crude shelter Malcolm had waded, carrying the brindle cow's young calf. Clambering half way up this peninsula of logs, the mother had taken refuge near her calf. Inevitably Juey's eyes turned to her as she stood there, a picture of the most hopeless dejection. Now and then she mooed mournfully and the sound echoed despairingly above the scene of devastation.

Equally forlorn stood Jill, the white sow who at the creek bed by Peace River Crossing had shown disdain of water and wild terrain.

"Oingh, oingh," she grunted pitifully as she crouched on the door sill of the abandoned home.

Already her litter of piglets had been swept away, and now, pigs of all animals being most poorly endowed as swimmers, it appeared that any moment might be her last.

An enormous ice-cake charged toward the small church. The watchers held their breath, expecting to see it ram into the side-wall of the building that had been Mr. Garrioch's special pride. Miraculously the battering ram stopped, only feet away.

Dusk began to creep over the scene of desolation. The two mothers tucked their children under blankets at one end of the attic. The men lighted candles, detailing Burton to keep watch on the still-rising water. Down the outside ladder he descended part way, to measure with a long pole the depth of the water.

Up he climbed back, calling to the bishop through the open window in his broad English accent, "It's one third of a fathom, sir!" Presently he clambered down again, and this time he shouted, "It's a 'arf fathom, sir!" Juey was too excited to sleep and she lay listening to his reports. As his performance was repeated, she giggled a little. She was vaguely aware that Burton's British ways were somewhat amusing.

At the far end of the loft away from the drowsing children by turns the grown-ups prayed and sang.

Often, afterward, Juey repeated, "I'll never forget that scene in that unfinished upstairs of the bishop's house,—the meagre candle light, and Burton making his queer nautical reports, and the Bishop and Mrs. Young and Father and Mother and all, singing hymns through the night and praying to ask God, if it was His will, to save us from the water."

In her memory was etched too, the roar of the waters and the crashing of the ice and the snapping off of the trees with reports that sounded like the boom of artillery, all reminding the prisoners of their plight. Added to these sounds were the forlorn bawling of the frightened cow and the weird calls of screech owls and the haunting cry of loons.

Tearfully little Osborne pleaded, "Mother, why doesn't God make the loons be quiet?"

Toward morning the water again began to recede. With another of his "fathoms-deep" reports, Burton brought the joyful news. Down river, the stubborn jam had collapsed a second time. Presently the men ventured forth to begin once more the gigantic task of clean-up and of salvage.

As the water sucked away, it left behind a slimy muck of silt and fallen trees and strewn logs and wrecked fences and buildings. Fortunately the exteriors not only of the bishop's house and the church but also of Juey's home and the Irene Training school-house remained intact. All of the barns, the small outbuildings, the fences, the woodpiles, symbols of months of toil in a land where mechanical aids were few and primitive, had disintegrated or been swept down

stream. Even the foundations of E. J.'s saw-mill shifted but
the big "boiler" that was beginning to spell a new way of
life had resisted the attack of the enemy. Flood-washed but
essentially unharmed, it stood defiant amidst imposing sou-
venirs of the onslaught. These were enormous ice pans
stranded by the retreating water. With chill faces they
towered over what gradually became again the site of garden
and of field and pasture.

Beside the church cowered the gigantic berg that had
threatened to smash it to splinters, and from its dwindling
bulk Malcolm chopped gleaming chunks to fill the water
barrels. Now while the Peace, their usual source of supply,
was roiled and unfit for use, like a kind of atonement this
melted ice from the "berg" provided drinking water that
was cool and fresh and lovely.

Before plunging too deeply into the work of rebuilding,
Bishop Young and the other men consulted with the Indians.
Never before in living memory, their native neighbors assured
them, had the Peace hurled such havoc upon them; never
before had a flood of such proportions occurred.

Unlike Noah, they could make no everlasting covenant
with God that the waters would not come again; their rainbow of hope lay only in these words of the Indians. Prayer-
fully they began to restore and to rebuild.

While Malcolm hustled with all the work at hand and
while his red beard became a restless will-o-the-wisp of flame
about the mission, he worried about the fate of the venture-
some family that was attempting to establish a ranch fifteen
miles upstream. Had they survived the terrific onslaught
of the waters of the Peace?

CHAPTER 9

On that fateful Sunday morning at the isolated home which the children christened The Riverside Ranche, Henry Lawrence and young Sheridan had risen early to do the chores. Before going into the house for breakfast, Henry stopped to admire the exquisite tiers of blue-lighted ice that were peering up over the bank of the Peace.

"Come and see the spectacle," he called to Maggie.

Maggie stepped out to gaze across the field to the channel of the Peace, about two hundred and fifty yards distant. Strange shapes shouldered above the bush-edged bank, shapes that were glowingly luminous in the morning sunshine.

"Thank goodness!" she exclaimed as she listened to the crunching, punishing sounds of moving ice. "The river's going out at last!"

During prayers Maggie remembered her two lads, sixteen-year-old Jim and ten-year-old Arthur, who were camped upstream another twelve miles at a strip of meadowland which they had named Prairie Point and where the boys were now pasturing the main herd of cattle. Then, following breakfast, the family walked over to the river's edge to get a close-up view of the spectacle.

For a moment they gaped at the amazing shapes and the awesome bulk of grinding ice being buffeted about by the swelling force of water.

Suddenly their awe and admiration turned to alarm. Already the crashing mass was beginning to overflow above the bank. Near-by stood the treasured mower that had accompanied them on the long trek in. To save it and other possessions more precious here than a Midas' sack of gold, they pelted back to house and barn.

With a lighted lantern Minnie and Harry ran downstairs to sack the potatoes, Grace and Isaac and Jack hustled bedding and clothing out of doors and up the hillside at the back to a point about three hundred feet distant, Sheridan and his father whipped a team of oxen through invading water to rescue the mower, and Maggie grabbed up provisions and kitchen equipment.

Next, Henry rushed to try to weigh down the enormous wood-pile that represented a whole winter's work and Sheridan ran down cellar to heft up the sacked potatoes so that his brothers and sisters could drag them up the hillside.

"By the time I had twelve sacks up, the water was all around the house," Sheridan wrote in his diary. "Then it was coming in the door, and I had to move more quickly."

Leaving their brother to rescue what he could from the home, the children flew to drive the cows and pigs to higher land and to entice the squawking hens to the safety of the hill. Somehow, while Maggie helped to supervise the flight, she contrived to keep calm. She was expecting another child within weeks and she was sick with worry over the fate of the two absent lads, Jim and Arthur. Already, as the youngsters pursued the terrified animals, they were wading in water up to their knees and now both parents joined in ordering them up the hillside to safety.

Resting a moment in her climb, Maggie turned to watch Sheridan's long legs wading toward his new dug-out. Only yesterday he had finished carving it in readiness for the river's springtime break-up and now she guessed that her resourceful oldest son was going to put it to good use.

Paddling through the open doorway into the log home, Sheridan loaded the canoe with dishes, utensils and provisions from his mother's shelves. He hurried this load to the rise of land behind; then he poled his craft back and into the kitchen for a second load. This time he almost stayed too long.

Now the water was so high that he had only to reach out to sweep the stuff from the topmost shelves. Hastily he steered for the doorway and crouched his lanky frame low to get clear, for already the water was lapping within two feet of the top of the door.

He paddled clear and watched for a few minutes. There was no hope of rescuing anything further; the water and ice were swirling upward so fast that the doorway was almost hidden from view; in his diary he recorded that "in just four hours, the water was up to within four inches of the top of the door." Already the huge wood-pile was afloat; chips, stovewood, and the logs so laboriously collected for further building became a part of the surging, foaming ocean of water.

While the boys herded the milk cows and the pigs and the chickens higher up the hillside and the girls helped their mother organize a temporary camp, Sheridan and his father set to work to build a poplar shelter for Maggie.

Below them all now the Peace, doubling its usual bulk, had become a devastating monster two miles in breadth. No matter how much Maggie worried about the fate of Jim and Arthur, it was out of the question to ask their father to try to reach them now. They themselves as well as the absent boys, if they were still alive, were completely isolated from help of any kind. If Henry were to make the attempt at this time, he too might lose his life, leaving his family in still worse straits.

For four days the flood of water filled the meadows and fields below the long ridge of hill. At night Maggie lay awake, gazing at stars that peered at them through the rude shelter. Were the awful prognostications coming true? Was it madness to try to continue farming and ranching here by this Peace that had at first seemed so helpful and friendly and that now seemed intent on destroying them?

At last the water began to recede and Henry decided to attempt to hike over the fifteen miles to Prairie Point to discover the fate of his sons. Leaving Sheridan in charge of the others of the family, he set out on foot. Sloshing through mud and water and slime and bucking deadfall in woods where the trail they had cut was utterly impassable, after several hours he reached the open meadow-land which they had designated as Prairie Point.

Emerging from thick brush, in dismay he gazed at the sweep of natural pasture which had seemed such a providential blessing for a cattle herd and which they had equipped with fences and corrals to control the animals, particularly at night when their herders were sleeping.

There was no sign anywhere of boys or of cattle. There

was no sign of their tent or of their pony, or of the corrals and fences, or of the haystack or the piled logs which they had collected there in readiness for removal to the main ranch buildings. Instead, everywhere gleamed the menacing water that was not yet ready to retreat from the land it had ravished.

For a minute it seemed to Henry that Maggie's worst fears were realized and that all the cattle and both boys had also been swept away. Anxiously he began to scan the upper woods. At last his eye selected an opening through which they might have escaped. As he worked his way toward it, he saw to his joy the tracks of the home-made jumper on which the pony had transported their tenting equipment.

He began to pick his way upward, following the tracks and hallooing at the top of his lungs. Within minutes there was an answering shout. The woods began to echo with a chorus of call and reply; then out of the bush two bedraggled lads came loping to meet him.

On the Sunday morning, they told him, they had been awakened by water soaking into their bedding. By the time they had scrambled into their clothes, a pair of ducks which they had shot the evening before were floating inside the tent. Outside, the cattle were milling about in alarm, for already they were standing in deep water.

The pair had rushed to harness the pony, hitch him to the jumper and heap on it their tent and equipment. With the axe they chopped down rails to set the cattle free. Wading knee-deep in icy water as their brothers and sisters were doing at their home, fleeing for their lives they drove pony and cattle into the wooded upland above. Here they set up camp and kept watch as best they could over the animals.

On his shoulder Henry had carried a knapsack of food. From time to time they interrupted the tale of their escape to wolf down chunks of their mother's baking. "The poor fellows had been practically without food since Sunday," their father told Maggie.

By the following Saturday, the river had retired to its normal channel. Like the little group down stream at the Irene Mission and Training school, Henry and Sheridan and the others plunged into the immense chore of reclaiming and restoring. The lovely hay meadow round about the dank ranch-house was dotted with enormous ice cakes, some of them twenty feet or more in diameter.

"Until they melted, our yard bore the appearance of a graveyard of giant headstones," Maggie noted. "Everywhere was silt and slime."

Indoors, the home-made furnishings which Henry and Sheridan had fashioned, tables that had been cut from tree trunks hewn on one side and attached with wooden pegs to tree-stump legs, benches that likewise were shaped from hewn logs and floors also of hewn logs with mudded cracks, all now had to be scraped and scrubbed to remove layers of stubborn deposit.

Henry Lawrence looked over all the desolation and for once his usual optimism failed him. "Shall we give up?" in despair he asked Maggie.

His wife shook her head and straightened her bulky body. "We simply have to see the game through now. Some way we'll win out."

Fortunately, smiled Maggie afterward in recollection of all the early crises, "though we were both distracted with worry, we seldom had our blue spells together." Her eyes, sapphire-hued as a mountain lake, lighted up. "Henry had such a wonderful way of jollying me."

Each spring and fall, during break-up and freeze-up of the Peace, they suffered a period of complete isolation from their downstream neighbors at the Fort Vermilion settlement on the south bank. Across from the settlement the trading post of the Revillon Freres perched high on the north side. So that they would in future be able to communicate with this latter post and thus would never again be so completely isolated, no matter if the Peace tried its utmost to drive them from its shore, Henry enlisted Sheridan's help in a mammoth cutting job. Through tall stands of poplar and spruce they hewed a road twelve miles overland, clear through to the post on the north bank.

"We were getting experience in frontier life," tersely Sheridan summed up in his diary.

There was no hay left for the animals and no grazing

in the river flats. There was some dry barley, but this must be hoarded for seed. "We did some scheming to bring our cattle through," Sheridan added. Fortunately, farther back from the river were marshes where a lush growth of the native red-top was fairly accessible.

Near at hand, the flood had left behind a two-inch layer of sediment, and the drying-out process was slow. Presently Henry set to work with his twelve-inch breaking plow and his team of ox and cows, and Sheridan paddled his dug-out downstream to help his uncle E. J. with his spring work.

Although the flood's aftermath resulted in late seeding of field and garden, again the growth was heavy, phenomenal in fact because of the enriching silt. This boded well for a lavish harvest; the prospect was especially cheering to Maggie, for on July the third she presented Henry with another mouth to feed, another sturdy son who would one day in return lend him a helping hand. Mrs. Mary Smith, a beloved Métis from Manitoba, attended Maggie and shortly this first white boy born on the lower Peace was christened Wilson by the Rev. Malcolm Scott.

In the little manse by the church, the missionary and his wife Anna had also completed the task of restoration following the flood; though Malcolm took her organ all apart and cleansed it thoroughly, never did it play properly again. Once again Anna established for the children a rigid routine which included school work and reading; each evening she set aside an hour when Juey read aloud to her brother from their modest collection of books. These, stowed in the upper story of the house, had remained undamaged by the flood water.

The summons to this chore Juey answered with pleasure; she was beginning to read voraciously all the volumes which her mother produced for her; in fact, she couldn't remember a time when she hadn't loved to read.

She reached for the current favorite, the tale of the Swiss Family Robinson.

"It's like us," she remarked with the wisdom of the pioneer child. Like the Robinson family, they were all re-establishing themselves from the havoc of waters.

Her father looked up from his work and his blue eyes

crinkled with smile lines. Gently he added, "Perhaps we may be able to profit from their experiences."

Certainly they were all coming to realize that, try as they might, they could not guess what contingencies the future might bring.

CHAPTER 10

For the young Sheridan, this year of 1888 was to enrich his experience in more unusual ways. And for serious-minded Juey, there were new ways of frolicking and new tasks to cram her days.

Leaping and dancing in the cool spring night, the aurora joined Juey and Osborne in their outdoor play. In its rich and restless rainbow of coloring, it transcended anything they had ever seen. It was like a troupe of dancers hurling multi-colored scarves across the sky and then themselves whirling, now near, now far, in unison with the sinuous movements of these floating fabrics.

In matching mood Juey and Osborne accepted the aurora as a playmate. They skipped about, tripping and leaping in time with the aurora's dancing. They listened to the faint swishing sound it seemed to make as it danced, a sound that was like a fairy's whistle or the fine rustle of skirts brushing the sky.

Finally gleaming-eyed natives visiting the Indian hall of an evening brought an end to their delight.

"No, no," they shuddered in protest to the Rev. Malcolm, and they tried to show him why it was wrong for the children to join in the dancing. "Spirits of dead dancing," they explained in muted voices. "They will pick up children, snatch them away."

Malcolm passed the word along to his children. "When the aurora is dancing, the Indians say that you should keep very still. They say also that you should keep your hand over your mouth and whisper only."

In their turn the pair protested. Dancing to the aurora was great sport. Malcolm compromised.

"All right," he smiled. "But no dancing when there are Indians about."

Whenever the northern lights made their outdoor world leaping and colorful, they continued to dance. With childlike hardness, they defied the spirits to snatch them away.

Sometimes, Juey became aware, she came off second best in this matter of respecting Indian custom and feeling. One morning just as she had finished scrubbing the kitchen floor for her mother, an elderly visitor shadowed the doorway. With his smudging moccasins he was about to step onto the still-damp boards. With one leap, Juey slammed the door in his face and fastened the wooden button.

Outside, the man scolded angrily. By this time the girl understood the dialects sufficiently to know that he was threatening her with "bad medicine."

A few days later, when she was burning with the fever of erysipelas, her puzzled father questioned her. A party of natives had recently spent some time in the Indian hall.

"Are you sure you didn't accept anything from them?"

"No, Father. They offered me gum but I wouldn't take that." The gum, from the fragrant spruce, was always pre-chewed, and the children had been warned always to scoop their own supply fresh from a tree.

Finally Juey confessed how she had offended the old man who threatened her with "bad medicine."

Like her parents and the Indians who came and went, Juey soon became proficient in a number of dialects. "Don't you think that the Cree tongue is the most musical?" her father asked the family as they practised speaking the Indian words aloud. "It reminds me of what I've heard of the spoken Welsh."

Even within the Cree tribe Malcolm found distinctions in pronunciation. For an example he quoted the word "house" which was pronounced "was-kia-gun" among the northerly Crees and was "was-kia-kun" by those dwelling in the Lesser Slave lake area. His own name in Cree, "Teeny-Muttiga-Mututully," became in the Beaver tongue "Te-Mutagoma-Tully."

While among themselves, he also discovered, the Beavers and the Slaveys, the Chipewyans and the Crees appeared fully to understand each other's speech, there were some sharp differences in word meanings in the various tongues. "Utlas," bread or bread of life in the Beaver dialect, meant in the Cree simply "ash." The way of speech of the former dialect was noticeably more guttural than that of the Crees.

Not only by tongue did Juey and Sheridan and their families learn to distinguish the peoples among whom they lived. Those tribes living to the west and the northwest, the Beavers, the Slaveys and the Chipewyans, tended to have broad almost bridgeless noses, with the bridge seeming to be completely absent in the young babies. Generally the Crees were taller and finer-featured than their brothers across the Peace. They were too, the Rev. Malcolm decided, often sunnier in temperament. An example of the stolid, almost sullen manner to be found sometimes among the Beavers was evidenced in a small girl whom he brought home to be treated by Anna and to be taught by Juey.

This motherless nameless waif was an abject picture of neglect. Anna cleansed her skin and her matted black hair and she treated her scrofulous sores with generous applications of ointment. Malcolm christened her Mary and gradually, as she became an accepted member of the family, Anna and Juey attempted to teach her something of the white woman's domestic chores. They were encouraged in this by the way in which Louisa, the broken-hearted Cree girl who in that first winter of semi-starvation was accused of cannibalism, had responded to loving care and teaching, and who had been sent on by Malcolm to make a new life for herself at St. Peter's mission on Lesser Slave lake.

"Go out now to the garden, Mary," directed Anna in the English tongue which she knew the Beaver child now understood. "Juey will show you where to weed."

In the garden as in the fields, a luxurious growth was following the flooding. Already Juey had coached the girl in the back-bending task of freeing the rows of lusty young vegetables from the equally lusty weeds. She pulled a few to show Mary where to carry on and returned indoors to do the sums which her mother had set for her.

Presently they looked out. Statue-still, Mary stood in the garden in the spot where Juey had left her. Again Juey went out to stoop and to set an example. Still the Beaver girl remained motionless and rooted to the spot, thus showing them in her sullen rebellious way that weeding was utterly distasteful to her.

Finally Anna herself gently but firmly indicated to her the plot where she must weed. When the child saw that there was absolutely no alternative for her, she knelt and busied herself with what to her was a foreign and hateful chore.

"Poor little Mary," sighed Anna. "She makes life so hard for herself."

For Malcolm, the red-bearded praying man, she was more tractable. For him she had a special feeling of devotion that was touching in the extreme and when he was absent on a visit to some far-flung camp she spent many patient hours by the river's edge watching for his return. At last she spotted his dug-out approaching. Racing up to the manse, she shouted, "Mrs. Scott! Mrs. Scott!" For once her smoky eyes lit with excitement and in a vivid English idiom that was all her own she cried out, "I see something red and shining like fire coming up the river. It must be Mr. Scott."

Thus did she single out the man whose resplendent beard was his one vanity.

Over at the Irene Training school Lydia Lawrence set aside five hours each day for the teaching of "school" and religion to her Indian pupils and her own children. Since her day was already so full, Anna Scott decided to take charge herself of the schooling of Juey and Osborne. Anna had been a governess in England and an instructor at the Miss Davis School which became the nucleus for the St. John's Ladies College in Winnipeg; now her daughter began to learn the role of monitor-pupil-teacher. Except for reading, to Juey's notion, school was a boring business; even more boring was the chore which her mother set her, whenever there were Indian children about, of teaching them syllabics.

Under her mother's stern eye, with pencil or charcoal Juey formed a letter-like syllable. Painfully a native boy

90

or girl strove to mimic her motions and to repeat after her the dull sounds, "bay, pay, say . . . ."

When the young blonde teacher and the black-haired brunette pupils alike began to fidget, Anna announced a recess. Then Juey and all scampered outdoors, plunging toward the river bank, their favorite stamping-ground. When she grew tired of the games, she searched out special stones on the edge of the great river or she sought in the low brush for the beautiful wild flowers or the nests of small birds.

"Don't let your breath reach the eggs," the Rev. Malcolm warned when the children came running with word of a newly discovered nest. "Or the mother bird will not come back to them."

Back of the strips of meadow and garden and field that hugged the river's edge were deeper woods where Juey hunted other wild flowers that her mother named for her. Here were the pendulous blue borage and the columbine, the shell-like pink twin-flower, the waxy wintergreen and many another exquisite blossom that made the shadowy woods a place of excitement.

Fringing these woods near the Irene Training school was a lush patch of greenery where Fennie Lawrence, E. J. and Lydia's younger son, was frequently sent to herd the hungry pigs. Bishop Young's children were younger than Juey; Fennie, a year older, made an ideal playmate.

"Come and play with us," the girl shouted to him.

When Fennie explained that he couldn't leave the pigs, the determined miss summoned Osborne to help. Dragging lengths of pole and small dead trees, the three children corraled his charges in a small enclosure. Presently the pigs, quite forgotten by the young people, escaped from their improvised pen; soon all available adults felt themselves obliged to join in the search for and round-up of the precious porkers; and Fennie was punished accordingly for his dereliction of duty.

Within weeks after the flood, so astounding was the fresh growth that shot up everywhere that the region became again an Eden of loveliness. At the same time for some of the junior residents who revelled in its delights there hung over it the shadow of an ogre. This monster's name was Going-Out-to-School, and somehow the Scott children sensed that they too were not safe from its threat. Now, as soon as the roiled waters of the Peace were safe for canoe travel, this ogre grabbed up Fennie's seventeen-year-old sister Susie and his fourteen-year-old brother Fred. It was arranged that Sheridan should come and take charge of the outdoor work while E. J. made the long journey outside to take his son and daughter out to school.

Meanwhile Sheridan found the opportunity to add to his river lore, for his uncle also asked him to accompany the trio as far as Peace River Crossing. Wide-eyed, all the younger children including a number of Lydia's native charges, gathered to watch while the youth stowed baggage and camping equipment and provisions into the long narrow dug-out and courageous Lydia bade her children good-bye.

By turns tracking and poling, the party fought their way up-stream over the three hundred sinuous miles to Peace River Crossing. E. J. suffered from pains in his arms, so where the river shore was passable on foot he tracked the canoe with the aid of a heavy rope. Then, when paddling or poling became necessary, Sheridan took over; guided by his uncle's teaching, he soon became adept at propelling the craft against the current. Fortunately, in spite of the great masses of debris that the break-up and flood had spewed into the water, now the main channel was free of obstructing tree-trunk and rock and earth slides. Within ten days they reached the Crossing.

Sheridan saw his uncle and his cousins safely on the next lap of the journey, which was by freighter's cart over the portage to Lesser Slave lake, thence by boat to Athabasca Landing, by wagon to Edmonton, by stage to Calgary, and finally by rail to Chicago where E. J. planned to place his children in school under the watchful eye of relations.

Then, mightily pleased with his new-found skill on the river, Sheridan made full use of its powerful spring-time current to speed his dug-out home again.

So well had his uncle instructed him in the use of the pole, he reported with enthusiasm, that before the up-stream journey was over his uncle had permitted him to pole all the time.

"Uncle E. J. was good with the pole. But with his arms bothering him, I would do more poling and he would do tracking. I didn't care for the tracking; since we could make better time by poling, we finally quit tracking altogether.

"I became real good with the pole," he bragged. He added in the confident tone of a veteran river-man, "It's the only way to get along with a canoe going up-stream in swift waters."

Sheridan described to the Rev. Malcolm, who was helping to lay plans for a synod meeting, how Bishop Young narrowly missed being able to attend. Near the Crossing, where the youth had met them, he and Burton had just had a narrow escape from death.

Burton had been standing in the bow of their canoe, poling it up-stream, while the bishop paddled in the rear. Suddenly the canoe shot into a swift eddy. In the violent lurch, Burton lost his balance, tumbling into the river and upsetting both bishop and canoe. In spite of the high water and the mighty current, both men succeeded in reaching shore.

Then, Sheridan related, Burton had sprinted down-stream trying to overtake the runaway canoe. Some four miles down he spotted it, its progress in mid-stream temporarily checked by floating debris. In haste, using his moccasin strings, he tied two logs together at one end. Straddling these to serve as a tiny makeshift craft and poling with a stick, the plucky Englishman manoeuvred himself into the racing current and retrieved the canoe.

"They were sure lucky to be alive," summed up Sheridan.

With varied feelings Juey and her parents recalled some of Burton's other exploits in the Canadian wilds. Thankful for the safety of both men, while Sheridan hustled to complete the seeding of his uncle's fields, the Scott family prepared for the synod at which the bishop would preside.

Twelve years earlier, at Fort Simpson on the Mackenzie river, Bishop Bompas had held the first synod or council meeting of the diocese. Presently, in this summer of 1888, the next diocesan synod got under way. At its meetings in St. Luke's "pro-cathedral" here at Fort Vermilion there were present, with Bishop Young and Rev. Malcolm Scott, Archdeacon Reeve from Chipewyan on Lake Athabasca, Rev. A. C. Garrioch from Dunvegan on the Peace, and Rev. George Holmes from St. Peter's mission on Lesser Slave lake.

"Ni-la oo-shoo-di," smiled Rev. Mr. Garrioch, the expert on the Beaver tongue, when, on meeting Malcolm's family, he held out his hand to Juey.

Understanding that these words in Beaver meant "shake hands," she responded accordingly. The gentle clergyman, who had set up the Anglican mission at Dunvegan just sixty years after his grandfather, Factor Colin Campbell, had re-opened the trading post there, had harrowing tales to tell of the sufferings there of the Beaver Indians, whose "hard lot" he sought to ameliorate. In the grim winter of 1886-87, he and his wife had shared their meagre supplies with the sick and starving, themselves sometimes dining on snowbirds. Soon Juey was exchanging "hunting" experiences with their friendly visitor, relating to him how she tried her luck with a bent pin baited with mouse-flesh as she fished at the water's edge and how Osborne and she too snared snowbirds to vary that winter's diet.

This matter of diet became a recurring theme of the synod, following close as it did upon the extreme suffering in that winter and spring of 1886-87 when measles and respiratory diseases had combined with shortage of food to empty many lodges and tents. Only by the growing of such crops as barley and potatoes and by the teaching of agricultural methods, the churchmen believed, could future starvation among the Indians be curbed. Sometimes there might be killing frosts; these, they believed, like the tremendous flood of the past springtime, were exceptional.

To demonstrate the possibilities of wheat-growing, Malcolm showed the visitors his patch of tremulous blue-green crop. In spite of the lateness, because of the flood, of this year's planting, it had put forth already tall shot blades with a speed that promised to defy the fall frosts and that would have been unbelievable back in Manitoba or Ontario. Partly because of the sediment left in the wake of the flood, the forty acres of barley which Sheridan planted on the Irene mission field also foretold of a bumper crop. Malcolm looked over the small patch which, in his uncle's absence, the youth had seeded to wheat and he thought of that heated debate in which E. J. had led the negative. Like a Cadmus crop this wheat too was springing tall and lusty, as if in defiance of the Roman-nosed schoolmaster.

Upstream at Dunvegan, Mr. Garrioch reported, he also had been successful in bringing wheat to maturity; nearby at the Shaftsbury mission his neighbor, Rev. J. Gough Brick, had tried his hand at wheat-growing and already was bringing notable credit to the Church of England missionary enterprise with his horticultural undertakings.

These experimental beginnings, Bishop Young forecast, boded well for the future carrying out of God's work in this land, and indeed boded well for the development of the whole area as a future home for the white man.

"It is very improbable,' he added in his prophetic address to the synod, "that the large extent of cultivable land . . . will keep this country sealed against the steady output of immigrants not only from England and Europe but from the eastern provinces of Canada herself."

Infusing the synod meeting with enthusiasm and with optimism, the tall forward-looking bishop at the same time directed the shaping of a special memorandum regarding the plight of the Indians. In this, which he caused to be forwarded to the Minister of the Interior at Ottawa, he called attention to the manner in which numbers of these native peoples were being reduced "by pestilence, starvation, and cannibalism."

Dispersing from the synod which, in Mr. Garrioch's words, "strengthened our faith, our courage and our sympathy," with rekindled zeal the missionaries hastened on to their program of visiting all of the summer camps accessible by water.

En route up-stream to Dunvegan, Mr. Garrioch paid a visit to the home of Sheridan's parents at The Riverside Ranche and to their enterprise and hospitality he paid tribute in his diary. He found the ranch "a splendid example of how a resourceful pioneer may build himself and his family a comfortable home with no other tools beside an axe and a hammer, and who by a little ingenuity in the use of a few other simple appliances may obtain from the soil a supply of food both palatable and substantial."

95

Before the Rev. Malcolm poled his canoe once again into the broad channel of the Peace, he conducted a church service that was preceded by food laid out in the Indian hall. This simple meal Anna always proffered to all who had journeyed a distance. Juey flipped sputtering pancakes when bannocks ran short; upon the floor of the hall she arranged pieces of clean sacking to serve for tablecloth; at the same time she remembered not to allow her full-skirted Sunday dress to rustle too close to them.

In her ears rang her mother's warning, "If a woman's skirt brushes near their food, the Indians will not touch any of it."

There followed the assembling in the small church and the faintly protesting melodies emitted by the organ as Anna played it. Unlike human beings, it had not fully recovered from the flood. The solemn service proceeded; here was heart-warming token to the missionary spirit that prompted all the vast undertaking reviewed by the synod in this diocese of some three hundred thousand square miles. Timidly Beaver and Cree and Chipewyan added their voices to the swell of sound; with eyes that, for the moment, seemed dark forest pools of happiness, each chanted the lines in his or her own tongue.

Never could Juey erase from her own heart and mind the picture of these services. Always she remembered how inscrutable faces relaxed their lines in this atmosphere of loving kindness created by the dedicated churchmen speaking the service of worship.

"The grace of our Lord Jesus Christ, and the love of God, and the fellowship of the Holy Ghost, be with us all, evermore."

Pronounced by the rich deep voice of the bishop or of her father, these lovely puzzling words that concluded the service were, Juey knew, intended for all, Indian and Métis and white. Sometimes these words seemed to suggest personal forgiveness for her own faults; sometimes her father's or her mother's vivid depictions of an all-seeing God came home to her at unusual moments or in the midst of drab unpleasant chores.

One morning she hurried through the hateful task of

scrubbing the kitchen floor because she wished to watch the solemnization of a marriage. The result was a badly streaked piece of work. Her mother refused to let her go across to the church until she had scrubbed the rough boards all over again.

"Remember, Juey, it may be that the eyes of Jesus are watching you too."

She kneeled again to the odious work, sulking bitterly. Gradually her mood changed; it seemed as if the eyes of Christ were truly upon her. Many times after, these words of her mother's became a kind of star whose luminous rays penetrated to her through all the clouds of her life.

When next her father returned from his out-voyage— with his guide the Métis Benjie Charles he had paddled a hundred and fifty miles upstream on the Loon river to visit the northern Crees in their sumer homes—he summoned his daughter to a chore that was more to her liking.

With sweeping strokes of the scythe, Malcolm began felling the patch of Ladoga wheat that in July had promised so fruitfully. Juey worked behind him, gathering the long stems with the full golden heads into small bundles. With a withe of pliant stems, she bound each bundle into a beautiful sheaf.

"I don't think the Robinson family learned to harvest grain," she remarked sagely that evening when she reached for her favorite book.

With a sisterly feeling of shared experience, she opened the book to look for further comparisons.

CHAPTER 11

Sheridan's tall frame blocked the doorway of his mother's kitchen.

"Hold out your hands, Mother. I've brought you a present." With a powerful forward heave, he swung to the floor before Maggie's knees a one-hundred pound sack of flour.

In Maggie's eyes floated a vision of rows of golden loaves of bread. Delightedly she thanked her eldest son for this treasure. This sack of properly-milled wheat flour had been imported from such a great distance that it was much too expensive a luxury for them to afford.

"My whole month's wages," Sheridan added. "And worth all of twenty-six dollars."

Often in the autumn of 1888 Maggie recalled this scene of the previous winter when her son, working for a month for the "Bay" had chosen to cancel wages paid in kind for this gift of flour. She had spun it out for many months, using it only for birthday cakes or for a loaf or two of bread when the bishop was coming to call.

But now she looked out to see Henry and their sons harvesting wheat, oats and barley on the fields of their new ranch and she anticipated at last a well-stocked larder. Downstream too, she knew that on his uncle's fields Sheridan, like the Rev. Malcolm Scott, was reaping and stacking an abundant crop of grain.

Then it was October and still there was no sign of E. J., the former school-teacher from Sorel who had taken his children out to Chicago. Already a skim of snow whitened the rock-hard ground and solid scallops of ice fringed the quietening river.

The lateness of her husband's return, so the anxious Lydia guessed, was occasioned by his decision to change his occupation. Like Sheridan's father Henry, he determined to set up operations on his own. Leaving Lydia to carry on with the teaching until such time as the Missionary Society could find a replacement, already on river-margin land adjoining that of the Training School he had sketched a beginning. Here with the assistance of the big "boiler," he planned to set up a ranch that would include a milling and sawing business.

At last one day, in the final week of October, his wide raft hove into view. On it he had jammed an enormous load of freight, including ten mares and eight cows which he had driven from Edmonton to Peace River Crossing.

The joy of his safe arrival was tempered by anxiety. Should the winter which was almost upon them be prolonged and bring much deep snow, how would they contrive to provide enough food for all the precious new arrivals?

At once Sheridan set to work. With the mower he cut a generous supply of the native red-top grasses that waved dry and tall about the frozen shores of Bear lake, a marshy body of water lying through the bush some distance back from the Peace.

"It was a cold tough job," he recalled. But it paid off. Again they were able to show the skeptics that even horses and cattle unused to it could survive a winter in this northerly latitude. "The animals turned out fine; we had no losses at all."

With the crops of vegetables and grains that the little community harvested, and with the natural increase in the livestock, compared with the privations of that very first winter, they were now living bountifully. Inspired by their example, a number of families of mixed Indian and white blood began to enlarge and improve their holdings and they began to plant grain and to buy livestock from the Lawrences.

"From this time on, 1888, times were much better. In fact, there were no more real hard times." With such cheery words did Sheridan record in his diary the change. "We all grew more than we needed for ourselves; we were raising hogs, making bacon, and breeding some cattle for beef."

Now it was that the big engine, which his uncle E. J. took over by arrangement with Bishop Young, began to play its part in the miracle.

The cost of imported flour was prohibitive; "the Lawrences changed that," wrote Sheridan. "After the winter of 1887-88 we never bought imported flour; we began to make and sell barley, rye and a good deal of straight flour from Nos. 1, 2 and 3 grain. Now that the other settlers could get Uncle E. J. to grind and to make flour, they started growing main crops of wheat and barley.

"In fact, Uncle E. J. with his saw mill, his grist mill and his shingle machine was a great help not only to the people who settled around but to the men from the different forts."

This reaching of a milestone in the development of the area took place exactly a hundred years after the first recorded visit of white men to the banks of the Peace. Alexander Mackenzie's records show that it was in 1788 that his assistant Boyer built a first fort and trading post on the river that was to carry the fur-trader-explorer on his way to Pacific-coast fame.

Maggie's diary also takes note of the new milestone that was reached in that year. "From then on, bread from our own wheat flour took its proper place in our household as the staff of life. In spite of the madness of what we were all attempting, our faith in the country augmented."

Already for her husband Henry and for their family of growing sons, Sheridan and Jim, and Harry, Arthur, Isaac, Jack and Baby Will, there loomed this problem of money and markets. The Hudson's Bay Company had first entered the region in 1803 and after years of warfare with Mackenzie's North West Company they had in 1820 finally bought out their chief rival. On the north bank of the Peace, Revillon Freres cornered a small share of the fur trading and provided a partial outlet for agricultural produce. However it was the giant "Bay," like the Peace itself, that was to become for the Lawrences both friend and foe. With its near monopoly, it set all the prices; yet its string of trading posts hungry for food for its employees and for produce to trade for furs furnished the only sizeable market.

Furthermore, since the "Bay" chose to pay for produce in goods rather than in cash, how could ambitious men obtain the money to raft in new equipment from the outside?

Again in 1889 the crops prospered. Already the Lawrences were learning what later geographers confirmed, that this valley of the lower Peace is a region of scant summer rainfall. Wheat ripened within ninety days but shrewd timing in the sowing of the seed and summerfallowing played an important part in bringing an abundant crop to harvest.

Late that same year there came to Sheridan an offer that promised both ready cash for him and a market for some of the produce of his father's ranch. Laboring still in the vast northerly diocese of Mackenzie river, the enterprising Bishop Bompas who had years before decreed the setting up of the Irene Training mission on the Peace, was still engrossed in extending his work in areas beyond the sixtieth parallel. He determined to set up a similar school at Fort Resolution on the south-easterly shore of the sprawling Great Slave lake; now, through Bishop Young, he extended an invitation to Sheridan. Would he and his sixteen-year-old sister Grace care to undertake the building and operation here of a training school?

Like her cousin Susie, who was now enrolled in medical school in Chicago, Grace had gained experience in teaching Indian children by helping Lydia Lawrence at the Irene mission; she too wanted to make the mission field her life work. Here was a wonderful opportunity, in a land where salaried jobs were almost non-existent, for both Sheridan and herself to earn the means to build toward the future. To Grace as teacher the bishop offered the annual sum of two hundred and fifty dollars, and to Sheridan as mission manager a yearly salary of four hundred dollars. They were to begin their work as early as possible in the following spring of 1890.

Wrote Sheridan simply, "We decided to go north and try it out."

Had they flown north with the migrating birds, their journey to Fort Resolution would have meant the traversing of only some two hundred miles of mountain and forest and swamp. By the circuitous water route which they must follow, the journey was at least twice that distance.

While they awaited the spring break-up, in their spare time the young pair began gathering together equipment for their undertaking. From his father's ranch Sheridan hauled barley to be ground at his uncle's mill; as soon as the rush of spring work was over, his brothers helped him with the shaping of a large sturdy raft.

When all was ready, they stowed aboard it the necessities which Grace needed to operate a boarding school, including a year's supply of provisions which Sheridan as manager was responsible for securing. Most of his basic wants he supplied from the Riverside Ranche by arrangement with his father Henry; these included, so he noted in his records, "a young team of oxen, a bull and two cows, 3,000 pounds of barley flour, 200 pounds of bacon, 100 pounds of butter and 25 pounds of cheese."

With pride and anxiety their mother Maggie watched the pair depart. To reach the scene of the new venture, Sheridan planned to guide the raft as far as the rapids in the vicinity of the Chutes, where portaging would be necessary. At the foot of these falls, he hoped to get passage for Grace and himself and all their equipment on one of the "Bay" freighters plying in summer between the Chutes and Fort Chipewyan.

"My intrepid son and daughter," Maggie wrote with bursting heart, "proceeded on their perilous journey, running rapids that would have made more experienced river men quail."

Aboard to help them past such difficult stretches as the area of rapids below Fort Vermilion was their brother Harry. Forty miles beyond the post, the broad bosom of water, already expanded with melting snows far back in the foothills of the Rockies, expanded further as it received the waters of the Loon or Wabiscaw river, up which the Rev. Malcolm Scott paddled to visit the Wood Crees.

Next the dancing excitement beneath the raft heralded the stretch of rapids foretelling the nearness of the Chutes, where in less than two miles the torrent of the Peace drops nearly thirty feet. Here Sheridan hired the services of two native river men and their boat; except for a half mile where the freight had to be portaged, and the boat lowered by line through the worst of the rapids, they transported it all by means of this craft to the top of the falls; the livestock they drove overland.

At the Chutes where along the south bank again they portaged, skilled "Bay" employees with long heavy ropes manoeuvred the boat down with the plunging waters and a few feet away pulled it in to shore at a landing footprinted by centuries of Indian portaging. While the party waited here for the steamer, for entertainment they turned their raft loose in the turbulent waters above the falls. They watched it whirl about through the rapids, and then drop down to the Chutes. Here the racing torrent up-ended it; with half of its bulk high in the air it cascaded its way merrily down the seething falls.

Finally the freighter arrived, gliding under the skill of its Capt. Sayers to within twenty feet of the Chutes. Losing no time in the process, its crew hustled to unload freight destined for Fort Vermilion and points up-stream, and to ship aboard all the waiting cargo, including the young Lawrences' provisions, equipment and animals. It turned about, chugging downstream in a north-easterly direction.

Now Sheridan found that the river with whom he had so far successfully contended zigzagged its sinuous way through an immense low land of forest and swamp. Gone were the mountain-like banks that had awed him at Peace River Crossing; gone too were the friendly ridges that made a companionable backdrop for his father's ranch; as the freighter passed beyond the boiling waters of the Boyer rapids, the Peace itself became less and less identifiable, branching out into several channels, the largest of which swung about to carry its water north-east and then north. Here, he found within a few days, the Peace was robbed even of its name, becoming known as the Slave river.

Capt. Sayers' first destination, however, was Fort Chipewyan, the busy distributing point near the northwest extremity of Lake Athabasca, and he now guided his ship through a channel leading into this lake. From Fort Chipewyan the two young people proceeded down stream a hundred miles on the Slave, the river which Sheridan always insisted should still have been called the Peace. They reached Fort Fitzgerald, the end of navigation for steamers from the south; here he hired a wagon and he and Grace proceeded to move animals and equipment over the fifteen-mile portage that bypassed the impassable rapids on the Slave river.

103

At the northern extremity of this portage stood Fort Smith, the journey's end for steamboats plying between this post and the Arctic ocean at the mouth of the Mackenzie. While the brother and sister were busy freighting their stuff, a south-bound freighter arrived; aboard it, the pair were overjoyed to discover, was Bishop Bompas. The energetic missionary had been bound for the outside, but now he altered his plans so that he could lend a hand in getting the new school started as quickly as possible. He made one trip in the wagon over the portage; then, while Sheridan proceeded to build a new raft, he returned on the boat to Fort Resolution to complete arrangements for the school and to collect, from farflung points, the pupils whom Grace was to teach.

Soon the twenty-year-old Sheridan was guiding his craft down the swift current of the Slave. At its mouth, the pair found themselves entering the frigid waters of Great Slave lake. Hugging close to the shore of this inland sea, thirteenth in size among the world's fresh-water bodies, they pushed their way southward some ten miles to Fort Resolution.

Here they were welcomed by the Rev. William Spendlove, who with his wife and family was established in a small building which served as church and dwelling. Sheridan's first task was to set up near by a second building and to furnish it with rudimentary equipment so that Grace could begin to conduct her boarding school.

To procure working credit for his enterprises, the youth sold one of his cows to the missionary; then he proceeded to scour about for materials. Across a small bay near the Hudson's Bay Company post he found an empty log house which he bought; with his team of oxen he skidded it down to the water, rafted it across the inlet, dragged it to the site of the new school, and then with his sister's help proceeded to make it a habitable nucleus for the institution. Following the example of his father at the ranch, he knocked together tables and benches and cupboards and in his spare moments turned his energies to chinking the building against the onslaught of the sub-Arctic winter. The raft he hauled ashore and with the logs from it he erected a stable for the cattle.

Already Grace had begun her teaching, her first pupils

being the two Spendlove children and Annie, the young daughter of Archdeacon McDonald. Presently Bishop Bompas returned, bringing Loucheux and Chipewyan Indian pupils from the Mackenzie river area lying to the north-west of the great lake. Apparently the ardent prelate was satisfied that this new project that was so dear to his heart had fallen into capable hands; for he soon departed for other points in the diocese.

Of his visit Sheridan wrote with satisfaction, "He gave us to understand that he would not interfere with us."

Already the brief summer was nearing its close and now the young manager had to delay further improvements to the combined school-dwelling while he set about procuring food for humans and animals. With his scythe he swathed quantities of the wild grasses that grew tall along the marshy bays edging the broad lake. Because mighty windstorms sometimes whipped water far inland in waves that built up nearly two feet in height, all of the hay which he harvested he had to pile onto stages that would keep it safe and dry.

Next he hired an elderly Indian who was adept in boat-building and fishing. Together they constructed a flat-bottomed craft that was roomy for fishing and that would not be readily swamped. Beginning in late September when ice was already fringing the lake, the pair ventured out three to four miles and here they set out eight fishing nets. Then, when advancing winter thickened and extended the ice so that it was safe to move over its near-shore expanses, they chopped openings in it to put down two nets for catching small fish for bait; the baited hooks they set beneath the ice to lure the tasty trout.

Even as the winter advanced, they had to beware the threat of the fierce gales that hurled with demonic force across the ocean-size expanses. "These storms," Sheridan noted, "would break up the ice and pile it up on shore ten to fifteen feet high. People would lose both nets and hooks; travellers never cut across from bay to bay until the ice got very thick, and even then they always kept fairly close to shore."

Yet fishing in these waters that by comparison seemed to shrink the menace that he had found in the Peace yielded

105

tremendous catches; presently he had a stock of between eight and ten thousand whitefish and trout. These he and his helper stored on high stages where they would be safe from both storms and predators.

Also urgently demanding a share of his time was the business of furnishing firewood to heat the school. With the help of Indians and of his ox team he hauled stocks of logs from the nearby woods; the better specimens he culled for the addition to the building which he planned to erect as soon as time permitted.

Again with the coming of spring the oxen, who like the other cattle wintered well despite the latitude, proved indispensable. Hitched to a small walking-plow, the team plodded back and forth until their master had carved a sizeable garden plot and field out of the virgin shoreland.

One day an incident occurred which, according to the account of a later neighbor, first gave the strapping youth the name of "Oochi Mow," the great white chief. Again and again one of the oxen rebelled at the tedious chore of dragging the plow. Finally Sheridan was provoked by its persistent stubborness to a terrible wrath; whipping would not budge it, so with his powerful arms he twisted the beast's horns until it half stumbled to the ground.

"An Indian passing saw the ox fall; he spread the report that the great white man had felled the ox with his bare fist, and Sheridan thereby gained the reputation as a Samson among the native people."

As with the untouched land along the Peace, this soil also yielded bountifully, providing splendid harvests of vegetables and of barley. "In the four years we were there, we never had a crop failure."

Nourished by the vigor and enthusiasm of its young teacher and its manager, the school throve. "Sister Grace was greatly taken with her missionary job," Sheridan reported, adding a trifle ruefully, "But it was hard work for me." He kept a written record of all his transactions and he found that financially he was getting ahead.

The Church of England Missionary Society, however, was perennially short of funds and after three years, in 1893, Bishop Bompas was obliged to notify him that he must cut the youth's salary to three hundred and fifty dollars per year and that Sheridan must board himself. Grace's salary was to be likewise reduced.

"I decided that I had better change my occupation. Besides, I wanted to get out and settle down."

Meanwhile, during his third winter on the lakeshore, he accepted another mission building chore. The bishop had determined to open a new mission at the mouth of the Hay river a hundred miles to the west on the shore of the same lake, and he invited Sheridan to undertake the building. Leaving Grace well stocked with fuel and with frozen fish and the animals with hay, accompanied by an Indian helper the young man drove his dog-team and led one of his oxen south-westward along the shore ice until he reached the new site.

First of all, this construction job was going to involve timber felling. Buckling on his snowshoes, he tramped upstream along the frozen Hay river searching out a suitable stand of trees. With his axe he cleared trails to several sites and these he tramped with his snowshoes to make them passable for the dogs. Then he felled the trees, prepared the logs and shaped a long flat sleigh sixteen inches wide over bunks that were six inches in height. Since he brought down the trees in line with the trails, the dogs had a straight pull to haul the logs by sleigh to the bank of the river. Here, after the spring break-up, he and his helper could tumble them into the water to be floated down-stream as they needed them.

This method of logging was, in fact, "harder work for us than for our dogs." In all he and his assistant hewed out ninety cords of timber, quite sufficient, he calculated, for a building twenty-four by thirty feet.

With the opening of water transportation in the spring of 1895 the first incumbent of the projected mission at the Hay River mouth, the Rev. T. J. Marsh, arrived at Fort Resolution. Completing his bargain with the bishop, Sheridan accompanied him to the new site, there to erect the mission building. This was an exceedingly fertile trapping area attracting many Indians; the man whom they too designated now as Kis-chi-oo-ki-mou, Big White Chief, had no difficulty in procuring assistance from among them and soon the project was complete.

Now Mr. Marsh offered to arrange to restore his salary to the original level if only he would stay on as mission manager. But he was now twenty-five years old and impatient to get on. So he thanked the missionary for his kindness and repeated, "I want to get out on my own."

At Hay River Sheridan traded all of the remaining provisions which he had transported there, as well as his equipment and extra clothing, in exchange for choice furs which the Indians here trapped in such abundance. Then he caught a ride with the first boat plying up the lake to Fort Resolution. By this time the Rev. W. C. Bompas had moved on again, to become this time Anglican bishop of the Yukon. His successor, the Rev. William Reeve, was now on hand at Fort Resolution and to him Sheridan sold his animals and all the balance of his equipment.

"I was sorry to leave my sister Grace," he wrote. "But she wanted to stay on in the work and I felt that I had had enough. The time seemed ripe for some travel."

With his bundles of prime furs he headed straightway by water route for Fort Vermilion and then up the Peace and outside. In Winnipeg, on his way to visit relatives in eastern Canada and the United States, he discovered that the girl of his dreams was the young lady whom he had first espied by a camp-fire nine years before.

She had been snatched away from the mission at Fort Vermilion by that ogre, Going-out-to-School.

CHAPTER 12

At first terror tightened Juey's throat every time she remembered that she must leave this lovely home by the Peace.

"If I could only stay here," she begged of her mother and she fought tears at the frightening thought of the far-away land whose memory was so shadowy as contrasted with the vivid present.

Her mother was adamant. More rigidly she began to set the fixed "school" periods in which she drilled both children in the rudimentary three r's.

Her father too would not yield. He dug out his old Latin and Greek text-books and began coaching the pair in elementary Latin and Greek. His wilderness children must be able to hold their own.

"Moreover," announced Anna, "you'll have to learn to sew better." Juey was not fond of sitting meekly stitching seams. She knew how to hem and to hemstitch and to knit and to do simple patching. But she greatly preferred activity in the great outdoors.

"Or you will be ashamed," her mother added. "Especially when you find that you don't know how to do what the other girls are doing."

Juey was not at all interested in clothes. But Anna realized that the time would come when her daughter, living with other girls in a residential school, would also be ashamed if she were not dressed like them. Word had finally arrived that she had been accepted as a pupil at St. John's Ladies College in Winnipeg, to be enrolled in the autumn of 1892, and that Osborne could enter St. John's Boys School. Therefore Juey must begin to prepare herself a wardrobe.

Anna's hands were now so afflicted with rheumatism that

she was unable to sew. But she contrived to show the girl how to cut down some of her father's long underwear for herself and how to fashion petticoats from her own supply.

Even in this domestic art, Juey discovered, her father could be a sterner taskmaster than her mother. From a bolt of yellow-sprigged navy material he himself cut out a pair of dresses for her.

"You are to make these frocks yourself," he told her. "No one is to help you. A girl of your age should be able to make all of her own clothing." Juey would be thirteen on her next birthday and she smarted at her father's rebuke. He reminded her that in their girlhood his sisters were adept needlewomen; they had been included among these women of Winnipeg in the bitter winter of 1870-71 who had knitted socks and underwear for Col. Wolseley's suffering soldiers and presently a family romance had developed—his sister Mary Anne married a member of the unit, Lieut. Robert Fisher.

When it came to the fashioning of a new Sunday dress for his daughter, Malcolm relented a little. He himself sheared it out of navy blue serge, and stitched it for her on the "hand" sewing machine. As he trimmed it with red velvet and narrow white braid, Juey helped him with the pinning and basting.

In the matter of knitting the young girl acquitted herself much better. As a lad in the pioneer Red River settlement, her father had included spinning and knitting among his accomplishments and he had been suddenly shocked at what he considered to be backwardness in his daughter.

"So you *have* taught this girl to knit," he smiled.

"No," answered Anna. "I couldn't manage the needles. She taught herself."

Juey's pride now went a long way to encourage her in mastering other distasteful phases of a needlewoman's art.

Following the springtime's annual upheaval of ice that in 1892 once again freed the spirit of the mighty Peace, there was tremendous upheaval too in the mission house on its bank. Because Malcolm was going to take time to shepherd his two children out to school, he compressed into the twenty hours of daylight the planting of garden and field, the curing of bacon and all the multifarious duties of a missionary in charge of an enormous area. Indoors, Anna supervised as Juey and Osborne and Mary, their Indian helper, packed clothing, bedding, and camp equipment, and boxes of provisions. It was decided that they would leave on Victoria Day, May the twenty-fourth, as soon as the annual picnic got well under way.

Juey dressed in her fine frock of flower-sprigged navy and donned a new hat that her mother had somehow acquired for the occasion—out of a missionary bale of used clothing, she guessed in later years. Just the same it was a proud piece of headgear, a brown felt with rolled brim and long ribbon tails, and of a sudden she realized that after all she did like pretty clothes.

In the midst of her daze and excitement, she remembered an oversight. The day before, she and Osborne had borrowed table knives and stuck them high in a tree back in the woods where they had been playing.

"Better go get the knives," she whispered to him.

"I'll fetch them when we come back," he answered. The present now was much too full for such an errand.

When Juey did return to the Peace, four years later, she discovered the knives, still high in the tree.

The wagon in which they rode to the picnic was loaded with supplies furnished by the mission house and by the Hudson's Bay Company, for the annual event was looked forward to as a great treat by all the native peoples of the area and every one lent a hand to ensure its success. Juey was obliged to squeeze close by a water barrel and the pleasure of the ride was spoiled by sudden anxiety for her new hat and dress.

At last, still with dazed feelings, she stepped into the canoe that was to take both her and Osborne from their mother and from their busy home. Quickly Malcolm and "Moyeese," the elderly Indian Moses Bottle, pushed off from shore, for Malcolm was anxious to make time before the melting mountain snows brought the turbulent high waters of June swirling down the broad channel of the Peace.

This was to be Juey's first long canoe voyage and soon she forgot some of her sorrow as she watched her father and Moyeese fight their way upstream. Their craft had been shaped from a huge balm of Gilead and it had a yaw or crook in it that made it difficult for Moyeese to steer.

Usually the sage Indian kept close to the bank, avoiding the powerful down-sweep of the heady central current. Sometimes, in order to circumvent uprooted trees or mud slides, he had to guide it out into deep water and the girl's heart seemed to leap in unison as the current flung the craft about like a bit of floating twig. Sometimes savage eddies drove it backward down stream and the two men employed all their strength and skill on the paddles to steady it and to impel it forward again.

A bitter wind sprang up and Juey, in spite of her father's long underwear, began to shiver with cold. A brief break came for the youngsters when they reached the landing pier at the Riverside Ranche of Henry and Maggie Lawrence. Malcolm decreed that they could go ashore long enough to say good-bye to the family.

Huddling close by the warm kitchen fire, the girl found her skin beginning to itch unbearably. Here, only fifteen miles distant from her home, already arose a dilemma attendant upon the business of going "outside," for she remembered the first of her mother's many warnings.

"Don't scratch ever," she had cautioned, mindful that people would probably be extra-critical of these wilderness children of hers. "Or they'll think you are an Indian."

When the bitter wind died down, a new curse in the shape of hordes of mosquitoes made her want to start scratching again. At length, on a Saturday afternoon, they reached Carcajou Point at the mouth of the Wolverine river, one hundred miles from their home. The two youngsters jumped for joy when their father announced that the overnight camp would be extended. The next day being Sunday, when he would not travel, for thirty-six hours they were going to be able to forget the tedium of the long hours of sitting motionless in the dug-out and the terror of the eddies and of the rapids.

Here by the Wolverine old Moyeese had a log cabin and near it the family set up their tent. Presently, after a meal at which Juey decided that her mother's cooking was the best she'd ever tasted, Malcolm became engrossed in his "spare-time" occupation, that of translating texts into the Beaver and Cree tongues. Left to their own devices, the young pair scrambled about, exploring along the river banks. Here to their delight they found several willow fish-traps left in the brush by Indians.

These were barrel-shaped containers three to four feet long and fashioned of willow saplings with partitions through the middle. The children removed their shoes and stockings and, with old Moyeese guiding them, they carried the traps into the edge of the Peace. He selected a likely spot where the fish might swim; there, weighting the traps with stones, Juey and Osborne placed them with open end facing down-stream. In June, Moyeese told them, the fish always swim up-stream.

Expectantly, next morning, they plunged into the water, to find that in the willow prisons they had trapped several jackfish. These they cleaned and cooked for breakfast and they envisioned an equally delicious meal on the following day. To their disappointment, their father would not permit them to re-set the traps. This was the Sabbath day.

At dawn on the Monday they re-stowed the dug-out. A strapping young man, old Moyeese's son Paullis, lent a helping hand.

"Paullis come, help paddle," suggested the old river man.

Malcolm thought of how, if Paullis were to accompany them, his meagre supplies would dwindle twice as rapidly, for he guessed that Anna's cooking was the enticement that attracted the youth. On the other hand, the young man's strength and skill would be of great help in fighting the long up-stream pull against the Peace.

"All right," he agreed with a smile.

Making better time now, they propelled themselves past endless silent woods sloping to the shores, past innumerable gullies and creeks that gaped wide-mouthed into the great river, past sand ridges and gravel beds and innumerable islands. Juey's scene-weary eyes brightened when any wild animals showed themselves along the banks, and she mar-velled at the alertness of Moyeese and Paullis and the speed with which they converted any wild game into a contribution toward the daily fare.

At one point the youngsters admired two adorable black bear cubs cunningly perched in a tree. That evening they all feasted on bear-meat and the two Indians continued the feasting through the night. Next day the children understood why there had to be many stops along the way.

At the end of seventeen days, the party reached Sagitawa, Peace River Crossing, almost three hundred crooked river miles from their home. While they camped here to await transportation over the portage, the children scrambled about exploring all the flat-land where the town of Peace River now is situated. In the six years since Juey had camped here before, so far as she could remember there had been no change at all. Still the deserted Hudson's Bay Company storehouse perched silent and lonely near the water's edge, three miles down-stream from the junction of the Peace and the Smoky.

When, in compliance with a request which Malcolm had made the previous summer, a Métis arrived with a rattling Red River cart, the young girl found herself accommodated in de luxe fashion. Her father stowed away a small portion of the remaining food for his return down river, for this crossing was reputed as a spot where no provisions were likely to be available. Then the men loaded the cart with the balance, adding tent and camping equipment and luggage.

"All right, Juey. Up with you now."

Nimbly the girl obeyed her father's words. The cart was pulled this time not by an ox but by a small pinto cayuse. Juey shook the lines over the animal's rump and firmly commanded, "Get up."

The Métis had brought also a "spare," another cayuse, which now provided a mount for Osborne. The two men, Malcolm and the Métis, travelled afoot beside them. Keeping an alert look-out for all of the uncertainties of the rough trail, the pair guided the tiny entourage up the great hill and out of the valley of the Peace onto the tableland above. Then they headed toward Lesser Slave lake.

Now Juey was enjoying herself, for this was a novel experience. At home at Fort Vermilion she had often stood in the haying cart and driven the oxen while her father gathered in the hay. Here, wedged between boxes in this

Red River cart, she quickly learned to let the pinto pick his own way through the muskeg of the portage trail. When the going was extra bad, her father's hand grasped the bridle strap to help the small pony; this gave her assurance that she also needed.

Before the week was out, they sighted the white buildings of St. Peter's mission. These had been erected on the bank above Buffalo bay, a pocket of the wide shimmering waters of Lesser Slave lake. Here the Rev. George Holmes and his English wife welcomed them, and again Juey and Osborne tasted the exquisite joy of freedom from the tedious hours of sitting still.

"Remember this? Remember that?" became a favorite game as they continued to retrace their path of six years before.

Soon, by York boat instead of by sturgeon-head they proceeded forward. They crossed Lesser Slave lake and wound along the Lesser Slave and the Athabasca rivers. At Athabasca Landing stood the grim skeletons that had been blackened by the fire on that terrifying day six years before, but Juey was able to discover other untouched samples of the enchanting balsam firs that she had fallen in love with when she was little.

In a heavy lumber wagon father and children rumbled over the one-hundred mile "Bay" trail to Edmonton. Here, in this year of 1892, the "mud-hole" of six years before was stirring with excitement; the railway that had by-passed it six years before was at last approaching from the south. Hiring a ride in a fast-travelling buckboard, Malcolm and the youngsters made good time en route to the Red Deer crossing. They were attempting to overtake the construction train, which had pushed north as far as the Red Deer valley and which was due to leave shortly again for Calgary.

At last the driver whipped his horses up to the brow of the hill overlooking the Red Deer river. The children's eyes widened at the sight of the huge construction camp. They widened further at the sight of the train which they were attempting to overtake and which began steaming away without them toward the distant southern horizon.

They swallowed their disappointment and Juey began

searching for their former camp-site that had been brightened by the beautiful rainbow. Their present camping equipment they had left behind in Edmonton, but now members of a detachment of North-West Mounted Police came to their rescue with the loan of a tent and blankets. Out of his personal possessions, each man furnished them with something, a fork or a knife or an offering of food. For all of this they refused immediate payment of any kind.

One of the red-coats, a Sgt. Ellis, beamed at Juey. "The young lady here can marry me when she finishes growing up."

Juey blushed shyly. The future was a shadowy dream over which she had taken scant time to ponder.

After two days of camping, there followed a ride on the "accommodation" or construction train which made any kind of dreaming quite impossible. No cart or wagon or buckboard could match this train for swaying and lurching and tossing one about.

"Osborne and I sat on the floor but we couldn't even keep our places there. We were thrown about right and left."

In Calgary the railway line on which Malcolm hurried to arrange transportation was now truly transcontinental, and the small foothills settlement itself had made progress. On the Sunday morning, during their stop-over, Malcolm preached in the Anglican church and in the evening he took the children to a service of the Presbyterian faith, to which his Scottish forefathers had stubbornly adhered.

Before she quitted Calgary, Juey had a humiliating experience which increased her life-long sympathy for her northern neighbors. With her father and Osborne she entered a small trading store and found her woman's shopping instinct aroused by the wonderful display of goods. Longingly she eyed a particular box of candy. Even with no means at all to buy, at least she could enquire the price and finally she conquered her timidity enough to ask.

"How many skins does this box cost?"

Other customers, hearing the young girl with the long blonde braids put her unusual question, turned to stare at her. Rudely they burst out laughing.

On the mammoth train whooshing its way eastward across the prairie, the humiliation and the bewilderment that accompanied this business of coming "outside" were softened by a delightful new friendship. On the train were another father and daughter; this was an Indian agent, a Mr. Brass, who was also taking his child out to school. Soon the lonely young ladies were sharing confidences and anxieties, and the new life ahead became less and less a thing of dread.

At last they were in Winnipeg and "ohing" and "ahing" at the changes that had taken place in the city that prided itself on being the giant gateway of the golden west. Soon they were down-river at St. Andrew's settlement and in the sturdy stone house where Juey and Osborne had been born and which was now in the keeping of their uncle Will.

The youngsters raced about, hunting out haunts that were familiar and dear on the narrow farm and the dwarfed river bank. Juey was dumbfounded; the farm, the trees, the creek, the river bank and even the winding Red river,— everything in fact—had shrunk so in size.

"Where's the river?" she demanded straightway of her uncle Will. The Red river that she remembered spread an enormous sheet of water before her eyes.

"But I mean the big river," she insisted when he pointed out the stream that lolled past their roadway on its lackadaisical way northward. What she saw before her, he assured her, was the "big river" of her memory.

"That a river!" she exclaimed in disgust. "Why," she scoffed, "that's only a creek!" Surely this wasn't the large river by whose side she had, as a small girl, felt the small crabs bite at her toes and where, barefoot, she had stood on the broad backs of slumbrous turtles, perching there patiently until they were ready to give her a bumpy ride over the pebbles.

Too quickly the days of re-acquaintance on the pleasant old farm passed. Both children were enrolled in St. John's college and thus domiciled in buildings that neighbored each other. Their father's friend, the Rev. W. A. Burman, the principal of the Indian Industrial school, and Mrs. Burman undertook to become their official guardians; then came the moment of parting from their father.

For a minute he knelt with them in prayer, entrusting them to the care of his God.

Then he hugged and kissed them both. "Be good children," he adjured once more.

He was gone and Juey tried to settle to the strange world about her. Homesickness wrapped itself about her like a shroud. She couldn't cry to relieve the numbness and she couldn't concentrate on the alien routine of the school day.

Each morning even before the rising bell rang at five, Juey, having been roused by an older girl, was already up and dressed. Her daily allotment of piano practice began at that hour and any missed time must be made up during the precious freedom of Saturday. To add to her mental depression, in all her schooling except Latin and Greek she found herself, a girl just turned thirteen, years behind others of her age. After years of comparative aloneness, of sharing her time with her mother and Osborne, of sometimes playing with Fennie and Clara Lawrence, and of only occasional visits to the big Lawrence family up-stream, to be surrounded by so many other girls was misery; especially eating with them in the dining-room was torture, and sometimes the head mistress, Miss Ley, sensing her predicament, invited her to supper in her room.

There was one happy spot in the daily routine, the period of the daily outing. Accompanied by a governess, the girls usually chose to walk along the creek bed that emptied into the Red river and where in autumn the scrub oak and the wild hawthorn blazed in a rich riot of color. The young ladies plucked and ate the acorns or indulged in the unladylike fun of throwing them at each other. With intense longing Juey savored of the healing balm of this out-of-door refuge and in her mind she saw her own bit of paradise on the Peace with its massive splotches of color, and her brown-eyed mother tenderly instructing her in some phase of nature lore.

With the coming of winter, she began to indulge in the outdoor sports that she grew to love, skating on the Red river and snow-shoeing at Silver Heights on the estate of Lord Strathcona. She found now, too, that her pioneering background brought her an advantage. Apparently because of the misdirection of an English architect, the pipes in the ladies' college were poorly placed and with equanimity she accepted the frozen pipes and their failure to bring heat or water to her shiveringly cold room.

Her first Christmas examinations awakened Juey from her lethargy and her homesickness. Not only were her marks poor but she was particularly reprimanded for her bad spelling.

"Remember, Juey," her master pointed out to her. "No one notices a good speller. But *everyone* notices a poor speller."

"What can I do about it?" she faltered.

"Get a small notebook and a pencil and carry them in your pocket. Jot down every new word you hear; find it in the dictionary and learn to spell it."

She did just that. Never again, she resolved, would this man be able to call her to task for poor spelling.

She began to apply herself in other subjects too. Soon, to her surprise, she discovered that she loved school. Gradually she began to catch up to her own age group, passing her examinations so successfully that in her first two years she was permitted to cover the work of five grades.

On Saturdays the girls were left largely to their own devices and presently Juey rejoiced that her wise mother had insisted on her becoming a competent seamstress. Mr. Burman arranged for her to have an allowance of seventy-five cents each month. Out of this she had to buy such necessaries as pencils and hair ribbons; the other girls seemed to have a great deal more money of their own. She began to do darning and mending for them and they gladly paid her for her work. When her enterprise began to include the making of aprons and blouses, she was permitted to make use of the college sewing machine.

At last came summer and the joy of returning with Osborne to St. Andrew's and to the happiness of their former haunts. Juey even recovered something of her old knack with garter snakes. Beyond the creek and fence bordering the Scott property a cheese factory now stood in the place of the home of a young playmate who had once treated her to a surprising supper of "clobbered" milk. The creek edging the front lawn was shrunken like everything else in the young girl's eyes. Still it ambled past tufts of coarse grass on its way to the Red river, and along its modest banks beautifully ornamented garter snakes still made their home. As a small girl, she had captured the snakes for playmates and kept them imprisoned in bottles in the "coach-house" until one day her father discovered them and insisted that she set them free.

"This year the cussed cutworms are that bad," her uncle Will complained now. "I'm afraid we'll have no garden left."

"I'll fix them," promised Juey.

That evening, equipped with empty bottles, she slipped over to the creek. Soon she had several prisoners, gorgeously patterned creatures from twelve to twenty inches long. Early next morning when globes of dew still lit sparks of fire on the grass, she carried these snakes to the far side of the garden and there she released them. To reach their creek-edge home, they were going to have to cross the garden where the cutworms feasted.

For several weeks she repeated her "cure" and the garden throve.

"Your snakes must have done the trick." Her uncle's blue eyes danced at her. "Seems now, so they tell me, I have the best garden in the whole settlement."

Earlier Juey had protested when her uncle had wanted to kill the snakes. With joy she smiled back at him, "So the snakes are some good after all."

Sometimes her grandmother, Anne Setter Scott, visited with her son and his family at the old home, and she and Juey began to share and to compare their pioneering reminiscences. The old lady's mother was Margaret Bates, the daughter of Sir Isaac Bates of the North West Company, and in her eyes her mother's chief claim to fame lay in the fact that as a youngster she had been stolen away by Indians who fancied her flaxen hair and fair blonde face. Now the still vivacious Anne loved to recall her mother's and her own experiences among the native peoples and her granddaughter Juey reciprocated with tales of the Beavers, the Slaveys, the Chipewyans and the Crees and of her father's work among them.

Her grandmother's stories of the old days among the Indians told Juey how times had changed.

"Without saying one word, sometimes the natives walked right into our home," Anne Setter Scott related. "If they saw something they liked and wanted, they stood and pointed toward it."

"What did you do then?" Juey asked.

"Gave them whatever they pointed to," the old lady answered simply.

Emphatically Juey shook her head. "Why did you do that? I wouldn't."

"I was much to scared to do anything else." Her grandmother's eyes, blue and wide-set between rosy high cheekbones, flashed at the chilling recollection. By contrast, Juey told of the now peaceable ways of all these tribes in the far North-west among whom she lived and who sought her parents out for guidance and for help. She described how Chief Keewaytin, whose name meant North Wind, came to sit at their table for dinner.

"Father said he'd never before sat at a table. But he carefully watched how we conducted ourselves." At the end of the meal, Juey continued, he protested in Cree.

"You are not treating me as your true friend. You have not shown me up your wooden road."

When he pointed to the stairway, her father realized what he meant and promptly he showed him upstairs.

One day a piquant reminder brought home to Juey how recent was, after all, the armed unrest among some of the Métis people. In Winnipeg she and a companion were passing a stall where a sign was prominently displayed. She stopped to read the words on it.

"Buy a piece of the rope that hanged Riel."

"Look," a bystander gestured toward a white-bearded man lounging by the edge of the sidewalk. "There's Lemereux. He was one of Riel's right-hand men."

Juey gazed curiously at the large heap of segments of tawny rope and she turned with a laugh to her companion, "It must have taken a lot of rope to hang Riel."

She glanced toward the old Métis. His eyes glowered upon her and she felt a sudden shiver in her spine. They

121

reproached her for her flippancy, just as her father would have done had he been present.

Especially when she visited the stone church of St. Andrew's which her father had helped to build did she suffer from homesickness for her parents and the mission on the distant Peace. Here in this church her grandmother showed her the record of her marriage to her grandfather, William Scott, who in 1833 had quitted his home in the Orkneys to enter the service of the Hudson's Bay Company and who had married her nine years later after having obtained a strip of land in the Red River colony on which to build a home.

Here, too, in this church Juey's own parents had been married and here she and Osborne had been christened. Here her father had wrestled with the decision as to which church he should offer his services. Though his whole boyhood and youth had been centred about this Anglican St. Andrew's, like his father he had still considered himself a Presbyterian. Finally, with a Christ-like humility, he had elected the Church of England.

There, he told his family, "it doesn't matter so much whether the clergyman is eloquent. The service is always beautiful."

Juey admired the hand-hewn beams of the old church and the neat gates opening into the pews. As she knelt on the buffalo hide that softened the kneelers, she agreed too that the service was beautiful. The ring in her ears of the beloved words carried to her the voice of her father, speaking messages of comfort in a small log church more than a thousand miles distant.

When in the autumn of 1895 there arrived the annual summer mail from her father, it brought with it no hint of destiny's arranging a special visitor for her. She was now an assured young miss of sixteen, with trailing pigtails that she could sit upon. So luxuriant was her crop of golden hair that one day on the street a woman stopped her with a fantastic proposition.

"Won't you let me draw a picture of your hair for my new advertisement for hair tonic?

Juey of course knew that the headmistress, Miss Ley,

would not permit a pupil to become involved in such an enterprise.

One late afternoon not long afterward she found herself incurring Miss Ley's displeasure. With the headmistress and her class-mates, she was riding a street car back to college following a Shakespeare matinee. She noticed an extra-tall young man board the horse-drawn car and presently turn to look and smile at her. When the passenger beside her moved and while the headmistress frowned, the strange young man came and sat beside her.

"Don't you remember me, Juey?"

It was five years since his raft had disappeared down the Peace. But of course she could not forget him. This was the youth whose very first picture in her mind had been framed by the rainbow's arch, the youth whom her father's Bishop had singled out as capable of building and operating a mission school in the sub-Arctic.

"You're Sheridan," she smiled shyly.

"I want to see you," the young man blurted.

"You'll have to ask," she answered in a low tone. She was still conscious of the disapproving frown on the face of Miss Ley. "This is our stop."

Sheridan jumped from the car and stood back while the young girls streamed to the sidewalk.

The headmistress turned to chide Juey. "You know you shouldn't speak to strangers."

"He's a neighbor," she explained. "From Fort Vermilion."

The seemingly offensive stranger stepped over and she introduced him. Miss Ley became more cordial and the young man pressed his advantage.

"I'd like to come and call on Juey. If I may."

Graciously Miss Ley agreed that he could visit her the next evening in the downstairs parlor.

In the course of the half hour which he was permitted to spend with her, what, the curious girls asked her afterward, did they talk about?

"Why, home. Of course."

Briefly, too, Sheridan told her that he was continuing all the way east to visit relations in Montreal and South

Stukely and Lawrenceville, and also in New York and Boston. She mentioned to him her dream of becoming a doctor.

When her genial guardian Mr. Burman heard of her visitor, at once he became suspicious.

"You'll be going to school for a long time yet," he warned. "Don't you go falling in love with that young Lawrence."

For ages, it seemed, the young man had been a shining ideal in the back of her mind. Now, she sighed dreamily, perhaps her guardian's warning had already come too late.

Afterwards Sheridan told her, "That day I saw you again in Winnipeg, I made up my mind. I was going to try to win you."

Juey was now thoroughly adapted to the life of a resident scholar. She enjoyed all of the curriculum except mathematics; her dislike of this subject, she realized later, was probably due to her compressed program of schooling.

"Here's where I get plucked," she remarked to a senior girl when she was about to face an examination in algebra.

The other student looked at her squarely in the eye. "You say that, Juey, simply because you do not know your basic theory."

There and then the girl took her schoolmate in hand, drilling her on all the fundamental principles. Juey profited both from the lessons, which enabled her to meet the dreaded testing successfully, and from the gracious spirit of helpfulness to others which her mentor demonstrated.

Encouraged by her successes, Juey settled with such determination into the scholastic routine that she achieved a special triumph. In the June examinations of 1896, she won the Bishop's silver medal for highest marks in the senior class.

"You're no brilliant star, Juey," smiled the truth-loving Miss Ley. "You've won through sheer hardwork."

"How the other girls laughed at these words," with a rueful smile she related afterward to her parents. "They never stopped teasing me."

In July when her father arrived, she was overjoyed to see him and she shed tears to learn that her gentle mother was now completely invalided with rheumatism.

It was a moment of heart-rending crisis for the girl. She wanted to study to become a doctor. Already she had consulted Winnipeg's only female practitioner and from her she had received a grim warning.

"If you don't have private means, you'll starve."

So far all of both hers and Osborne's college fees had been furnished by a kind patron in eastern Canada who made a point of assisting the children of missionaries. But she could no longer expect this kind of aid.

Her thoughts turned next to missionary nursing. Perhaps, with some training in medicine, she could work near her father's field. He consented to her presenting herself for an examination.

"You are not old enough to enter a training program for nurses," she was told. "Nor are you physically strong enough."

Many many times in days to come the irony of these last words flashed a lightning spark of amusement through her mind and brightened sombre moments of trial or ordeal.

Sheridan sometimes shared her enjoyment. "Just think," he teased her. "If those doctors had passed you, what a lot of trouble it would have saved me."

In this period of decision-taking, while her father talked to her and while she still cherished her own private dreams, she became aware that he had his heart set on his own firm plan. In four years of separation, she had matured and changed.

Now she looked on this man who was almost a stranger. She saw that the blue eyes shone out of his ruddy face with a zealot's intensity; his red beard, untouched by grey, still flamed like a token of that zeal. He told her of the progress which he felt that he had made,—so many Indians helped, so many baptized, so many given a rudimentary education or being guided a little along the path toward better self-help.

Juey was vitally interested. After all, she wanted to use her life, as she had been taught, in the service of others. But she was now seventeen and she wanted to work out her own destiny. She felt that she could not commit herself.

Then her father played his last card. With sadness

spreading over his weathered face, he spoke of her mother and of her continuous suffering from crippling rheumatism.

"We need you at home, Juey," he pleaded.

Juey made her decision. She would turn her back on her ambitions for further study. She would go home.

"If she falls in love with that Sheridan Lawrence," teased her kindly guardian Mr. Burman, "send her back here to me."

Juey pretended not to hear. Sheridan had made a final call on her in the previous summer when he had returned from the east.

He had said to her only, "Dad wants to buy a small grist mill. I think I'll go home and help him run it. It's time I settled down."

CHAPTER 13

With the return to the ranch of Sheridan, his eldest son, for Henry Lawrence the geese honkod still higher. Now at last came the fulfillment of a cherished dream. Every spring as he had watched the water tumbling down the near-by creek, he had envisioned a mill that would produce their own wheat flour on their own premises. But the practical mind of his first-born saw only objections to such a venture.

"I was sure there wasn't enough water in the creek," he wrote afterward in his diary. "And I thought we weren't capable, nor had we enough experience, to operate it."

Sheridan had also come to believe that if a thing could be done at all, persistence and ingenuity would ferret out a way. So he finally concurred in his father's scheme and during that return trip of his in the late summer of 1895, he bought from the Waterous Engine Works in Winnipeg a two-inch stone burr mill complete with smut mill, cleaner and water wheel. The company arranged to have it shipped as far as Edmonton and from there Sheridan paid for its transportation by trail and water to Lesser Slave lake post at the western extremity of the lake. From there he himself freighted it over the portage and rafted it down-stream to the Riverside Ranche.

During that next winter, with Sheridan assuming charge, father and sons worked together on the grand project of setting up the new mill. They felled logs for the mill building, erecting a two-storey structure twenty-eight by thirty-two feet; they whip-sawed lumber for the roof and the penstock flue; they built a dam on the creek, with a flume fifty-five feet in length to a penstock and a second flume one hundred and ten feet long to take care of the overflow.

The hustle of that winter rewarded them amply. By the time the snow started to melt in the spring of 1896, they had the wheat cleaned and the machinery all installed and they were ready to begin operations. Water began to rise high in the pond and they started up the mill.

Now all Henry Lawrence's splendid optimism seemed justified. Their mill began turning out chop and shorts and precious wheat flour, all the product of their own grain grown on the fertile flats of the Peace.

Alas, as Sheridan predicted, within a fortnight the level of the water in the pond sank too low to turn the wheel. They had to wait for it to refill.

Ruefully Sheridan shook his head. "It was a great deal of work with little return."

He had to admit that there were bright spots. "We did get a lot of enjoyment out of it. We surprised some of our friends with our work, and we were getting experience in building and handling machinery."

His independent mother Maggie was delighted. After years of hand pounding of grain or of contriving to get grist and flour at E. J.'s mill, to have a mill of their very own was a joy indeed. She envisioned endless golden loaves of bread and dainty cakes all the product of their own efforts.

With a shrewd practical note she commented, "It'll help to bring the exorbitant price of flour down a bit further."

Next, Sheridan turned his restless energy to the matter of erecting a new dwelling house on the ranch. As yet, his family still made do with the crowded log building they had thrown up nine years before. The Rev. Malcolm Scott came periodically to conduct church service for them in this home; he was going out shortly, he told them, to bring his daughter back from Winnipeg. Already Sheridan's parents were proposing that they turn the ranch over to him. But if he were going to plan definitely to marry and settle here, there would have to be many changes.

He could not ask a young wife to face the many privations which his mother had known.

Having agreed to return home, Juey too pondered over

the changes that were so rapidly flooding into her life. En route from Winnipeg all the way to Fort Vermilion, often she recalled the words of old Moyeese, whose weathered skin seemed ancient as the Peace. Like the Peace was that venerable river man, self-contained and sure. Four years before, he had waved toward its water.

"You drink. You come back. Always."

Unmindful of her private dreams and of her torn heartstrings, the train propelled her back through Calgary and Edmonton. Soon youth's resilience diminished her sorrow and she began to look with something of her usual perceptiveness at the landscape that streamed past.

In this summer of 1896 she noted how, a little more than ten years after her first initiation into travel in the northwest, new life was quickening in the land. Along the rail route west to Calgary and north to Edmonton, spread restless waves of growing grain. On the Athabasca trail, here and there raw log cabins staring out of the bush made her feel that already she was an old-timer.

At Athabasca came the most joyful highlight of the journey home, a re-union with her godmother Julia Young. Because of the building of the Canadian Pacific railway through Calgary and of the subsequent rail extension to Edmonton, Athabasca Landing rather than Fort Vermilion had become the most central and important point in the diocese. Hence, in 1893 Bishop Young had moved his family here from the log dwelling on the Peace.

Crowded into the hospitable Young home at this same time were Bishop Reeve of the Mackenzie, and Rev. W. G. White and his fiancé, the mission teacher Miss Wooster. Unruffled by the arrival of three more house guests—Osborne had a year's leave from college and was accompanying his father and sister—the hostess somehow found sleeping quarters for all and then went on to complete arrangements for the wedding of the affianced couple.

Presently the Scott family resumed their journey, the newlyweds travelling northwestward with them on the same convoy of boats. Again Juey found herself enjoying the antics of the river men, both Indian and Métis, as they tracked sturgeon heads up the Athabasca and the Lesser

Slave rivers. Again she found herself enjoying the deep silent woods of the north and she basked in their spell of loneliness and mystery.

Arrived at the portage, instead of by Red River cart this time she found herself beginning to rumble along the trail leading to the Peace in a settler's lumber wagon. On the way, in this land of great waters, there was no water to drink. The rain poured down and from deep puddles by the trail she dipped their requirements for tea.

From the heights she gazed at last far down upon the Peace and she knew more happiness. Tranquilly it flowed, majestic and self-contained and every bit as magnificent as her memory of it.

Next, floating upon its back on a raft, she renewed a more intimate acquaintance. Her father had secured a passage for the three of them with a family of Indians whose name, translated into flowery English, was Belrose. It was now September and the tall balm of Gileads seemed to wave great banners of gold in welcome to her.

Soon she found that she was going to have an abundance of time to marvel at the panorama of color sweeping back from the water's edge to the far horizons; in the slower-moving waters of autumn the Indian raft was gradually becoming water-logged and she wakened in the mornings to find cakes of ice formed along the floor beside her blankets. Finally Malcolm, who by this time had learned many devious ways of coming to terms with the Peace, persuaded his native pilot to make camp. Here he and Osborne assisted in cutting fresh poles and laying a new floor above the sodden logs. Then they pushed on, and Juey enjoyed the pleasure of sleep on a bed that no longer glistened with ice.

Surprisingly, she found herself adapting with ease to the ways of the north. When with incredible quickness the Indian father spied and shot a pishew or lynx lurking in brush by the water's edge, almost as speedily the mother skinned and cooked it over the fire that smouldered on one corner of the raft. The Rev. Malcolm would not touch the meat. But the young college lady who had once dined on mice and snowbirds rapidly recovered her pioneer's appetite;

she ate the lynx and discovered that it tasted just as delicious as it had smelled in cooking.

At last loomed familiar landmarks, the twin islands marking that section of shore that fronted the Lawrence home. Here they stopped for dinner and for church service.

It was a time of reunion, they found, at the Riverside Ranche. Grace had at last returned from the mission at Fort Resolution; in the next spring she planned to go outside to Montreal to begin her nurse's training. Meantime Sheridan and his six brothers and sisters were all at home with their parents.

Unflurried in her restricted quarters, Maggie proceeded to prepare the meal and Juey puzzled, "How in the world can she squeeze us all in?"

A few yards away from the ranch-house, Sheridan and Jim toiled at the building of the large new home. While resourceful Maggie and her girls were contriving to find food and places for all, Juey happened to look out and to see that the eyes of the young carpenters were upon her. They both flushed guiltily and her curiosity was piqued.

Presently she asked Sheridan, "What were you and Jim speaking about just now?"

He flushed again. "I can't tell," he stammered.

She tried to insist. She guessed that it must concern herself.

"No," he repeated. "I can't tell you." He added with a sheepish grin, "Some day I will."

Later, persistent Juey reminded him of his promise.

"We were drawing lots," he smiled. "We wanted to see which of us would get you."

When Juey saw her mother, her heart told her instantly that she had done the right thing in forgetting her splendid dreams and returning home. Pretty little Anna was bent like an old woman and so crippled that she could not stand alone. Pushing a chair for support, she hobbled about but she refused to utter a word of complaint. Night and morning she had to be carried up and down stairs. Stubbornly she rejected Juey's suggestion that she go "outside" to seek medical help.

"Your father loves his work here. I am going to stay with him."

Anna had trained two young Indian girls in the routine of housework and Juey, taking over the management of the mission home, found everything spotlessly clean.

There had been, during her four-years' absence, a number of changes in the mission lay-out. Her parents were now living in the larger house that had been vacated by Bishop and Mrs. Young. Attached to it were rooms which served as sleeping quarters and school-room for the Indian pupils. In charge of teaching the children was the Rev. A. J. Warwick, who had undertaken this task when Lydia Lawrence had eventually to give it up. She and E. J. lived a few rods down stream where the former schoolmaster now devoted all his time to farming and milling on his own.

With a will Juey settled into the mission routine, which now involved caring for the physical needs of all attending school. She cooked and cleaned and supervised for her big "family" and guided the young Indian girls who were living with them to learn the life of a domestic. The native dialects, she found, returned quickly to her tongue. She helped her father make ready for his journeys into the camping grounds of his people; she administered medicines as her mother had done; under Anna's guidance she gave nursing care to the ill and she assisted at births; with solemn concentration she listened to all the problems that were brought to the mission.

One of the most tragic of these last in which it fell to her father's lot to lend a hand, involved a robust woodsman named Tall Cree. This man and his two brothers, Horseman and Nanooch, dwelt in the Wabiscaw area some eighty-five miles south-east of the mission; he, the eldest and the tallest of the trio, was the chief of the tribe.

With smouldering eyes and distraught features, Tall Cree one day brought to the Rev. Malcolm a harrowing tale. His son-in-law Norbert had repeatedly shown himself to be utterly indolent; he sponged on Tall Cree and his family, refusing to do his share of the hunting and the trapping. Because of the young man's laziness there had been a series of quarrels. At last Tall Cree had uttered a final command:

"If you can't work, you must leave your wife and go."

Norbert had slunk to his teepee. Presently they heard the blast of a gunshot. Rushing to the tent, they found a fearful sight. The young man had propped himself up on his bed roll, first having placed his gun barrel so that it pointed at his head. With a string looped at one end to the trigger, he had contrived to fire the gun and to blow off the top of his head.

Malcolm did his best to comfort the self-reproaching Tall Cree. Together they knelt in prayer and Malcolm agreed to go and conduct a burial service and to try to comfort the unhappy family. The ground was snow-covered; as he reached down his snow-shoes and readied his gear, Juey rushed to prepare cakes of frozen stew and dry bannocks. Accompanied by the Swampey Cree, Ben Charles, they set out for Tall Cree's camp.

Much sooner than Anna and Juey had expected, Malcolm returned home again, and his bleared eyes bore witness to his explanation for the rapidity of the trip. Each night, following the all-day tramp through bush and over muskeg, he had looked forward to a sound sleep. But Ben Charles refused to sleep; while he, Malcolm, took only the briefest midnight nap, Ben Charles sat staring moodily into space.

"He dared not sleep, nor even lie down," explained Malcolm. "He was too terrified of the dead man's unhappy spirit."

At home now, after a sound sleep, Malcolm was restored in body and mind; it took longer for Ben Charles to return to his silent but usually unruffled self.

As the season of Christmas festivities approached, for all such dark musings Juey now began to plan the healing and fellowship and fun of a giant party. To all and sundry within the area, traders, trappers, the Lawrence families, Métis and Indians she sent out invitations. Her father lent enthusiastic support; each Christmas he tried to fill with both meaning and pleasure and annually out of his modest seven-hundred-dollar stipend he sent out for small gifts for all of the children. Her spare time during the day Juey filled with baking; using dried apples and the native fruits, raspberries, saskatoons and blueberries, she prepared forty pies. In the evenings, sometimes with the aid of young men

133

callers, as a gay but thoughtful Santa Claus she sorted and wrapped and tagged a multitude of tinsel-bright packages.

Early on Christmas day helpers arrived to peel potatoes, to cut cakes and pies, and to lay a long ell-shaped table in the school-room. Serving in three relays, they accommodated eighty adults and Indians who elected to sit on the floor. The great dinner began with grace pronounced by the Rev. Malcolm and concluded with a giant sing-song to the accompaniment of Juey at the organ. That unfortunate instrument, her ears told her, still wheezed complainingly of the damage it had received during the flood; soon the chorus of hearty voices swelled to drown its plaintive tone as it had once been drowned by the waters of the Peace.

When the magnificent party concluded, an exhausted Juey was warmed by the obvious pleasure of all and by her father's words of praise. As she reviewed in her mind's eye all the dozens of dark eyes gleaming with happiness, momentarily she was content. Her mother shared their feelings; always she taught, "You must do your share to help keep the world turning."

Perplexed, Juey pondered. She had been forced to forget her dreams and her ambitions. Could it be that even here in these backwoods, life could be sufficiently rich and meaningful? Here for a young girl life certainly abounded in opportunities for male companionship; there were always Lawrence boys about, Sheridan and Jim and their brother Harry and their cousin Fennie; as for marriage, right now she was not in the least interested.

With the passing of the Christmas recess passed also idle moments for such puzzles. At the spring break-up, the Peace renewed its shuffling of the lives along its shores. On its north bank young Fred Brick was established in a trading post. He was a son of the Rev. J. Gough Brick whose horticultural exploits brought him fame when Lydia Lawrence's brother Albert Kneeland submitted a sample of his wheat at the Chicago World's Fair. Now on Fred's fur-laden scow Osborne took passage, bound for Winnipeg and university. On it also Jim Lawrence accompanied his sister Grace; she was setting out for Montreal to begin her training for the medical missionary field.

Anna and Juey did not have long to lament Osborne's going; the Peace was due to bring them soon a prolonged visit from the Bishop and Mrs. Young. Malcolm hurried with his spring planting and paddled away to the Chutes where he expected to meet their guests. Soon he was back again, worried and alone and having found no trace of them.

Presently, in shocking condition, they arrived. Juey could scarcely believe that this was the handsome couple with the unquenchable spirit that she had known since her babyhood. The jolly robust bishop was emaciated and ailing and gone was the buoyancy of the lively woman who was her godmother. With them was their son Frank, a youth of about eighteen, who had become violently ill from the hardships of their journey.

Instead of following the all-water route via the Athabasca and the Peace rivers, the visitors had portaged overland from their home at Athabasca Landing. They had reached the source of the twisting Loon or Wabiscaw river, only to find it in low water and full of treacherous boulders. Forced many times to unload their canoe and float it empty or to carry it along with their packs, they had fought their way through swamp and forest along its devious three-hundred mile course until they reached the mother-Peace.

Juey flew about to do her utmost for their starved guests. She asked Mr. Warwick, the school-teacher, to kill several chickens for her. When he was slow in complying, the urgency, she felt, was so great that she wielded the hatchet herself. "The only time ever in my life I cut off chickens' heads."

During a week of illness in bed, young Frank's whole body broke out in painful abscesses. To provide other light but nourishing food for the sufferers, several times Juey paddled down river to her favorite fishing haunt where she caught a number of toothsome gold-eyes; at night she heated milk and poured it over broken-up bread which she served with sugar and cream.

For Bishop Young this journey was doubly tragic,—just as, for Juey, it was to be doubly challenging. His enthusiastic plans for the great work of his church had centred here in Fort Vermilion, his first home in the northland. Now he had to break the news that he no longer had sufficient funds to maintain a teacher for the Irene Training School and that Mr. Warwick was going north to Chipewyan.

"What do you think, Juey?" he asked the young girl. "Could you manage to carry it on?"

Juey took a deep breath. She had come to help her crippled mother but perhaps under her supervision the Indian girls alone could carry on the household routine. There were, she knew, some eighty names on the register and one teacher alone could not possibly manage that number.

Fortunately, attendance was never anywhere near one hundred per cent; pupils would become so homesick that they would have to be sent back to their parents or mothers would grow so lonesome for their children that they would take them back to the woods; or boys especially would go to join in the hunt or on the trap-line.

Even so, to operate the school and to act as general supervisor for the whole home-mission establishment would be a challenge more of the stature of her dreams.

She looked at her father. His blue eyes twinkled affectionately and steadily. To close the school now would mean a partial negation of all the years of toil.

"I'll try it," she smiled at him and the bishop.

During the summer recess she worked with and supervised her young Indian helpers as they scoured out the dormitories and the schoolroom and cleaned and repaired all the equipment. Straw-filled ticks laid in rows along the floor provided places for sleep; home-made tables and chairs and benches furnished the large room which served for classes and for meals. Most of the clothing and bedding came in bulky "bales" supplied by the Church Missionary Society. Life in St. John's College had taught Juey how to organize a school week. So, in September, when her new pupils duly streamed back to school, she was ready for them.

As at St. John's, Juey began the morning routine at five. While she took charge of cooking breakfast, preparing a huge pot of porridge, the older girls set the tables and washed and dressed the little ones, and the boys turned out to help with chores in the stables.

Following the advice of Mr. Warwick, Juey confined

her teaching to the rudimentary mastering of the three r's. One special factor affected her time-table. This involved the daily selection during the morning period before recess of a topic which she could teach sitting down. Always at this time she nursed in her lap a pan of potatoes which she peeled in readiness for the noon meal. At recess she would rush to the kitchen to put them to boil and to pay a brief visit to her mother.

Whenever her father was available to help, he called the huge class to order and attempted, following opening prayer and songs, to teach in Beaver or Cree or English some of the simple Bible stories.

Juey sensed that the children loved her father and she tried to follow his method. "With his knowledge of their languages and his sympathetic understanding of their ways, he had a wonderful knack of winning their hearts."

Lacking her father's awesome stature, augmented by the flaming beard and by his depth of experience, Juey found her path sometimes as uncertain as the Peace in early spring. She could recall no example from St. John's College of the problem of communicating with little ones who knew no word of English. She was thankful that in her own earlier days her mother had insisted on her drilling children in syllabics; she remembered how cruelly the routine and isolation of her first college days had made her suffer and she understood that these children of the wilderness would have even more difficulty in adjusting to a white man's school. To lighten their days she varied her program frequently and the afternoon she devoted largely to music and needlework and art, in all of which they showed great aptitude.

Often alert-minded pupils surprised the father-daughter team with their quick answers and their perceptiveness.

"Mr. Scott," spoke up a vivid-eyed lad barely a moment after the Rev. Malcolm had suspended from the blackboard a picture displaying the sturdy bearded figure of Abraham with his son Isaac. The boy was pointing at Abraham. "What big muscles that angel's got!"

Pleased with the interest, Malcolm continued with the story of how Abraham promised to find a wife for his son.

"What did Abraham promise to find for Isaac?" he asked.

"A gun," shot forth the practical answer from another quick-tongued lad.

With her older pupils, Juey presently ventured into the abstract world of fractions. Successfully she carried them through the adding and subtracting of halves and quarters and thirds. When she tried to introduce them to mixed and vulgar fractions, they grew confused.

"I try and try," she complained to her father. "I seem to be up against a stone wall."

"Don't worry," soothed Malcolm. "Do what you can." He smiled wryly. "When they return to the forest, it's not likely they'll need vulgar fractions."

In spite of Juey's five-foot-two stature, problems of discipline were surprisingly few. In these the parents sometimes delighted her by supporting or even doubling her punishments. One small spoiled boy she finally spanked with her hand.

"I'll tell father," he sobbed angrily in Cree. The youngster and his sister returned to their home for the week-ends.

"Did you tell your father?" Juey asked him the following Monday.

Silently the child put his dark head on the table. His sister spoke up in Cree: "Father said you didn't spank hard enough. He spanked him again."

In the disciplining of the motherless Beaver lad Johnny, Juey was able to rule by love alone. Usually Malcolm would not accept a child under five years, but luckless Johnny, who was only three, was large for his age, slow of speech and comprehension, and obviously unfitted for the rigorous life of the bush. Between him and Juey there soon developed a great love affair.

She cut his hair and kept him clean. Even at his best, with his pouting lips and his wide flat nose he was anything but beautiful. His great dark eyes glowed with affection for her.

"A-na!" My darling, he called her, following her about like a faithful dog and refusing to obey any one else's wishes. He could manage a few sentences in the Beaver tongue.

"Ma-chase-tonny!" he shouted at every one but Juey. "I hate you!"

"Teen-put." I am hungry, he announced meekly to her near meal-time.

Of all the children who, in three years of teaching, came under her charge, Johnny was the only case of mental retardation. Physically, too, his resistance was low, and when finally he succumbed to influenza, she was heartbroken.

Where in the early years Anna and Malcolm supplied medicines whenever they could out of their own or out of mission supplies, now the Department of Indian Affairs helped them out. From the Indians as well as from her mother Juey tried to learn more of the healing arts in order to meet the almost daily calls upon her.

In summer the native people collected the dainty blue-eyed grass in quantity; the whole plant they soaked in water and the resulting liquid they treasured as medicine; she could not discover what it was intended to cure. In autumn they made a frothy red mash of the scarlet buffalo berry.

"Eat them," they instructed Anna and Juey. "Good for blood."

For ointments they blended bear's grease with pitch from the evergreens; following their example Malcolm made a healing salve that combined animal fat and pitch; because his blonde skin suffered much from the vagaries of the wind and the weather, a can of this always accompanied him on his journeys. Ancient rural lore also taught him to preserve the thick gall from the bladders of butchered animals; one and all applied this to soothe chilbains and frost bites.

From these proud resourceful people who, as Anna reminded her still, "had so very little," sometimes Juey became aware that the imbalance was probably on her side. Earlier, Mr. Garrioch had called attention to that spirit of stoicism and strength which somehow they conveyed when they reached forth a hand to shake, saying "Nwas-tych," "I like you," a spirit which sustained them so that even in the end "they would die game." To Juey it became immensely gratifying to see bright eyes gleam with pleasure and to catch flashes of quick understanding lighting a dark face.

For some time the certainty that she was bringing

139

enrichment to youthful lives was all the reward that she was to earn. When Bishop Young brought word of his curtailed funds, there had been some talk of governmental assistance. In the summer of 1898 when a "treaty" party comprising representatives of the Department of Indian Affairs visited the land of the northern Peace, Juey made formal application for a grant of money. Not until her third year of teaching did any "salary" reach her pocket.

By no means, for the dedicated Juey, was life one long routine of toil. As the only "white" girl of the immediate settlement, there was also for her the exquisite pleasure of being sought after by several young men. Sometimes on a week-end evening three or four would be present at one time, Sheridan and Harry Lawrence and their cousin, her old playmate Fennie.

Then the Peace, silent and inscrutable, began carrying young men hopefully north toward the rainbow that planted a golden foot in the Yukon. Presently, as the rainbow vanished, it ferried them south again. A number of these "Klondikers," pausing in Juey's vicinity, added the spice of their presence to her informal court and their hearty voices to those of the young men already circled about the organ which she played for them.

CHAPTER 14

It was April the first of the auspicious year, 1898, the year marked with the golden circle in the northwest, the year marked with the signs of an era concluding and of a new one beginning.

A warming sun sparkled down upon the snow and ice of the still-imprisoned Peace and the Rev. Malcolm was treating Anna to a sleigh-drive over its surface. They were bound for the Riverside Ranche, fifteen miles distant. Juey sent the school children out to enjoy the sudden feel of spring in the air and began to scrub out her father's study.

There sounded a knock at the door. Juey went, expecting to see an Indian child or parent. A six-foot-two figure, swathed in Arctic dress, filled the doorway. Sheridan's blue eyes blinked down at her.

"Welcome back," she smiled. He had been in the sub-Arctic again, building another mission. Of this much she was aware.

He inquired if she knew of a chance to catch a ride up-stream or perhaps borrow a team. "I've had a rather long walk," he explained.

As she made haste to set a meal before him, he told her about it. Bishop Reeve had written to him, she also knew, telling of his great misfortune in the loss by fire of his mission and residence. This was at Fort Simpson, near the mouth of the Liard on the Mackenzie river and some two hundred and fifty miles north-west of Sheridan's previous building project at Hay river. Would the young man return north and replace it for him?

Again Sheridan had set forth with provisions and equipment from his father's ranch. Again he journeyed circuitously by water, reaching the site of his former mission enterprise at Fort Resolution, on the steamer crossing the lake to Fort

141

Rae, next turning about to head for the mouth of the Mackenzie, stopping over at Fort Providence, and finally arriving at Fort Simpson.

Here the youthful builder of missions hurried to make up for lost time. In the last hours aboard the steamer he began searching for and spotting likely stands of timber; he must get his logs cut and rafted down river before freeze-up.

With a party of Indian helpers, up-stream he cut and hewed some five hundred logs; these he rafted down river over water that was swift and shallow. At Bishop Reeve's landing he put down skids and hauled the logs up the slope to the site of the re-building. Here, in a niche that offered the most shelter from the early winter winds and snowfall, with hand and rip saw he prepared lumber for floors and siding and roofing.

From all this hustle he took a brief holiday, turning to lend a practised hand with the harvesting of the bishop's fine crop of potatoes and root vegetables when the first sudden bitter snowstorm descended on the Mackenzie. At the same time he noticed how the more experienced men at the "Bay" post misjudged the harvesting; from their large field of potatoes they had dug only two hundred bushels before the weather closed in. However, their loss of some six hundred bushels left in the ground to freeze solid proved to be the Indians' gain.

"It was poor weather for moose hunting and times were hard," related Sheridan. "So the Indians trudged into the potato field, shoved the snow from the buried potatoes and dug them up. They took them to their camps and ate them frozen."

Meantime, the word "gold" had extended its spell even to the remote posts on the Mackenzie river. Somehow word of that fabulous strike of August 17th, 1896, on the Yukon's Klondike sped across the sub-Arctic and southward through the Territories. At Fort Simpson Sheridan received a letter from his brother Harry inviting him to come home and join with him in a venture to Dawson City. Just as he had completed his undertaking there and was preparing to turn homeward, a Capt. Walker made an appeal to him for assistance.

This Capt. Walker was an American who had journeyed from Point Barrow, Alaska by way of the Mackenzie and he was bound for Seattle, Washington, where he planned to inform the Steamship Whaling company that three of their ships had been crushed in Arctic ice floes. He offered Sheridan the payment of four of his dogs if he would accompany him as far as Fort Chipewyan.

This time Sheridan had planned a more direct journey to Fort Vermilion, following the Hay river out of Great Slave lake and then hitting across country by Indian trail. However, he agreed to change his plans, even though he knew that the more circuitous route meant many more miles of trudging behind dog teams through deep snow and winter cold.

Now, as he recounted his experiences to Juey, he summed up with a pleased grin.

"It's been quite a walk, Juey. Eight hundred miles, I figure. Made it in one month less one day."

Afterwards she learned that this was something of a record.

He looked quizzically down at her. "Have you missed me?"

"I've been much too busy," she teased.

"Harry wants me to go with him to the Yukon," he told her. But he wanted to talk plans over with his father before he came to a decision.

In Sheridan's absence, Harry had been one of Juey's most frequent visitors. So far she had made them all understand that she was completely engrossed in her teaching and that she wasn't ready yet for marriage.

As soon as the Peace shook itself free of all the throttling ice and whenever circumstances permitted, the Rev. Malcolm resumed by canoe Sunday visits to the Riverside Ranche to conduct a service of worship. Usually Juey accompanied him and she found the sabbath quite astir now with plans.

During this spring period of high water, the new mill was producing more lovely flour and for guests Maggie produced with bursting pride sumptuous cakes and loaves. To hungry people who had known what it was to exist for months on potatoes and mashed barley, every bite, every mouthful was a miracle of delight.

The family's achievement with the mill weighed large in the decision which Sheridan now had to make. Should he join Harry in the rush to the Yukon? His father Henry suffered badly from asthma.

"Dad wants me to take over the outfit," his eldest son told Juey. "He'd like to go outside to be near a doctor."

If he declined Harry's invitation, he himself would have have to go outside to bring in up-to-date equipment. For years they had been managing along with makeshifts; for years, for instance, they had depended on the slow labor of oxen; for years they had even depended on the trampling of the lumbering beasts round and round the circular stacks to thresh their grain for them. Should he, Sheridan, spend all his savings on new equipment, on engine, thresher, saw mill, binder, disc, harrows, seeder? Or should he head for the Yukon?

Already, in this hectic open-water season of 1898, when thousands were joining the scramble to discover a quick route to the goldfields, sometimes motley crews of starving strangers came sweeping down the Peace; sometimes the gold of Maggie's loaves of bread came to mean much more to them than all the fabled treasure of the Klondike, and she and the families down at the settlement found themselves literally casting bread upon the waters.

Confident that they had selected the best and the quickest route to the fulfilment of their golden dreams, voyagers paddled canoes or they poled rafts which they, like the Scotts and the Lawrences years before, had built for themselves at Peace River Crossing. Maggie's lonely youngsters hailed them all and the hungry among them welcomed the excuse to make a stop.

"We spared what we could," said Maggie. "Then we sent them down stream to the 'Bay.' Many had already exhausted their supplies."

In their headlong rush others, she recalled, would not spare the time to stop either at the ranch or at the trading post.

"Unaware of the dangers ahead, some of them were

swept right over the Chutes. Later their bones washed ashore."

Heeding the warning of what lay before them, one party paused long enough to hire Harry Lawrence to guide them past the rapids and to help them portage round about the Chutes. At that point, during the height of the "rush," the expert rivermen William Flett and Ben Charles set themselves up as guides and portage-men to all "Klondikers" willing to pay for their services.

"Would you wait for me?" Harry asked Juey as he made ready himself to go gold-seeking.

His party planned to cut across overland to the Hay river, follow the river to its mouth portaging around falls reputed to be the highest on the continent, travel northwestward for a distance along the shore of Great Slave lake, eventually crossing the mountains to reach one of the tributaries of the Yukon river. Other gold-seekers reaching this area of the Peace, they knew, selected an alternative route when they headed for the Hay river, choosing to go up this stream and overland to Fort Nelson and the Fort Nelson river.

Juey was not yet ready to give Harry a definite answer. "Perhaps," she countered. Marriage was not yet important to her. Her school still ranked first in her life.

Months later she heard from him. Klondike fever had carried him all the way. As yet he had found no gold and he could not ask her to wait for him.

At his home his younger brothers maintained their vigil on the river. Presently came word by moccasin telegraph that a real English peer, Lord Ravenhurst, was on his way down stream.

"I sure hope he stops at our place," sighed the lads. Excitedly all the family agreed that to have a real English lord among the Klondikers who paused at their home would afford a true thrill.

One afternoon ten-year-old Will came shouting to the door, his blue eyes ablaze. "I think Lord Ravenhurst is here," he panted.

Maggie hurried to throw off her apron before she went to the door. Toward it were plodding three bearded bedraggled men. They wore long tattered coats that taggled down about their bare feet.

Alas, they were not Lord Ravenhurst and his party. They were three exhausted Americans from Connecticut, dead beat and near starvation. After eating heartily and thankfully of Maggie's food, they looked with amazement on the interior of the cheerfully painted home and the organ that was now its special new treasure.

By this time Jim Lawrence had married Florence Lendrum of Edmonton, whose father was one of the earliest surveyors in the North-West Territories. The young couple made their home upstream at Prairie Point on the spot where, ten years before, Jim and Arthur had retreated from the great flood. One Saturday evening Florence stepped down to the river's edge to fetch water and her red dress attracted the attention of a craft manned by more hopeful Klondikers. After so many hundreds of miles of lonely forest, these men were so startled by the sight of a white woman in a gay dress that they made an excuse to land.

They also were Americans, this time from Chicago, and they welcomed the hospitality of the community. It, in turn, welcomed them for a special reason. They were all musicians and they carried their instruments with them. When they visited Maggie and Henry Lawrence, they were directed downstream to the post.

Next morning they appeared at the morning service in St. Luke's church and during the offertory, accompanied by Juey on the organ, one of the youngest of the party played a solo on his piccolo. There followed a hearty dinner for all at the home of E. J. and Lydia Lawrence and a round of hymn singing to the accompaniment of their instruments, piccolo and violin and accordion.

"Always wear a red dress when you go down to the river," they bade young Florence as they said good-bye. "You'll cheer the hearts of other lonely wayfarers."

Next morning they resumed their quest. In farewell, as they began to drift down-stream, they played their instruments and from over the broad Peace floated the strains of a familiar song.

Another and more impatient party of gold-seekers carried grain which they had been told they could have ground at E. J. Lawrence's mill. E. J., whose great engine and grist and saw mill had been so helpful in the area, was prepared to grind their grain. But only in his own good time would he bestir himself. In their pelting rush toward the Yukon, they would not await his pleasure. During the evening, with a young lad who worked about the place to guide them, they started up the mill for themselves and ground their grain. Then on they hurtled down river to join the mad chase for gold.

Whether the most of these treasure-seekers ever found their heart's desire or even themselves, the little settlement did not learn. They brought to the community a strange new feeling, a feeling of being part again of the far-away world. Because they were a motley crowd, they brought, too, a many-sided picture of the civilization that had grown so distant. As with the party of musicians, they gave sometimes more than they received.

One gentle Klondiker of this latter sort was a well educated man, a Mr. Vietz, who had formerly been a jeweller in Digby, Nova Scotia. On his way down river, the slight elderly adventurer had been advised not to continue. Presently he was back, defeated by the cruel hardships of the journey and by a defaulting partner. At the mission the Rev. Malcolm gave him shelter for the winter and he puttered about, doing what chores he could in return for his keep.

He was a mine of information about all manner of topics and to Maggie especially his tonic conversation became a healing and a blessing. For the arrival of the mail late in 1898 brought letters from her daughter Grace in Montreal and the same packet also brought word that in the course of her training the young woman had contracted pneumonia and died.

Surprisingly, the small Nova Scotian proved apt in the handling of machinery. So the following spring Henry employed him to help operate the grist and flour mill set up near the mouth of the creek. Finally he had earned sufficient to enable him to make his way back to eastern Canada.

"We're going to miss you," Maggie told him truthfully.

To her family he had brought a whole book-case of information.

Word came later that their gold-seeker who carried his mine in his head had found employment in the parliamentary library at Ottawa.

Meantime Sheridan too had recovered from Klondike fever. Briefly he told Juey of his decision. He had agreed instead to comply with his father's wishes and to take over the ranch. He was shy and reserved as ever, but she sensed what was in his mind. She sensed also that he would say nothing further, even if he wanted to, until he was able to offer a comfortable home. First he was going outside to buy equipment that would re-outfit the place in line with some of his dreams.

Already, in this open-water season of 1898, as he began to cope up-stream with the tortuous Peace, he saw evidence that reassured him that his decision was right; already the quest of many of the gold-seekers was symbolizing endings and beginnings; they too having been cured of their fever were searching for land on which to settle or new ways of wrestling a living for themselves.

During his journey Sheridan took charge of a trading scow belonging to Twelve-Foot Davis, whose unusual name helped to develop him into a north-country legend. With Métis he hired to assist him, in seventeen days of poling and tracking the energetic Sheridan guided the scow to Peace River Crossing.

At the end of the portage to Lesser Slave lake, Sheridan saw awaiting there a restless motley crowd. "They were all people who had gotten over their Klondike fever and who wanted to get back outside and settle down."

Here, at this Lesser Slave lake post at the western end of the lake, Davis had cached a boat which he had had built for him the previous year. Sheridan supervised the repairs to this craft and the loading of it with the bales of its owner's furs. Then he accepted a number of the stranded gold-seekers as passengers with the understanding that all would take their turn at the oars. Presently a fair wind sprang up and they rigged out a square sail to speed them across the lake. Next, with Sheridan steering, they proceeded to run the rapids in the Lesser Slave river.

"Most of the people aboard enjoyed themselves," he remembered. "Though some were pretty frightened."

Where the river joined forces with the Athabasca, a dark ugly head bobbing in the water made the passengers forget their fear and remember their hunger. It was a moose —alas, out of season. Obligingly, a mountie aboard the boat shot the animal and the whole hungry party camped to feast on moose meat.

In Edmonton Sheridan found that here too the gold rush had brought a great stir and that a boom was in progress. Here also he met his cousins Fred and Fennie, who were returning from school to take over their father's outfit. The three discussed plans and Sheridan proposed that "we take the lead" in the Peace country by forming a partnership. However, E. J.'s boys rejected his offer and Sheridan went on to Winnipeg there to look over the newest in farm and ranch equipment.

"I wanted a steam engine, a threshing machine, and, if possible, a saw mill. I was tired of hand-sawing all my lumber or of working for other people in order to get ready lumber."

In Winnipeg he found equipment that he felt would meet his greatest needs, among other things a Waterous No. 0 sawing rig and a wood-burning steam engine or "boiler." These he arranged to have shipped on to Edmonton. Then, back in that town, he proceeded to hunt out an opportunity "to go to school." If he were going to operate intricate machinery some seven hundred miles distant from expert mechanical know-how, he himself must learn details of procedure. So, to gain experience he hired himself out on the large farm of George Long, a productive spread fanning out on the banks of the Sturgeon river. There he stooked grain behind a five-horse binder and when threshing began he worked on the outfit as bagger and as oiler.

The thresher on the Long spread was powered by horses. The young "student" mastered the details of its operation and decided in favor of a steam-driven machine. This latter type he also studied how to operate; then he sent his order to Winnipeg for a thirty by forty-two Peerless separator equipped with a hand-fed straw elevator. He also ordered among other implements a binder, a seeder, a disc and harrows.

All these machines, along with the "boiler" and the saw mill which he had already purchased, he planned to freight over the winter trails as far as Peace River Crossing. His shopping also included four hundred bushels of oats for which he paid fifteen cents per bushel and which he hoped to sell at Athabasca Landing at ninety cents, thereby earning himself cash to pay wages to his helpers. He hired an American, Adam Herbison, who had his own team and sleigh, and three other assistants. Then he proceeded to assemble his purchases at Strathcona, now Edmonton South, on the south bank of the North Saskatchewan river where all his freight from Winnipeg had been detrained.

The giant moving job he planned to undertake in stages, making two trips between each stage, and finally gathering all the bulky loads together on the shore of the Peace ready for rafting down stream after the break-up. The whole operation, he calculated, he could complete within five months. With good luck he should be home in time to thresh the past season's crop and with the fresh seed thus readied and his other new equipment, turn at once to the re-planting of all the fields.

As he completed his final arrangements, Edmontonians by turns scoffed and marvelled. Those who knew something of the difficulties and the distances involved shook their heads at the sheer improbability of his ever reaching his destination with such a bulky accumulation of freight. Those who didn't know sensed the challenge involved.

To transport the heaviest piece, the "boiler," he built extra-wide sleigh bunks with wide planks on their underside to help them keep the road. The combined weight of sleigh and boiler alone was sixty-five hundred pounds or three and a quarter tons. Eventually he manoeuvred boiler and threshing machine down and then up the banks of the North Saskatchewan and with his brigade of four loaded sleighs set forth on the trail.

"We left Edmonton on January 20th, 1899, taking with

us a tent, a tent stove, large extra blankets and nose bags for the horses. We had to camp the first night out. Of course that was the coldest night of the winter and I was suffering from what is now called flu—then we called it grippe— though it is equally distressing under either name.

"The trails were poor. My team hauled the separator. I put a pole through between the separator wheels and wherever the trail wasn't level I rode on the end of the pole on the upper side. My illness lasted three days—but what a three days! I felt so weak and tired; I couldn't eat; I wanted to lie down and rest all the time.

"After unloading at Athabasca Landing, one hundred miles north, we returned to Edmonton for the balance of the load."

On the second stage of the freighting, from Athabasca Landing to Lesser Slave lake, they had the good luck to follow a Mr. Carson, who had taken over a freighting outfit from the Hundson's Bay Company and whose men drove both oxen and horses. Since there were no stopping places at all on this stretch, this was a considerable blessing.

"Some of his freighters were experienced men from around the Sturgeon; he had cut some new trails, avoiding the Lesser Slave river above the rapids, where several people had lost horses and freight through the ice; travelling behind his men made our going simpler and easier, for following him meant that we were spared the task of spotting new camp grounds, cutting new trails, finding adequate fuel supplies, cutting water holes for four teams with an axe and shovelling off snow for camp grounds."

Along the shore of Lesser Slave Lake it was a different story. "There it was always quite a heavy job chopping out ice for water holes, shovelling snow, finding dry trees in the woods for fires at night and then cutting our wood." They unloaded their first consignment at Bishop Holmes' mission on Buffalo Bay and headed back for the balance of the freight.

Next came the business of moving the heavy engine and separator over the worst section of the road, the portage from the lake to Peace River Crossing. Mild days smiled ironically upon them, pleasantly foretelling spring but softening the trail so that the heavy freight became unmanageable.

"In many places on the old trail we had to do a lot of work with axe and shovel to keep from going sideways. Finally, on the prairie east of Peace River Crossing, the engine cut off the road so badly that I had to put on two teams and make a new road all the way to the next bush area."

At last they neared the final critical hurdle, the eight-hundred-foot hills that towered above the Peace. "About a mile from the top of the Peace hill, we cut the separator off the road. Underneath it, the back sleigh slid right off the trail and it started to tip."

Sheridan went around to the side to check, only to discover that the snow was drifted so deeply that it was impossible to work there. So he brought a load of freight along the upper side of the road. "This we hitched by block and tackle to the back sleigh and pulled it back onto the trail, after which we proceeded down the hill." This journey down the long hill to the valley some eight hundred feet below they achieved by rough-locking chains around the sleigh runners.

Although there was still another load at Buffalo Bay, it was now time to prepare for raft-building and the final lap. Sheridan sent two of his men up river with one team; there they were to cut and haul logs ready to be floated out at break-up time. Meanwhile he walked the ninety miles back to the mission to fetch the balance of his freight.

At nearby Lesser Slave Lake trading post he met three prospectors who were searching for a means to reach Great Slave Lake. He made an agreement with them, undertaking to give them transportation as far as Fort Vermilion if they would assist him back over the portage, join in the building of two rafts and aid in the management of them on the Peace.

Even with the extra assistance he thus received, because it was break-up time this transfer of the final consignment of his freight as far as the shore of the Peace was man-measuring experience.

"Travelling was tough. If we started too early in the

morning, the ice on the water and the mud holes hindered us. We would get stuck and all hands would have to join to help push the wagon up the hills."

Twenty miles from Peace River Crossing their trail approached Hart river. Here they found on this usually modest tributary of the Peace that both the ice-pack forming the winter crossing and, a short distance away, the summertime bridge had been swept downstream.

Gathering together poles and sticks, the men tied them together to form a rough raft. Then Sheridan, armed with the advantage of his great strength and his six-foot-two height, stripped off part of his clothing and stuffed a complete change into a sack which he tied high about his neck. Then he waded throught the ice-dotted water, carrying a line across to the opposite shore.

"Now using our harness lines and bed ropes, my men pulled the raft back and forth until everything was taken across."

Next they secured the wagon box to the wheels so that it could not float away and swam the horses over with the empty wagon. They re-packed their freight and proceeded toward the Peace.

Already this gold-rush era was making known to the world outside the possibilities of the Peace region that lay hidden beyond the tremendous barrier of muskeg and swamp and dense wood. "Winter freighting increased," Sheridan noted. "And it wasn't long before various people along the river and lake shores built bunk houses and stables for accommodation of freighters and their horses. The steamers did some of the hauling. But until the railway came through during the First World War, most of the hauling into the Peace country was done by freighters over the winter trails."

Arrived once more at Peace River Crossing, Sheridan received shocking news. The two men whom he had sent with one of his teams to cut and haul logs for raft-building reported that one day they had put nose-bags on the two horses and left them, still hitched together with the neck-yoke, standing by the edge of the river. Meantime the men crossed on the ice to inspect timber on the opposite shore. When they returned, the horses had disappeared. They followed their tracks on the river to a point where rapids made the ice weak. Here a fresh hole told the tragic tale. Because the pair were linked together by the neck-yoke, they would have been completely helpless in the swift current beneath the ice. They were never seen again.

Dismissing his negligent workers, Sheridan proceeded up river himself to make ready a stack of logs. Soon, with the help of the three prospectors, he had a sufficient pile awaiting the pleasure of the waters. When the break-up finally shoved the ice downstream, he floated his logs to a suitable building site, hauled them out of the current and constructed two rafts each twenty-four by forty-five feet, floored with four to six-inch dry spruce poles and with oar-locks fitted at each corner.

In the vicinity of his stock-pile of freight, next he selected the most likely-looking loading point. Here he and his assistants cut away the low bank and braced the slope to the water's edge with heavy planking. Then they contrived to manoeuvre the engine and the separator, each on its own wheels, down the slope and aboard the anchored rafts. Next morning they stowed aboard all the balance of the freight, led the teams of horses aboard and hove to.

A strong west wind blew continuously, making it difficult to keep the two rafts in the main channel. But they kept moving and within four days they had breasted three hundred miles of sinuous river. Sheridan and his prospectors poled their "ships" into the mouth of the creek close by his father's pride, the nearly "home-made" mill. Here they unloaded the whole outfit.

"Not one thing was broken. All of it was in tip-top shape. Everything in the whole experience would have been fine except for the team that went through the ice."

The prospectors, empty-handed, went on to their own way of seeking out the wealth of the north. Beside the water-mill, the acme of Henry Lawrence's achievement on his ranch, spread a new potential of local riches for ranch and settlement, wondrous up-to-date equipment for the generation that was taking over.

The enterprising representative of this new generation arrived at a critical juncture. Henry, his father, was still in poor health and anxious to get outside; Juey's father Malcolm wanted to move because of Anna's rheumatism; and E. J. Lawrence's family became involved in double tragedy. Lydia had become ill; there being no medical help, the neighbors gave what assistance they could. When Juey could spare the time she lent a hand to Clara, Lydia's younger daughter. One Sunday morning as she sat playing the organ in the church she glanced out the window in the direction of E. J.'s home. She was startled to see that the signal meaning trouble had been raised, a red rag tied high on a pole.

"Excuse me," she said, stopping her playing. "I must go. There's something wrong at the E. J. Lawrence's."

She hurried out, to meet Fennie coming for her with a team. He raced the horses back, but already his mother was dead. Juey weighted her eyelids and presently she prepared her for burial.

Movingly the Rev. Malcolm commended Lydia's faith and fortitude and her devotion in the service of others. As a young school teacher and mother eager to add her contribution, in the first place she had been the moving spirit in wafting the Lawrence family into this remote corner of the Territories.

"Aunt Lydia had been in the country all those years," Sheridan wrote of her in his diary. "And she had never once had a trip outside."

Before she died she had the joy of knowing that her elder daughter Susan, who had gone out eleven years before, had become a medical doctor and with her husband Dr. Skinner was continuing in China the missionary work that was so dear to the heart of her mother.

"A good woman who loved the Lord," summed up the Rev. Malcolm as she was laid to rest beside the river that had watched her work for almost twenty years.

Then, when E. J. was on a trip outside, a second disaster struck. Sheridan was on the river, homeward bound with his two great rafts in that spring of 1899, when he learned of this fresh tragedy. "I met my brother Jim and he told me that Uncle E. J.'s whole outfit was burned up, along with over four hundred bushels of precious No. 2 wheat. I was sure that Uncle wouldn't come back when he heard the news."

As his nephew predicted, E. J. then decided to settle in the Edmonton area so that his daughter Clara could attend school. His sons Fred and Fennie, having declined to share with Sheridan, decided to order fresh equipment and to rebuild. So Juey's former playmate became again a frequent visitor at the mission-house.

But now Sheridan too was once more on hand. Fairly bursting as he was with his energetic plans for the new century about to be born, quickly he let it become obvious that the winning of young Juey Scott was a definite part of his grand dreams.

PART II

*"He . . . had the faculty of beholding
at a hint the face of his desire
and the shape of his dream, without
which the earth would know no lover
and no adventurer."*
—LORD JIM

CHAPTER 1

Sheridan smiled down at Juey. A dance was in progress and she had sunk down to rest after the breath-taking whirl of a Scottish reel.

"You need a breather," he said. "Come outside and look at the northern lights."

She went with him and saw that they were as magnificent and as mysterious as when in her childhood she and Osborne had danced to their magic.

It was a perfect moment. "But if he tries to kiss me now," thought Juey, "it will spoil everything. It will be all over between us.'"

Sheridan made no attempt to kiss her. He sensed that the moment transcended passion. It became one to treasure, a kind of symbol of their love, of a partnership which would respect the independence of each.

Sheridan had read her right. Juey was a young woman with a strong streak of self-reliance and determination. He proceeded warily with his wooing, perhaps of an evening helping her with her many "children," perhaps waiting on the helpless Anna and carrying her up to her room. Sometimes Fennie was already on hand, milking the cow and "separating" for her. Then Sheridan would arrive.

Once Juey heartlessly left Fennie choring for her while she went for a walk with the more favored suitor. With resident pupils constantly besieging her, there were very few opportunities for them to be alone.

While his wooing of Juey proceeded with hesitating steps, his plans for conversion of the Riverside Ranche advanced with giant bounds. Within forty-eight hours of the time when the powerful Peace co-operated to bring his two burdened rafts to the creek mouth in the spring of 1899, he had the new threshing machine pouring forth a stream of grain.

The brisk throbbing of the engine driving the belt seemed to banish the air of stagnation that hung about the whole valley of the ranch. All of the previous year's crop was still unthreshed and grain was badly needed for flour and for seed. The stands had been cut with a mower, then raked and stacked after a fashion into beehive shapes. Because the stacks had not been sufficiently domed, snow had melted on them and tough kernels began to flow from the thresher spout into the sacks.

"Even with what I learned at Mr. Long's, I had had very little experience in actually operating the machine. It kept clogging up on us."

Fortunately for the baffled young man, Juey's father paddled up stream to see the "wonder" machine in operation. Malcolm's early experience on the Red River homestead in Manitoba now proved a blessing; he recommended setting the "governor" higher to speed up the engine, thereby increasing the speed and power of the new separator; this change at once improved its efficiency.

"We learned too, after that, always to give it a little spurt when the grain was wet."

Next, with Sheridan leading the way, he and his brothers knocked the two rafts apart and used some of the logs to build a foundation for the saw mill. In his absence the boys had cut and hauled over four hundred logs and these also awaited the new equipment.

"I had little trouble running the saw mill," Sheridan noted. "We cut both lumber and shingles. Although we had to employ natives and inexperienced people, no one was ever seriously hurt. At first, I hadn't been careful enough about watching the man who was at the tail saw. Shortly after we got started, he let a two by four touch the saw. It caught the board and flung it just past my head, hurling it fifty feet away. After that I watched more carefully."

Presently he tackled and mastered the process of planing boards. At the same time, he set men to work on the land with the new machines, plough and disc and harrow and seeder. Soon the fourteen-inch share of the husky breaking plow was biting into more and more of the fertile virgin soil of the river basin and presently the newly-tilled earth

160

was being seeded with the freshly-threshed grain. Near the old log barn the boys also erected a fine new horse barn; durable oxen had been the mainstay of Henry Lawrence, but now horses symbolizing the changing era of progress were being introduced in numbers by his oldest son.

"Breaking-in bucking bronchos became a specialty with the boys," Maggie recalled. "I have seen beasts so tired from trying to throw them that they would have to lie down."

Sheridan found that the persuasion of Juey to his way of thinking was not so easy a task.

"You make it difficult," he complained to her one evening as he towered over the organ while she played and sang to her dark-eyed charges. "You never give me a chance to talk to you."

Her blue eyes danced with mischief. It was true. She could guess what was in his heart, but she was so very busy. She knew that he was now twenty-nine and impatient; she, only twenty, was in no hurry. And the certain knowledge of being wanted by him kept a singing in her own heart.

One evening she noticed an especially resolute expression on his tanned face. He had given up hope of obtaining privacy for what he was determined to say to her. Indifferent to the gleaming pairs of brown eyes all round about them, suddenly he reached out a powerful arm and curved it about her tiny waist.

Will you marry me, Juey?"

He spoke quickly, knowing that at any moment a demand might be made upon her which would divert the attention he jealously shared with her pupils.

Juey looked up. For once her eyes were solemn. So long he had hovered in the background. So long, as far ago as that distant evening under the rainbow's arch, he had been her ideal. Even now, in these years since she had returned from school, she could not remember when first she had secretly begun to love him.

"Yes," she answered, just as quickly.

Indifferent to all the watching pairs of young eyes, at last he took her in his arms to seal the promise with a kiss.

"When can we be married?"

"I don't know." Juey couldn't honestly say. "I can't leave Mother yet."

She consulted with her family. Because of his wife's continued ill health, the Rev. Malcolm had already asked to be transferred to a church outside, preferably in Manitoba. Anna now thought of a probable solution to Juey's problem. In England she had a niece who had expressed a desire to to come to Canada.

"Perhaps Alice would come and stay with me."

When word finally arrived from Bishop Young that the Scott family was to be transferred to the village of Westbourne in Manitoba, Juey wrote inviting her cousin to make her home with her parents.

One new phase of all the changes in the north involved the mail service. Replacing the old routine of mail out one year and replies in the next, now trader Jim Cornwall had secured a contract with Ottawa. Four times yearly this enterprising "Peace River Jim" brought the mail in, packing it on his back when other means was unavailable. Presently there arrived word from Alice that she would join the family in the summer of 1900.

"Splendid," beamed Sheridan. "Now we can be married very soon."

Fired now with more determination than ever to make a success of his enterprises, in that autumn of 1899 Sheridan flung himself into the business of demonstrating what modern methods could do for the country. Inspired by the example of the little group whose presence there had stemmed from Anglican missionary enterprise, quite a few families of mixed blood were now cultivating small holdings and growing wheat, oats and barley on fertile stretches of valley land sweeping back from both sides of the Peace. One of these areas, called Stoney Point, lay almost directly across from the Riverside Ranche, a name shortened at this time simply to The Ranch. Further down stream, also on the south bank of the Peace, Juey's father had an excellent stand of wheat, as did also Sheridan's cousin, Fred Lawrence. So then and there Sheridan made up his mind.

"I decided to raft my threshing outfit across the river to Stoney Point, do the threshing south of the river, then

162

come back, load my outfit on the raft again, drift down about two miles, then thresh on the north side."

By the time he had completed the threshing at North Vermilion, the co-operative Peace would probably be frozen over and unable to help him further. But cold would also freeze the muskeg and swampy areas on that trail from North Fort Vermilion—which he and his father and brothers had cut following the great flood of 1888—making it usable for the moving of heavy machinery.

"That fall, 1899, we threshed eleven thousand bushels, most of which had been cut by hand or with a mower. Some was grown on new land and some was very rank growth. Part of it also was frosted or frozen badly, making much of it difficult to thresh. However, we were able to help the settlers greatly."

By the time he had completed his circuit, snow lay deep on the ground. Since the crops had been stacked in readiness, he had been able to carry on. Next he put the engine to use grinding grain for chop, shorts and flour. Once again he demonstrated that modern machinery could make this northern countryside self-supporting.

Again he urged Juey to set a date for their wedding. A mutual sense of obligation to their parents became a bond of shared understanding between them. Paradoxically, it became a bond that also divided them.

They could not be married, insisted Juey, until she saw her mother settled outside in the new home.

"Perhaps," Sheridan worried, "you won't want to come back here."

They could start afresh somewhere else, perhaps in Manitoba. "But then we'd be giving up everything we've done here," he reflected. "I guess it's my duty to stay and make enough money to help Mother and Dad get out."

On her part Juey too wavered. She accompanied her parents on their difficult transition, stepping from the train at Westbourne on July the first, 1900. Here was another significant transition. They had come from the North-West Territories, where the queen's birthday, Victoria Day, was still the important "political" occasion to be marked with an annual social gathering. On the day of their arrival at the little Manitoba village northeast of Winnipeg, the Rev. Malcom's new parishioners were all out of town, attending a picnic to celebrate Canada's birthday.

The new manse was a small two-storey building sturdily shaped of oak logs but in a sad state of disrepair. While her father and Osborne attacked the exterior, Juey set to work scrubbing and re-papering the interior. Soon Sheridan arrived and she was overjoyed to see him.

He soon learned one reason why she welcomed him. His height and his long arms were the very things she needed to complete the papering, even though the job nearly destroyed the romance. In the fuss and mess, tempers became short and affection was strained to the breaking point. One afternoon an exhausted Juey let fall a strip of freshly-pasted paper. Angrily she stamped her foot on it. Sheridan looked quizzically at her but he said not a word.

Immediately, she was ashamed. "You'll never be able to say that you didn't know about my bad temper," she observed ruefully.

He comforted her with a kiss and the papering proceeded. Love survived the trying task. Still Juey hesitated about leaving her mother.

Sheridan was adamant. "It's you I want, Juey, and I won't wait any longer. If you won't marry me now, I'll find some one else."

She set the date and went to Winnipeg to acquire a trousseau. During her third year of teaching, Bishop Young had made over to her the full grant of two hundred dollars which the federal government had allotted to the Irene Training School, and every penny of this money she budgetted carefully.

First she commissioned a dressmaker to fashion her a dove-grey tailored suit, a dark green riding habit, and a wedding dress of French organdy over satin with demi-train and ornamentation requiring thirty yards of narrow French lace. Her other shopping included staples such as bolts of white flannelette, lengths of cotton prints, white mull, nun's veiling, navy serge and fine red cashmere, as well as twelve pairs of sheets, two dozen pillow cases, a number of linen tablecloths and yards of embroideries and trimming laces.

In Winnipeg her former guardian, Mr. Burman, coaxed her to see a doctor. "You don't look well," he told her.

The doctor told her what she herself knew to be true. She was "run down" from overwork. "You had better postpone your marriage," he advised. "For at least one year. Preferably two."

Without his parents, without her, it was going to be so lonely for Sheridan in the long northern winter. She knew that he had reached the brink of his patience. She decided to go ahead with her plans, even though her mother's warning words rang still in her ear, "It's a hard life, Juey, that you're choosing for yourself."

The sun beamed down upon the little log church at Westbourne as Juey walked down the aisle on the arm of her red-bearded father. Children of the parishioners had decorated the setting with lavish masses of sweet pea blossoms, and relatives and friends were present from Winnipeg and from the parish at St. Andrew's.

Almost stealing the show from the small bride was her eighty-year-old grandmother Anne Setter Scott. The old lady was desperately afraid of trains; besides, the jolting of these new-fangled monsters was thought to be bad for one who, like her grandmother, was supposed to have something wrong with her heart. So she had ridden all the way in a buggy pulled by a skittish young horse that was driven by her brother, John Setter. Still spunky and still sure of herself, she arrived at the church door all gorgeously arrayed in voluminous black silk. The performance of disembarking her while someone managed the nervous prancing horse rivalled the bride's appearance as an attraction.

With a candid eye the plain-spoken lady swept her glance over Juey in all her glamor.

"Fine feathers make a fine bird," she smiled waggishly. "There's only twice in your life you can be told you look pretty."

Juey's kindly Uncle John was loath to see her return to the wilderness. "I'll sell Sheridan a quarter section of my land," he offered. "And I'll make you a present of another quarter if you'll stay in Manitoba."

She passed her uncle's offer along to Sheridan, saying

nothing about the second quarter. She would not become involved in bribery.

In the northern land of the mighty Peace were his father's extensive fields and pastures and all the improvements, representing fourteen years of toil, of clearing and development. There were all the buildings, and the livestock and the mill, and back of it all the potential of a vast virgin land with its wide marginal river areas for free grazing and for hay-cutting and with its wealth of firewood and timber and wild game and its streams rich with fish and fur-bearing muskrat and beaver.

"Even if he weren't too proud to accept a gift," Juey told her uncle a little regretfully, "he would see a half section in Manitoba as far too small."

Here in Manitoba there were cleanliness and order and the niceties of civilization, with well-dressed people going about in a pleasant routine of living. So it seemed to Juey.

"We'll stay in the north five years," decreed the bridegroom.

They caught the train rocking west to Calgary and there they turned their faces to the north. Now Juey was about to participate in a second "Swiss Family Robinson" tale the outcome of which she could not begin to guess. Like the family of the Wyss story, the bride and groom were soon to be buffeted by the seas of fate. Like them, they went forward with no clear purpose other than to survive and to better their position.

At first, as a honeymooning couple, they did not pursue destiny too anxiously. The thrice-weekly train service now established between Calgary and South Edmonton on the North Saskatchewan river was leisurely, but not as leisurely as their mood. There was a two-hour mid-day stop at the half-way village of Red Deer. Over a meal they reminisced about the rainbow-brightened scene near the present vicinity when they first met fourteen years before.

"You were so cold and wet," laughed Juey.

"And you were so little," Sheridan teased.

They emerged at last from the restaurant to see the train puffing northward.

"Oh, Sheridan," cried the bride as she watched the dark

shapes of the final cars becoming pinpoints in the northern distance. She thought of that time, eight years before, when her father's driver had raced to try to catch the "accommodation" train. She seemed fated to miss trains at Red Deer. "What will we do?"

"Go to the hotel," was her bridegroom's prompt reply.

The proprietor of the small hotel seemed vaguely familiar. As Sheridan signed the register, he took a look at Juey.

"Aren't you the former Miss Scott?"

The bride acknowledged her identity. Now she remembered. The hotel-keeper was the former Sgt. Ellis of the mounted police, one of those who had befriended her family on that previous train-missing and who had suggested that some day she marry him.

Two days later, she and Sheridan caught the next train north.

In Edmonton Sheridan assembled more equipment and supplies for the ranch and arranged for it to be hauled to Athabasca Landing in two wagons. For his bride and himself he acquired a buggy, a tent, a stove and "a good camping outfit."

Bumping northward in the heavily-loaded buggy, along the Athabasca trail the newly-weds took fresh stock of the change that was everywhere rearing its head. More and more tiny clearings, dotted each with its log cabin, were gouged out of the bush; at Athabasca Landing a whole settlement replaced the fragrant wood of balsam fir that once served as Juey's special cathedral.

More prompt transportation by water was available too. On September the fourth Sheridan sought for his bride and himself a sheltered spot aboard one of "Peace River" Jim Cornwall's crowded York boats. So much were the niceties of civilization catching up with them that now Mr. Cornwall made Juey a wedding gift of books to read during the journey. The vagaries of water transportation, however, had not changed; so low were the levels of the Athabasca and the Lesser Slave rivers that the journeying on them involved, Sheridan recorded, "all tracking and no poling."

The weather, too, showed itself incapable of improvement. In the buggy the couple had been pelted with snow and sleet; by the time their York boat reached the vast sweep of Lesser Slave lake the bad weather worsened. Bitter winds and swamping waves tossed the bulky craft like a chunk of cork. Quickly the crew furled the sails and rowed for the shelter of the shore.

That night while the crew and the other passengers, all male, sought shelter in an Indian encampment, Sheridan and Juey remained aboard. With boxes of freight and with poles from the bush, they built a nook which they roofed over with a tarpaulin.

Wakening early, Juey hungered for breakfast. Several times she nudged her new husband, suggesting that it was high time to eat. Drowsily he mumbled an answer and slept again. At last, about nine o'clock, she sighed, "I certainly wish I was a man."

The wish brought instant action from the bridegroom. In a minute he was rummaging in the freight for tent and axe. Under driving rain he scrambled ashore. In the dripping marsh he chose a site and put up the tent.

His bride followed and quickly discovered why her husband had been so loath to start the day. If she stood still even for a minute, water oozed up all round her feet; in the sopping earth the pegs refused to hold and the tent toppled drunkenly. She joined in a search for dry twigs and presently a sulky blaze in the tiny sheet-iron heater brought the first shred of comfort.

On the lake whitecaps danced to the wind's tune and the boat shuddered restlessly. Obviously they were going to have to spend a second night storm-bound by the shore. So, while Juey cooked breakfast, Sheridan axed spruce boughs and at one end of the tent shaped with them a pungent mattress.

She had just stowed the breakfast paraphernalia back in the food box when the tall "Peace River" Jim arrived with several more passengers.

"Mm," grinned the big trader. "This is the coziest spot I've seen on the whole trip."

It was so much more comfortable than the rain-swept open boat or the drenching forest, that hospitality demanded that

168

the reluctant honeymooners make room for their uninvited guests. When some one mentioned food, the bride felt obliged again to make the right gesture. The men slipped out of the tent and came back with their arms loaded. Each one had raided his own freight, presenting her with cans of meat and vegetables and fruit. Her slim stock of bread she supplemented with hot-cakes.

The day became a kind of sample and a symbol forecasting the pattern of their lives. Regardless of race, color or creed or of the hour of the day or of the night, always Sheridan extended the hospitality of home and meals, and her parents' training taught Juey to share his generosity.

At first, the rugged northmen stood a little in awe of Sheridan's five-foot-two bride. After all, she was mission-raised and college-educated.

"I suppose you want us to sing hymns," teased "Peace River" Jim.

Soon they were all joining in both hymns and songs and swapping stories that she knew were being censored sufficiently to be acceptable to her.

That night Sheridan praised her for her efforts. "It did my heart good to see them tuck away all that food," she sighed with pleasure. As she basked in the warmth of her husband's approval, she sensed a pride in the way his new wife's presence had woven a kind of charm into a bleak storm-bound camp.

By the time they reached Buffalo Bay, and the hospitality of the Rev. George and Mrs. Holmes at St. Peter's mission, the weather too had grown friendly again.

Here they lingered for several days; Sheridan insisted on harvesting their host's potato crop while Juey filled her time with blueberry picking. One day as she made her way to the berry patch a solemn-eyed Indian woman approached her.

"You Juey Scott?" the stranger asked carefully.

"Yes," smiled Juey. "Juey Scott Lawrence now." The dusky face confronting her and the soft almost-pleading voice were shadowy-familiar.

"Me Louisa." The dark eyes seemed to beg for a sign of recognition. "Your father save my life."

Juey remembered. Instinctively she threw her arms about the black-braided woman. It was the unhappy youngster who, in those early bleak days of near-starvation, had been accused of eating her sister's flesh and becoming "weentigo," devil or witch.

Tears filled the sombre eyes. "Your father, I never forget," she repeated over and over. "He save my life." Softly she stroked Juey's hair.

In answer to her halting questions, the white girl told of her family whereabouts and of her father's new work and in her turn Louisa informed her of her own husband and children.

"Your father do this for me," she said again.

In the midst now of Juey's own overflowing cup of happiness, this chance encounter with Louisa came as a timely reminder to her of the example of her parents' lives. Indeed the lesson it blazoned forth to her stood her in particular good stead as she and Sheridan proceeded next to venture over the portage to the Peace. After weeks of summer rain, freighters reported that it was almost impassable. Gambling on his man and his final supply of cash, Sheridan offered it to the determined and discerning teamster Jake Hudson to move all his freight to the shore of the Peace. His stock of provisions included three hundred pounds of salt which he was taking to the ranch, his mother Maggie having sent word that she was obliged to store all her butter on ice, as there was no salt available at the trading post.

In exchange for some of the blueberries which Juey picked, Sheridan obtained the loan of a pair of lively cayuses from a nearby homesteader and he proposed that they two would drive in their new buggy over the portage.

Reports about the condition of the trail, they soon discovered, had not been exaggerated. It was indeed the worst they had ever experienced. Being still but a narrow cut through bush, the sun's rays could not penetrate to dry it out. They began to pass freighters whose wagons were mired to the hub in water and mud and Juey worried secretly about the fate of all her treasured purchases, which like the bulk of their supplies were all entrusted to Jake Hudson's care.

Finally they reached a section of the trail that had become one long silver-topped swamp of sluggish water.

"Here, Juey." Sheridan was handing her the reins. "You'll have to drive. I'll walk ahead and check."

Here and there along the portage previous drivers had criss-crossed all the worst of the myriad of mud-holes with crude corduroy lengths of rough logs or jagged sticks. These posed a constant threat of death to the horses; suddenly up-ended by a hoof, their spear-like ends tore gaping wounds in soft flesh and many a suffering horse had to be shot.

"Drive slowly," cautioned Sheridan. "We've got to be sure that we don't stake the horses."

Nervously holding her breath, Juey guided the sopping team where her husband indicated. Up on a hidden stump one wheel rose and the heavily-loaded buggy tipped crazily. Down in a deep pocket the other wheel dropped. Water began to ooze above the floor boards and to swirl about her feet.

"Good girl," Sheridan turned to grin encouragement each time they reached almost-dry ground again.

All the way to the Peace scenes of magnificent beauty were marred by the discomfort and even danger of the trail. By this time the autumn colorings of the deciduous bush and trees, yellow and orange and crimson, were beginning to lighten the great sombre spreads of evergreens; when they reached the plateau above the Peace Juey had her first sight of the breath-taking loveliness of the mountainous hills robed in their broad tapestry of fall hues.

Next morning they crawled from their tent to discover that the scene was still awesome in its loveliness but distressingly uncomfortable for camping honeymooners. Everything but the silver-streaked water of the restless river below was swaddled in a four-inch-thick wrapping of snow.

Soon they had quitted their breakfast camp-fire and were creaking down-hill to the flats bordering the Peace. Because it was trading time, the lonely little "Bay" post was open; because of the condition of the portage there was almost nothing to trade. Sheridan was able to procure only a little flour, some salt, a few pounds of dried beans and five pounds of rancid bacon. With these supplies and with the little he

171

had cached there on the way out, Juey was going to have to "make do."

Next morning her husband had another test awaiting her. Sheridan had borrowed a canoe and a wagon which he dismantled. He proposed to move up-stream twenty-five miles to a large island where girdled spruces were still plentiful and where he would hire the Indian, old Akernum, to help him build a raft.

Into the bottom of the dug-out he stowed the supplies as well as the pole, the reaches and the axle of the wagon. There was barely room for a bride and the four wheels.

"You sit in the bow," he directed. As she settled herself he laid two wheels across the canoe. Where was he going to place the second pair?

"Woud you mind?" he smiled as he swung one of them above her head.

"Oh, all right," she agreed. He lowered the wheel over her so that her head stuck up between the spokes. Carefully he placed the second above the first and began to pole out into the Peace.

"I feel so insecure," she complained presently. Surely, if the dug-out were to tip, she would be trapped under the pair of heavy wheels.

"Don't worry," grinned her confident husband. "There's no danger."

Highlighted by baking-powderless bannocks, the meals for the week's camping were far from idyllic. In spite of them it was an interlude of enjoyment. The snow had slipped silently away and the September sunshine filtered through woods both green and gold; while Sheridan worked to build the raft, for Juey there were at last hours of leisure to read or to knit or just to tease and talk.

It became a week to remember. They were deeply in love with each other and with life and with the northland. At last Sheridan was taking home the girl for whom he had waited so long. Far ahead, he knew, lay tremendous challenge and problems galore, problems with which the current of this Peace would confront them all too soon.

Even here in this autumn tranquility he suffered many an anxious moment. He had gambled on Jake Hudson, paying out to him his last two hundred dollars on the guarantee that the hardy freighter would win the battle with the portage. In his freight were not only his bride's whole trousseau but so many necessities for converting the ranch into a successful venture.

While he worried about the fate of Hudson, he completed the finishing touches on the raft. His helper Akernum agreed to manoeuvre it down-stream while he and Juey rode in the wagon back to the meeting point on the river flat. Just as they came in sight of the eight-hundred-foot hill down which the portage trail wound, they made out dark specks that grew into wagons beginning to descend its slope.

Sheridan hustled the Indian cayuses. They rattled forward and he saw that the wagons indeed belonged to Freighter Hudson. This was an omen of good luck; Sheridan had measured his man correctly.

They pushed the new raft across the river and Juey watched with delight while Sheridan assisted Hudson and his men to load all their freight straight from wagons to raft.

"Took us nine days, though," commented the freighter. "And I didn't count how many times we got stuck." Repeatedly he had had to take off half a load, pull the other half through, unload that portion, then return for the balance. That, he told them, had been the routine all along the portage.

Sheridan anchored the tent on the raft, and secured the stove in place in the bride's kitchen corner. Then he poled their "ship" out into the central channel of the Peace.

It was October the first, 1900, and the river had reached its maximum low. Within an hour, Juey discovered that there were many living creatures aboard other than herself and her husband. During the transfer of the freight, they had also taken on dozens of hungry mice.

Together they contrived a trap, a half-filled pail suspended over the side of the raft. Over it they balanced a stick temptingly weighted with cheese and presently this "trap" disposed of all the extra passengers.

Progress down river was slow and, for Juey, very different from that first racing voyage of fourteen years before.

With low water and long hours of darkness they dared not attempt to move by night, so each evening Sheridan sought out a suitable spot to tie up. His bride dipped into the crates of canned provisions to provide variety for their suppers but soon she longed for the taste of fresh meat.

"Where's the moose you promised me?" she teased.

"Coming soon." Sheridan smiled with assurance. He turned to survey the passing landscape, with which by this time he was quite familiar. "It'll be round the next point," he guessed.

They curved round the next point of the tortuous stream and there, as if raised by a magician's wand, on the brow of a rise a moose was feeding.

Sheridan grabbed his gun and launched the dug-out. "You'll have to guide the raft," he shouted as he shoved toward the shore.

Juey stepped forward to grasp one of the long sweeps. With alarm she gazed ahead. As luck would have it, they were heading straight for a sizeable island planted right in the midst of the river's main channel.

From the canoe her husband saw her predicament. Frantically he signalled for her to steer to the right of the island. She looked where he pointed. Surely the right channel was too shallow.

She made a quick decision. In spite of his signal, she steered for the left channel, which appeared so much deeper. Pushing with all the wiry strength of her small body, she manipulated the heavy sweep as she had seen Sheridan and her father doing. As the raft nosed close to the gravel bar edging the island, she succeeded in forcing it into the left channel.

If this were another omen, at the moment neither recognized it as such. Sheridan's quarry had turned and fled without his even reaching firing range. When he scrambled back aboard, he commended her choice.

"You did right, Juey," he said, sealing his praise with a kiss.

As they twisted and turned over the many zigzagging bends of the now-placid Peace, Sheridan began to check the calendar. His brother Jim was still living with his wife Florence at Prairie Point.

"I'd like to make it there by the fifteenth, Jim's birthday," he planned.

Finally ahead loomed Oliver's island, so-named, it was said, because a man of that name cutting wood for the "Bay" was drowned in its vicinity. Sheridan pointed out other familiar landmarks, the shelf beyond indicating Prairie Point and, ahead on their right, the area of the Waterhen lakes where he and his brothers crossed the river to harvest timber and hay.

Next morning, after an over-night stay with Jim and Florence, they concluded their travelling honeymoon. There limned into view the treetops on the triple islands that obstructed the mile-wide channel fronting the Ranch. To inform the family of their approach, Sheridan boomed forth a pair of double volleys on his gun. Because at this late-autumn season the left channel was too shallow to accommodate their bulky craft, he proceeded to "shoot the snye," manoeuvring round about on the right side of the first island. He poled toward the landing stage and Juey looked with fresh eyes upon the land that was once more to be her home.

It was October the sixteenth. Already the sun, reflected upon the pellucid water of the Peace and in a hundred soft shades upon the rocks and pebbles lining the shore, shone also in rainbow refraction upon ice patches fringing the water's edge. A few golden leaves still clung to the great light-loving balms and brightened the reassuring deep green of the tall spruces. There was a suggestion of oriental coloring that reminded the young woman of an Egyptian etching that she had admired back in Manitoba.

Soberly, as she watched her husband's competence on this water where he was so much at home, she pondered. Here were contradiction, puzzlement, paradox. From this imperious river that seemed to command their lives stemmed a spaciousness and a freedom and a challenge. This was the northland that they both loved. This was home.

Surely this restless river, if it could speak, would welcome them back. Surely its song, telling of the rich magnificence of this great empty land of which it was the pulsing, life-sustaining heart, echoed upon their own heartstrings a melody vibrant with hope and with promise of achievement.

CHAPTER 2

Again Sheridan announced something of the time measure of his dream.

The first few hours ashore told Juey that this five-year plan of her husband's was going to bristle with problems.

The large ranch-house that was to be the new home of his bride was still not entirely complete; he and his brothers hadn't yet had time to roof over the upper storey. His parents were planning to leave in due time but, meanwhile, they were still established on the premises. Sleeping arrangements were therefore sketchy, with Henry and Maggie quartered in one curtained-off end of the living-room and Sheridan and Juey accommodated similarly, on the floor, at the other. Minnie, the second daughter, was keeping house for her uncle E. J. at Edmonton, where he had retreated after Lydia's death. But all of the younger boys, Isaac and John and Arthur and Wilson, were still at home and slept in the crowded bunk-house with the two hired men.

Warmly hospitable as always, Maggie welcomed her new daughter-in-law with motherly affection. After the staggering load of the school and the mission-house, to Juey the fresh routine of the Ranch was by comparison a light affair, and she set to work with a will to do her share. Afterward, Maggie confessed to having had her eyes newly opened.

"You were such a dainty little thing when I first saw you," she mused, remembering that evening long ago by the Red Deer. "Just like a little flaxen doll."

She went on to add with a rueful smile, "I didn't think you were the right wife for Sheridan. Yet you get far more work done around here than I can."

Juey laughed at Maggie's confession. She had half suspected her disapproval. She was delighted now that the passing of her probation test was accompanied by such words of candid praise.

Out-of-doors, the presence again of the organizing spirit of the eldest son stepped up the whole pace of progress on the Ranch. Impending winter demanded haste, so Sheridan tackled all the tasks awaiting in the order of their greatest necessity.

"The boys had dug the potatoes and had put them in covered piles in the field. My first job was to finish the big cellar in the new house, then line the walls with tamarack poles in order to make them frost-proof. After that we collected the potatoes and put them in the root cellars. Then we finished stacking the grain and got ready to start threshing."

Before he set the thresher humming, he took time to complete the roof over the new home. The upstairs also he partitioned in two, and now he and Juey moved to sleep in one room, "still on the floor," Juey noted, "but with so much more privacy," and the two hired men were transferred from the over-crowded bunkhouse to sleep in the other.

Again this season there came requests from neighbors across river at Stoney Point and down river also, to do threshing for them. Now in 1900, at the beginning of this new chapter in his life, Sheridan determined that a different order should reign in the district. Because there was little or no cash in the area, a sloppy system of credit-giving prevailed both at the Ranch and around the countryside generally, and wages were frequently paid as credit notes on a trading store, usually that of the Hudson's Bay Company.

First, with the help of his brothers and the two hired men, he threshed quite a good home crop of wheat and barley. Then he was ready to challenge local custom and to thresh for the neighbors.

"How'll you carry on without a crew?" his father Henry asked him. "The men won't work unless you pay cash. Or unless you give them an order on the Hudson's Bay store."

"In that case, we'll neither thresh nor grind their grain," announced his son.

177

He was as flat broke as every one else. But he was determined.

"I was on the war path, and I decided to see the thing through," he noted afterward. The new order must prevail.

With a half crew, he started up. To have his marvellous machine pant noisily to their modest holdings and replace the ox-trampling or the hand-flailing methods of threshing grain that dated back to antiquity, would, he guessed, be quickly coveted as a mark of prestige among his Métis neighbors.

"If I thresh you, you must pay me with furs," he decreed. "Or you pay me with work on the outfit. There's not going to be one dollar in wages going in orders on stores. And we're not giving any more credit either."

Despite his father's bleak prediction, his new policy paid dividends. He rafted the big separator and "boiler" across to Stoney Point, taking along as well his grain crusher and his wood-sawing rig. Soon he had a full crew and "a really good business."

He moved on down to the mission area and even included his cousin Fred Lawrence in his transactions. Fred had been forced to sell wheat at a dollar a bushel to the "Bay" to get supplies; now Sheridan offered him a dollar and a half. Because the grain was stacked, again he was able to carry his operations into the winter months. For his customers when he came to thresh their grain, he was also able to crush feed and to saw wood right in their farm yards. The season's harvest of wheat, oats and barley that poured from his separator spout totalled some fourteen thousand bushels.

"It was a really good business for us and excellent training for the young men in the country then," he noted with satisfaction. In this land the threshing-machine had finally supplanted the flail and the oxen.

By the month of March Sheridan's enterprise involved more work with his new saw-mill. He and his helpers hauled and sawed a thousand logs and prepared hundreds of shingles; then with all this added building material they hustled on to complete the big ranch-house. This achievement marked another milestone on the road to modern methods, for the back-breaking chore of whip-sawing was now also banished into the past.

178

While Sheridan lunged forward from one gigantic undertaking to the next, all the while blissfully happy with married life, Juey struggled to conceal her distaste for it. She was expecting her first baby and her surroundings did not ease her discomfort.

"Ugghh!" she would sigh in secret, thinking of the clean gentle home over which her mother ruled. Here there were so many big careless men, smoking and spilling ashes about the rooms and tramping thoughtlessly through the house with manure on their boots. The example of her mother's cheerful acceptance of the role of wife lighted her darker days and steadied her so that she could still lend a hand in time of serious need.

With two families managing the Ranch, there sometimes resulted a clash that produced unfortunate results. Perhaps because more than once, both back in Ontario and here in the north-west, Henry Lawrence had seen the grim spectre of starvation shadowing his family, he had a mania for planting too many potatoes. The frozen surplus, of course, was always fed to the animals, but his children came to dread "potato-pickin' time." One summer they heard the adults discussing a prediction that the world was soon coming to an end.

"Gee whiz!" sighed young Will, the first white boy born in the north Peace. "If the world's going to come to an end, I sure hope it does before potato pickin' time."

One evening now Sheridan made the rounds of the barns, shovelling out to the stabled animals generous portions of frozen potatoes. Presently his father, not knowing that the beasts had already been fed, served them all with second liberal helpings. The oxen, loving the special treat of frozen potatoes, soon gorged themselves with them.

When Sheridan discovered the error, he hurried the beasts out of door and began to exercise them. All through the night he walked them, back and forth, back and forth. Early in the morning, one ox was still so bloated that death appeared imminent.

Sheridan rushed upstairs to Juey, she who had administered first aid to one and all.

179

"Where," he wanted to know quickly, "is an oxen's stomach? Would you come and show me where to pierce it?"

At home in the mission Juey was thoroughly familiar with two much-fingered books, "The Family Physician," and "The Farmers' Guide." As she flung on some clothing, she concentrated on diagrams in the latter book, which also gave directions about piercing a bovine stomach.

With a ruler the young couple measured a line from the the animal's hip bone to a rib in the region of the flank and thereon Juey sketched a triangle.

"That's the spot," she pointed.

With his sterilized pocket knife Sheridan punctured the tough ox-hide at the apex of the triangle. There was a terrific outrush of gas and then he washed the wound with turpentine.

The suffering beast lived and Juey's stock rose accordingly on the bustling Ranch.

Then there was the sickening moment when Sheridan rushed the "tail" sawyer into the house with blood streaming from his hand. The saw had sliced off his thumb at the main joint. Maggie turned away, looking suddenly ghastly ill.

"You'll have to help him, Juey," she gasped.

Juey stanched the flow of spurting blood and dressed the wound as best she could. There was now a trained nurse in attendance down-stream at the Roman Catholic mission, and she persuaded the man to go with Sheridan to get further attention from her.

Already the new order which her husband's taking over of the Ranch was bringing about involved Juey in more and more responsibility. With the break-up of the Peace in the spring of 1901, for the price of six thousand dollars his father turned over the major share of his holdings to him. Then Henry and two other of his sons, Arthur and Will, left to establish themselves outside. Following the old pattern, Maggie was to join them later when Henry would have found her a new home.

If Sheridan were going to convert the Ranch into a profitable enterprise, he was going to have to find more markets or to force the "Bay" to give better prices. Freight rates for bringing goods in were high, seven dollars per hundred pounds, or one hundred dollars per ton. And prices for produce, so Sheridan insisted, did not measure correspondingly.

"The 'Bay' had not played fair with father," he wrote. Henry had sold them butter at twenty-five cents per pound, fresh bacon at ten cents and beef at six cents. The "Bay" needed produce for trade and for the use of its own men, both at Fort Vermilion and down-stream and further along at the various sub-Arctic posts. So in this year of 1901 Factor Wilson finally met Sheridan's price demands, buying from him fifteen hundred dollars' worth of bacon and butter.

Then a small competitor of the great trading company, George Carter, who was acting for Bredin and Cornwall, purchased from him five hundred dollars' worth of flour, bacon and butter. There was one hitch to the deal; Sheridan must agree not to sell flour to the all-mighty "Bay." The small mill which he had set up for his father on the creek he now operated by the steam engine. Still it was small, producing only one hundred pounds of flour in a whole hour's operation. Yet flour was a key factor in the conflict arising from trade.

At this time dire rumors began to spread. The "Bay," so reports said, saw in Sheridan's determination a growing threat to their near-monopoly and they were planning to spoke his enterprise.

Presently Juey turned her attention from this vital conflict in the matter of markets and trade to a vital problem of her own. It was September the thirteenth of 1901 and the birth of her first baby was imminent. In spite of all the vicissitudes Maggie had known, she was the most nervous person present. "Isn't the room going round?" she asked amid the confusion.

Having delivered a number of infants for her Indian and Métis neighbors, Juey herself directed the young woman Charlotte Flett, who assisted her. Though it was a Friday, the only bad luck evident was a pair of tiny thumb-like appendages hanging by a thread of skin outside each of her new daughter's little fingers. She was sure that the superstitious would associate these with the sawyer's lost thumb.

With strangers Sheridan was still shy and reserved. But

181

this small stranger he took at once to his heart, demonstrating an intense affection for the tiny child that delighted Juey. On the little one's third day of life, she noted on his face a mask of suffering. Shortly she discovered the cause—he had nipped the thumb-like bit from one of the baby's hands. The other was presently to drop off of itself.

As Baby Hester throve and grew fat, her only flaw was a persistently "teary" eye. This too was cured in pioneer fashion. During a lull in his feuding with Post Manager Wilson at the "Bay," Sheridan had agreed to sell him a load of grain. Juey bundled up the child and with her went along for the ride.

Within a day or two after, the infant's eye stopped overflowing. "That jolting over the river ice was good for Hester," she told the doting father. "It has cleared her tear duct."

Because Sheridan dealt sometimes with the "Bay's" competitors or was himself obliged to become more and more involved in outright trading, accepting furs in exchange for the produce of the Ranch or for the services of his machines, frequently Factor Wilson refused to buy from him at all.

Sheridan scoffed at this. "He's hoping to drive me from the country."

In his determination not to let the powerful concern force him to quit, Juey backed him to the hilt. All her life, in fact, she had been familiar with aspects of this trading conflict; her father Malcolm used to relate how his father, struggling to make ends meet on the narrow strip farm in the Red River colony, engaged in freighting and trading down into American territory under the very nose of the monopolistic Hudson's Bay Company who had once been his employer.

If there were no butter anywhere available except that made at the Ranch, Post Manager Wilson protested that his own family didn't need butter and that bear's grease was quite good enough. Juey knew that his wife loved butter and from time to time she would sell or make small presents of some to her.

She was present at their table once for a meal when the factor spied butter.

"Please pass the butter," he requested.

"Oh," teased his wife. "I thought you preferred bear's grease."

The two women were fast friends, and Juey always returned from a visit with her inspired by her great compassion for one and all.

"Such a marvelous humanitarian," she reminded Sheridan, who saw her husband in a very different light. "Always helping the Indians in every way she can."

Presently the "Bay" showed that it did intend to stiffen its competition with Sheridan. It shipped in an up-to-date flour mill, many times larger than his modest outfit. Again Sheridan accepted the challenge; this kind of competition whetted his determination to succeed.

"In those days I was fighting mad," he told his family afterward. "I'd rather fight than eat."

When later friends asked him why he stayed so long in the north, he threw back his head and laughed.

"Why, it was the 'Bay' that was responsible. They made life so interesting I just couldn't leave."

When his first son arrived on the Ranch in December of 1902, his mother Maggie had gone out to join his father in Boisevain, Manitoba, and Juey could get no help at all. In spite of Factor Wilson's opposition to him, Mrs. Wilson arrived to lend a hand. She assisted at the birth and remained with Juey for two days.

"Which showed," wrote Juey in her diary, "how in the pioneer days women would help one another even over the heads of their husbands' feuding."

That winter neither she nor her compassionate neighbor saw any other white women.

The new baby, named Malcolm for Juey's father, continued cranky and scrawny and it wasn't until long afterward that she realized that he hadn't been getting sufficient food. In desperation one evening she boiled cow's milk and, diluting it with water, fed the mixture to him from a cup. She had no such treasure on hand as a baby's rubber nipple. That night, for the first time, the child slept through until four in the morning. His young mother was overjoyed.

Next day she continued the mixture of boiled milk and

water. That second night she lay awake in terror, fearing fatal convulsions.

"I was just too tired to think of that last night," she told her husband.

There were no complications and she began to strain whole wheat porridge into the infant's milk. From then on, he throve.

It would have surprised Maggie and those medical men who twice had pointed out to her her physical frailty—so she smiled to herself sometimes—to discover how she too throve under the stern discipline of ranch mistress and mother. With no household help, she cared for the children, and regularly she prepared meals for six to nine men. Spring came gently with no flooding and she added gardening to her program. Like the fields of grain that Sheridan and his men planted, under the long slanted rays of sunshine her vegetables and flowers sprang up like Jack's beanstalk.

Similar to the wild game, the wild fruits followed cycles of sparsity and plenty. During this summer of 1903 the strawberries, lush and abundant, hung in fat red droplets and Juey, in spite of two hampering babies, could not bear to see them all go to waste. Pushing Malcolm in his buggy and with Hester toddling beside her and the dog Prince cavorting near, she tramped forth to the river flats where the crop was most prolific. Down in the buggy she tucked both children, and she shook a warning finger at the dog.

"Now, Prinney, you stay right beside them."

He understood and lay in the tall grass beside the buggy. Presently she heard a child's cry. At the same time Prinney came galloping to call her. If she did not hustle to them at once, he would run back and attempt to soothe the baby by licking his face. That made him yell all the louder. The worried dog rushed to grab Juey's skirt, trying to inform her how urgently she was needed.

There was small danger of the children's being molested. Occasionally during saskatoon-picking Juey would find herself sharing a patch with a black bear feasting on his favorite native berry. Upon discovering her presence, the animal would plunge back into the woods, obviously much more alarmed than she.

By August of that summer of 1903 the branches of the

184

fruit-bearing shrubs were bowed low with the weight of an extra-bountiful crop. She envisioned dozens of containers filled with jam and preserves but meantime she had told Sheridan that a third baby was on the way.

"No more berry picking," he dictated. With his men he was hurrying to complete the haying. "One of these days it will rain. Then the men and I will pick the berries."

Sure enough, soon rain pelted down for several days. Sheridan and his men tied ten-gallon cream-cans to their saddles and rode off to the berry patches. They rode home with gallons of fragrant saskatoons and raspberries and blueberries and cranberries. Juey dried and canned and packed and her shelves in the dark ice-cellar grew into a treasure-store of red and purple-filled jars and cans.

If it were love that gave life meaning, late that same autumn she had a heart-warming illumination of its value. Down at the Anglican mission now, Miss May White kept house for her brother the Rev. Alfred White, and taught the Indian children in Juey's place. In response to a pressing invitation, the young mistress of the Ranch carried off her little ones Hester and Malcolm to her former home; she planned to remain a whole week.

The visit was proceeding with apparent mutual enjoyment. Her hosts were well-educated English folk who were born in India to an army colonel, five members of whose family gave a total of one hundred and ninety years to mission work in the Peace country. Juey savored with relish every minute of their company. She even treated herself to a special purchase, an extra-large and magnificent home-made quilt that had arrived in a mission bale. When she thought of the number of times that she awakened shiveringly cold after Sheridan in his sleep "cocooned" the bedding about his six-feet-two frame, the extravagant sum of nine dollars which she paid for it did not seem a penny too much.

On the third day, Sheridan appeared. His face was so woebegone that at once she sensed disaster.

"You'll have to come back," he blurted. "I just can't stand it without you."

At once she cut short her visit. On the way as he put his arm tightly about her waist, he repeated, "The house is just too empty. Seems life's got no meaning without you."

She heaved a heavy sigh of resignation.

He had prepared a home-coming surprise. Day and night in her absence he had bent to the task and with the speed of the shoemaker's elves he had fashioned and planed to a creamy finish a high chair and several cup chairs and a long settee. In her turn, to add to the joy of the reunion, she produced her treasure, the gay quilt.

For several years it warmed her outwardly and it warmed her inwardly with the memory of those brief words that told of his desperate need for her. One day an unfortunate who had lost his bed-roll happened along. Sheridan, who had been nurtured on Maggie's pioneer teaching of "share and share alike," handed his wife's quilt to the luckless traveller to warm him on his way.

Presently Juey had again a special reason for being grateful to the jolly Miss White of St. Luke's mission. It was now March the 17th of 1904 and she was expecting the arrival of her next child. Because she herself was about to give birth, the native midwife Mrs. Charlotte Flett declined to come. So off through the extra-deep snow Sheridan drove to fetch the gentle Englishwoman.

On the fifteen-mile return drive one mare played completely out and refused to move a step farther. Sheridan unharnessed her and she staggered through a drift to lean against a tree. He was wearing his beautiful musk-ox coat that had been fashioned in Montreal from skins he had brought back from the sub-Arctic. Pulling it off, he tucked it all round about the small shivering Miss White, and proceeded to lead the second horse.

Step by step he coaxed it through the drifts, sometimes himself lending a hand to help pull the sleigh. To lighten the load, from time to time the kind-hearted passenger jumped out and trailed along behind. Once, when the exhausted beast stopped dead and refused to budge another inch; she grabbed up the oat bag and rushed up to the animal's nose.

"Would you like some grain?" she pleaded in her soft English voice.

In after years, among the growing Lawrence family the words, "Would you like some grain?" became a sort of happy byword in moments of predicament, a byword that was guaranteed to produce gales of hearty laughter.

It proved after all a lucky St. Patrick's day for Juey. Fortunately Mrs. Flett relented and travelled the two miles across river to be with her. Discovering that the cord was twisted about the infant's neck, the experienced midwife was able to slip it free and to bring about a successful birth.

Next morning, carrying hay and oats in the sleigh, Sheridan set forth to search for the exhausted mare. He half expected to come upon her carcass, buried in snow. He met her, head on, plunging with dogged steps along the homeward trail.

With the new baby Margaret, there was to be a second equine association. The child was extremely fussy and at last her anxious parents tried her on a diet of mare's milk. On this she throve for three weeks. Her mother pored over articles on infant feeding and next came up with the suggestion that they offer the little one a mixture of milk from several cows. This now, too, seemed to agree with her.

From a pinnacle of after-wisdom Juey later concluded, "The truth of it was that the poor wee thing simply did not get enough to eat."

The irony of this situation, on a ranch where disposal of masses of foodstuffs was a growing and disturbing problem and where already its master was handing out great chunks of frozen skimmed milk as free gifts to the Indians, brought a wry smile to her lips.

Unexpectedly the "Bay" contributed toward helping to solve a portion of Sheridan's marketing problems. In order to be able to move the flour which the company expected to grind in the new mill, it hired men to cut a road between Fort Vermilion and Little Red River in the vicinity of the Chutes. Here flour could be stock-piled until summer, when steamers could distribute it to the company's posts down the northern waterways as far as the Arctic ocean. During the late winter of 1903 Factor Wilson paid Sheridan to break out the road and then, at ninety dollars per ton, to freight ninety tons of flour as far as Little Red River.

In the matter of wheat-buying the two men also came to terms and in the years 1903-04 the master of the Ranch sold the post manager over two thousand bushels at a total of $4273.

Then, before all the snow melted in that late spring of 1904, there came another offer which Sheridan accepted with satisfaction. The company decided to build a boat of spruce lumber right at Fort Vermilion and Factor Wilson invited him to get the timber out for it. A boat plying between the Chutes and Hudson Hope in British Columbia on the upper Peace could mean new markets for produce from the Ranch.

Packing camp equipment, sacks of frozen food and tools, with a gang of helpers he set off up the Peace to search out suitable timber.

"It was getting late in the season. But we were able to move most of the logs for the boat to the river. After the ice went out, we landed a raft of logs measuring over 60,000 board feet at the company's mill at Fort Vermilion." In a spirit of fairness he added, "And we were well paid for it."

The achievement he viewed with special pride.

"This raft would be considered a small one in the east," his notes added. "But it was a good size then for our parts. There were no power boats at our disposal; there was swift water; besides, we could not get experienced river men."

Those five years for which he had planned were drawing to a close. His brothers John and Isaac were still sharing the work of the Ranch, but they were anxious now to go outside and start on their own. The year 1903 had seen a harvest of some six thousand bushels and another big crop was in sight.

"We can't leave yet," he told his wife. "But if the boys would wait till next spring, you and I could take a trip out together."

Juey agreed that they must stay on a while longer. Jubilantly she began to make preparations for the holiday even while she continued with the regular ranch-house routine. Indoors as well as out the problem of getting and keeping help was continuous. Also continuous was the preparation of meals and, in winter, if Sheridan and his men were going to be away hauling freight or cutting timber, a kind of large-scale stock-piling of food for them. For such occasions her program involved the filling of one-hundred-pound sacks with doughnuts, which could be eaten without being thawed, and with innumerable stewed minced-meat patties containing also potatoes, onion and carrots.

John and Isaac agreed to take charge of the Ranch over winter, with their oldest brother promising accordingly to pay each of them two thousand instead of one thousand dollars for their interest in the property. For the trip outside Sheridan rented a large Peterborough canoe and he and George Bristow, a hired helper who was leaving for outside with the family, stowed in it a load of freight including camping equipment and provisions. Into a nest of bed-rolls in the centre of the craft they tucked the small children, Hester, Malcolm and Baby Margaret; Juey squeezed herself in beside them and away they paddled up river. It was September the 14th of 1904 and already the early mornings were bitterly cold.

"We arose each morning with the sun, had a cup of tea, fed the baby, and stopped at ten for breakfast, at one for dinner and at four for tea and to feed the baby again; at dusk we stopped to put up the tent."

Meantime Sheridan watched for a sheltered spot for the night's camping. As soon as he had erected the tent, he made a wall of stones to keep the small children from falling into the numbing Peace and George Bristow selected a niche for his bed-roll away from the family's tent. It was Juey's sixth journeying over this tortuous three-hundred-mile stretch of the Peace and she had prepared for it with the experience of a veteran. She had brought plenty of canned tomatoes which she mixed with mashed potatoes or cooked rice or sago to feed the little ones; at night over the camp-fire she baked bannocks for the following day and washed clothing, using the baby bath-tub that had been presented to her mother by J. H. Ashdown, Winnipeg's first hardware merchant, when she herself had been born.

The children throve on this camp diet but the adults were overjoyed when, on the fourth day out from the Ranch, they sighted a moose. Juey stuffed the children's mouths with candy to keep them quiet and her husband knocked the animal down with one shot from his rifle. In great haste they put in to shore and Sheridan followed the wounded beast over a ridge. When it saw him, with a rush it turned and charged him. He dropped it with a second shot.

After several more days of up-stream paddling and poling, they met more good fortune. As they were putting in to find a camping spot for the night, an old Indian woman, Mrs. Cardinal, paid them a visit. Beaming on the little ones, she brought a pail of fresh milk for "Mr. Scott's grandchildren." She insisted on the family taking shelter overnight in her cabin; she was both clean and intelligent and Sheridan and Juey thankfully accepted her hospitality. "Surprisingly enough, she was of the Roman Catholic faith. But in those days, differences of color and religion meant little."

Next morning before they resumed their voyage, their hostess baked bannocks enough to last them for a number of meals.

As they neared Peace River Crossing, Sheridan had the good fortune to bag a second moose. This time he kept the hide; the bulk of the meat he gave to the Indians.

On their last night along the river, they camped on a gravel bar. Here, as the moon came up, it lighted the majestic evergreens blanketing the sides of the steep cut-banks above the Peace. Juey lay in the tent listening. Out of the stillness came a weird sound, a kind of moan proceeding perhaps from the throat of some one in dire trouble. Again and again it was repeated.

"Sure it's some man in distress who's seen our campfire," concluded Juey.

She wakened Sheridan; he listened for a minute. Then he pulled on trousers and jacket and paddled quietly across the river in the direction of the sound. His anxious wife added wood to the slumbering coals and suspended the kettle over them as she strained to watch him disappear in the dusk.

In a few minutes he was back with the single comment, "The next time you get me up to hunt out an old screech owl, I'll be a lot older."

Juey hurried to make him a soothing cup of tea. Actually the owl's call, echoing through the trees and bouncing off the cut banks, seemed so different that neither of them had recognized it.

After fourteen days on the river, they thankfully accepted the hospitality of Herbert George, the Hudson's Bay Company representative at Peace River Crossing. Mr. George was also a lay reader or catechist in the Anglican church; he and his wife, a full-blooded Cree woman, made Juey and the children welcome while they waited for Sheridan to complete arrangements for their further journeying.

This next lap, over the portage, was true to form again in its testing of human endurance. First Sheridan hired a ride with a Mr. Robinson from the Shaftesbury Mission and for a few rods all went well. Then, about half-way up the steep hill-side above the Peace, a wagon wheel locked. The luckless horses pulled and strained in their traces and pulled again; finally they panicked. The men tried in vain to remove the wheel so as to regrease it and the frightened animals swung over to the side of the sharp incline. Sheridan hurried to block the wheels and to help his wife and little ones clamber from the wagon.

Next, hunting out a Métis called Benjamin, he hired his team and wagon for the journey.

Now the weather had turned rainy and again this portage to Lesser Slave lake was nearly impassable. "It was, in fact, one mud-hole, ninety-eight miles long," recorded Sheridan.

The entire valley flat of the Hart river, three miles wide, was flooded. So once again he fashioned a raft and on it he transferred his family. Then the men lashed the wagon-box to the wheels so that it couldn't float away and the horses waded across.

As they proceeded, Juey knew more worry. Surely the jolting of the wagon was going to pitch Baby Margaret from her lap. Finally she bundled her into a fine cashmere shawl and slung her over her shoulder; she tied up her own long skirts and petticoats, slipped off her shoes and stockings and, wearing only rubbers on her feet, she tramped a good part of the way.

A slight little clergyman, Mr. Williams, was crossing the portage with them. From time to time he did his best to encourage the young mother.

"Mrs. Lawrence, if it's of any reassurance to you, I am walking right behind the wagon. I shall hold it down if it starts to slip."

She was also delighted with her chivalrous friend when the wagon got mired hopelessly on a stretch of corduroy called Crooked Bridge. Said he, "Mrs. Lawrence, if I were Samson, I would love to lift you from the wagon."

As the men struggled to free the vehicle, an end of heavy stick up-ended in the mud, whacking Sheridan's heel. He turned white with the extreme pain; as he hung onto the wagon his wife tossed a cup of cold water over his face, shocking his color back. He broke then into a drenching sweat, so he told her after, but in a few minutes he had recovered.

Presently they reached a stopping-place operated by Pete Leduc, a former hired man of Sheridan's. With a wide-mouthed grin he welcomed "Big Boss," and soon the family basked in the warmth of his cabin. At the end of the portage there were more welcome and warmth, in the hospitable St. Peter's mission where the Rev. Robert Holmes and his wife made their home.

The pioneering flavor of the holiday continued as they travelled by wagon fourteen miles to Willow Point and forward from there by York boat. At this Willow Point anchorage on Lesser Slave lake, sixty passengers were distributed in the three Bredin and Cornwall narrow vessels, but departure was delayed until a party of mounties arrived with a prisoner. The captive, whose name was King, was being brought out on a charge of having murdered his partner. He had been arrested, Sheridan was told, after an observing Indian boy noticed that he was obliged to keep his missing partner's dog on a leash.

It was now October and each morning until about ten o'clock the oars were sheathed with ice. When a wind sprang up, sails were unfurled and in spite of the bitter cold Juey admired the stark magnificence of the scene. "With the sun blazing on the wide waters and on the full white sails it all looked so beautiful."

At night she and the children slept in the stern sheets of the boat and all of the men except the mounties, who took their prisoner ashore, bundled themselves into bed-rolls out in the open. Even with partial protection from the biting breezes she suffered from the cold because she covered the children with part of her own bedding; at the end of the water-journey over lake and rivers, and the two-day trip by freight wagon from Athabasca Landing to Edmonton, she was looking forward with eager anticipation to the prospect of at last banishing the chill from her bones. Alas, the management of the hotel where they sheltered had not yet begun to fire the furnace.

Eventually they reached the heart-and-body-warming welcome of the manse at Westbourne in Manitoba. Juey found her mother still happy and still belittling her suffering, and her father as exuberant as of old. The fiery beard he had reduced a little in length not long after an impertinent woman's query.

"Mr. Scott, how do you keep your beard in such beautiful condition? Do you sleep with it in a bag?"

Via the grapevine his daughter heard too that he had been seen racing home from a funeral which he had conducted and she charged him with this transgression. She knew that, like the pedlar Sam Slick, he still dearly loved good horse-flesh.

Malcolm smiled delightedly. "Well, that *is* a smart horse I've got there. At first the farmer wouldn't sell him to me; he said preachers starved their beasts. I told him I'd once been a farmer and that I looked after my horse better than myself."

"But, father," persisted Juey, "is it true about the racing?"

At the recollection, mirth pranced in Malcolm's sea-blue eyes. "Mm. We were coming home from Mr. M . . .'s funeral. One of my neighbors wanted to pass me. Well, my horse didn't want to pull over. That was all."

Later on, returning from Manitoba, Juey herself became involved in a different kind of race. Meantime, in her parents' home, she feasted on the warmth and the sleep that she craved. The doctor whom she consulted about her hacking cough and chest pains mentioned the word "tuberculosis," insisted that she hire a girl to care for the children and prescribed prolonged bed rest for her. Sheridan saw her comfortably established in her parents' home and returned to the north alone.

With the arrival of March in the early spring of 1905, Juey set forth to rejoin Sheridan. The newly-building Canadian Northern rail line was soon to furnish a direct route between Winnipeg and Edmonton and she was impatient at the circuitous journey she had still to make to reach the latter city. As a result, she was a day late in her rendezvous with her husband.

With a young assistant, Grace Munroe of Winnipeg, who was accompanying her to help with the children, she peered from the window while the train jolted to a stop at the South Edmonton station. With relief and joy she caught sight of Sheridan's tall figure and she couldn't understand why his face looked so crushed with despair.

"Thank God!" he exclaimed as his powerful arms enfolded her. "Mother said you'd never come back to me."

In a democrat they set forth for Athabasca Landing; the Lendrum family with whom they stayed in Edmonton expected that the weather and the condition of the trail would turn them back. Their forecast proved correct as far as Sheridan was concerned. Again he was sending north a caravan of freight wagons; presently, while his wife and family camped in a shack at Lily lake, he hurried back to the city for replacement of a broken wagon wheel. Then at top speed at the Landing he set to work to build a caboose*. Ahead, the rivers and lakes were still locked under the winter's ice and he planned to race the spring break-up all the way to the Peace. Haste was of the essence, for if the ice became unsafe they might have to camp for at least a month until the waters became passable for the York boats.

With Sheridan himself driving the caboose, their brigade set forth. It consisted also of three hired teams and drivers, the freight having been transferred from wheels to sleighs. Snug in the stove-warmed caboose, Juey listened to the music of the creaking runners beneath it as they slid over the ice of the Athabasca river and she exulted in the beauty of the

_____

* caboose: a small one-roomed cabin built to travel on wheels or sleighs.

never-ending walls of sunlit fragrant evergreens. Here and there swatches of open water were beginning to appear; one night they awakened to a sound of gurgling and crashing and the men leapt from their bed-rolls in time to pull to safety a sleigh that was beginning to slip into the water.

After that, each night the drivers took turns sleeping and watching, and Sheridan would permit no more stops for lunch or tea. At Moose creek they left the Athabasca and turned onto the ice of the Lesser Slave. The weather warmed considerably and he encouraged the horses to their utmost.

"Every minute is precious," he observed.

Juey kept silent but she noted in her diary, "We were the last team coming off the ice of the Slave. Water was oozing into our tracks as the runners passed over the ice."

This was Saturday night. On Sunday morning the Rev. Malcolm, who had now been re-assigned to the mission field and who had met them at Athabasca Landing, held a thanksgiving service. Now when they looked back on the Lesser Slave river, the ice was out as far as they could see.

Juey grew more anxious when they ventured onto the vastness of Lesser Slave lake's ice-pan, but Sheridan was unworried.

"We had a fine trip across the lake," he recalled afterward. "We stayed at St. Peter's mission for several days before going on to Peace River Crossing. The trail on the portage was rough and stump-filled but still firm. There was snow in the bush but on the prairie there was none. We transferred our freight from sleigh to wagon as required and got along fine."

At Pete Leduc's stopping place the Métis again hailed the "Big Boss" and his family with the warmest of welcomes. Here there were so many freighters that "people lay like sausages on the floor of his small cabin. In the night his seven cats started to fight; he called to the dog to chase them out. Such a scramble and yowling there was all over the bodies of the sleepers in the dead of the night!"

To the young city girl Grace Munroe the preparation for the night's rest had been even more disturbing. Because all were obliged to sleep close together in the one room she became quite overcome with modesty. "She thought it just awful to sleep in a room with men." But Juey gave her a lesson in how a lady contrived to undress in such circumstances, slipping her nightgown over her head, removing her clothing underneath it and stowing her garments under her pillow so that they would be both handy and warm in the morning.

There was another prolonged disturbance through the night, the persistent coughing of the cheery Pete. Next day Juey told the "Big Boss" that she was sure their host suffered from tuberculosis. Her bleak diagnosis was confirmed the following spring; word reached them that he had died from this disease.

At Peace River Crossing Sheridan calculated they might have to make camp for a whole month while he built a raft and while they awaited the full break-up of the Peace. Again the kindly Hudson's Bay Company factor Mr. George came to their assistance, arranging for the family to make temporary home in his freight shack. This building, solidly constructed of logs, consisted of one large room with two bunks installed at one end. Here Sheridan set up a cook-stove which he was freighting to the Ranch and knocked together a table and a pair of benches.

Next morning early he left to hunt for logs for the raft and his wife and Grace set to work on the cabin. Raiding their freight, they covered the rough table with red oilcloth, the bunks with Hudson Bay blankets and the centre of the ugly floor with bearskin rugs. Like her mother before her, Juey was travelling with plant cuttings; now she hunted up discarded tins and planted her slips in soft earth.

"Grace and I really felt as if we were playing house here. We put up shelves under the two small windows for the plants and brought a rocking chair from the freight." By four in the afternoon, when Mr. George paid a call to see how his guests were managing, they had just completed the whitewashing of the walls and were hanging up pictures which Juey had brought along.

Except for one terrifying incident, this last month of the extended holiday passed happily. One evening as they were about to begin supper, three-and-a-half-year-old Hester came rushing into the little shack. She was so excited that only

196

her mother could understand what she said. Juey didn't pause to explain but pelted from the cabin and down the slope toward the creek. Here, a hundred or so yards distant, a barrel had been set in a shallow well so the water could drain in it and settle. There on his head in the barrel was two-year-old Malcolm.

"I pulled him out, saw that he was purple, slapped him and shook him and gave him artificial respiration to start him breathing again." Then in the warmth of the shack she hurried him into dry clothing and in a few minutes he was clamoring for his supper.

On a memorable Sunday while they awaited the pleasure of the Peace, the Rev. Malcolm, who was now established with Anna at St. Peter's mission, journeyed over the portage to pay them a visit. He conducted a divine service and in the evening the family, including Sheridan and his youngest brother Will, paid a call on a near-by encampment of mounties. The party possessed a clarinet as well as some fine voices, and soon the strains of the instrument were accompanying the chorus that rose from round the campfire. A glorious spring sunset reflected on the sombre spruces and the giant hills.

As the stately words of the old hymns swelled and echoed across the broad river, to Sheridan and Juey they seemed an echo of early Sunday camp-fires that had first lighted their way into this land of the Peace.

The holiday ended with two extra items of pioneer luxury. Sheridan was taking north a small amount of finished lumber; on the raft with this he laid a floor under the tent. He had also purchased a small tin heater which he rigged up inside the tent. Juey's "cook-stove" was of course the open fire set up in one corner of the raft.

The couple were agreed that they must give their northern ranching another five years' trial. Did such comforts on the raft as these portend a profitable sojourn for them? In their five days aboard, Juey pondered.

Once again the powerful current was sweeping them toward a future they could not foresee. Was her husband's dream to become in a modest way a kind of empire builder in the north?

CHAPTER 3

Glancing out the ranch-house window, Juey saw that the wagon was stacked high with unexpected freight. She had only a few minutes to wait before she would know if she were guessing its meaning aright. Home from still another raft trip to Peace River Crossing, her husband was already at the door.

"I've bought a cat in a sack," he smiled.

Over at Lesser Slave lake a "small" trader, Isaac Gagnon, had died and from his family Sheridan had purchased his basic stock of trading goods.

"You can see, Juey, that we've simply got to trade. Or we can't break even."

In this new era ushered in with 1905 she could understand that he was right. No trading company had any longer a single monopoly and any man who cared to compete was free to do so. Years before, when in 1870 her home province of Manitoba had entered the Canadian confederation, in a vastly profitable exchange the mighty Hudson's Bay Company had ceded its exclusive privileges to the federal government at Ottawa. But its long established empire still kept its firm hold on the giant's share of the fur trade. In the struggle that was now bound to follow between her husband and the "Bay" in their area, she was prepared to support Sheridan to the limit.

In a lean-to adjoining the "drying" house were a number of rough shelves which the men used to air damp grain. She helped him set up "the cat" in neat rows and their trade battle was joined. More settlers and trappers would, they expected, be attracted to the Ranch when they learned that they could obtain "store" staples there as well as produce.

In this year of 1905 a new era was beginning, too, for the whole of the north-west. Acts had been passed at Ottawa creating two new provinces, Saskatchewan and Alberta, and their Fort Vermilion area fell within the boundaries of the latter. The change meant an increasing blessing to the Ranch. Formerly most of the mail had been handled through the Hudson's Bay Company and it was not to be expected that service could be counted upon if one's business mail passed first through the hands of one's chief competitor. Now the hardy Métis Louis Bourassa secured a fresh contract to carry the mail, in summer by water, in winter overland or upon the ice.

Paradoxically the "Bay" became more and more both friend and enemy. To survive, since the price of shipping to far-away markets outside was prohibitive, Sheridan must still grow all of their own necessities, exchanging by barter for any extra needs. At the same time he must dispose of all of their extensive surplus to the sprinkling of settlers and to the trappers and trading posts. It was especially the accepting of the money-making furs directly in trade exchanges with the trappers that began to bring him into more and more bitter conflict with the "Bay."

Bestowing on him also a kind of bonanza, when the great company became compelled to buy from him it now furnished him with large sums of coveted cash. During his sojourn with his wife and family in Manitoba, his brothers Isaac and John managing the Ranch in his absence sold over six thousand dollars' worth of wheat, beef, butter, and bacon to the wealthy "Bay." From this sum Sheridan was able to send a payment of two thousand dollars to his parents on account, to buy out both John and Isaac and to settle in full with his brother Jim. The latter, planning to try out working as his older brother's foreman, now moved his family from Prairie Point to his former home, with Sheridan taking over his holdings at Prairie Point.

At the beginning of this second "five-year-plan" on his river-valley ranch, its hustling master looked over the cattle herd. From the tiny nucleus of animals brought in by Mr. Garrioch twenty-five years before and those which he as a lad had helped to drive in, there were at the moment one hundred and fifty grazing out on the native grasses.

"Means too much hay-cutting for winter," he decided. Following a series of butchering bees, he sold off beef to the value of one thousand dollars, again to that very good customer, the Hudson's Bay Company.

On their return Juey too flung herself into all the matters awaiting her attention. With horror she looked upon the interior of her usually spotless ranch-house kitchen, which according to her housewifely notions had suffered extremely from "a whole winter of batching men." With the help of Grace, who stayed on with her for two years, she planted a large garden. Although she was expecting another baby, her energy burgeoned with her garden; she was out picking saskatoons on July the first when her labour began. The new baby was a husky son whom they named Osborne after her brother.

"We should really call him Chipomasos," she teased his admiring father. "Chipomasos" was "little owl" in the Cree tongue; she was reminding Sheridan, he knew, of that night in the previous September when she had roused him to investigate that human-sounding and deeply-moving cry of distress that had echoed from the bank of the Peace on their journey outside.

The baby flourished; his mother, having benefitted from the long rest in Manitoba, soon settled back into the busy routine. Within her special domain, more change was under way, for during this summer of 1905 Sheridan constructed a large addition to the ranch-house. This addition, he calculated, would make it easier for her to handle the growing operations. Its chief feature was a huge kitchen eighteen feet wide by thirty long with an adjoining pantry all in proportion. In it he erected six-foot-high movable cupboards to divide the eating area from his wife's working theatre. Now the family began to take their meals separately in the dining-room, while they served the ranch-hands in the kitchen.

While the master viewed with special pride this big addition that was all of frame and all of lumber produced entirely by their own mill, to Juey the older main building brought a particular blessing. Because it was of log, in it she was able to keep green and blossoming throughout the winter not only the lilies that she inherited from her mother but as well her gay geraniums, her rich-leafed begonias and her fragile fuschias. In the new frame addition, these delicate plants would have perished.

Long before, her father had learned from natives how to make a pleasing white finish for a log interior and now she followed his practice. The Indians brought her a whitish powder which had been deposited in ages past from millions of snail shells and which they dug from areas of dried swampland. This powder she blended with skim milk, adding blueing to keep it from yellowing too quickly, and all the squared logs of the walls she coated with this mixture.

On the exterior of the logs treatment was a must if the rooms were to be warm in winter. This treatment consisted of an annual "mudding," the forcing into the chinks between the logs of a mixture of mud and straw. For this messy chore Sheridan wore sturdy mittens with no thumbs.

Already ranch-hands were cutting, curing and stacking hay in readiness for winter. Next he supervised the preparation of the sheds and stables for the winter sheltering of all the animals; by this time there was the crop to be harvested, the cattle and horses to be rounded up, and preparations made for butchering and for the running of the mill, for grinding grain, for milling flour and for sawing wood.

Then it was threshing time and again competition with the "Bay" added spice to the proceedings.

To outdo him, so he believed, in the matter of threshing as well as of grinding and milling, in 1904 the company had sent for an outfit of its own.

"With a big machine of our own, we'll hang that Sheridan's hide on a fence." So rumor reported words of "Bay" men. "And his little old outfit will be lying useless somewhere in a fence corner."

The new thresher proved to be, upon its arrival, a splendid piece of equipment. The separator was an up-to-date Sawyer-Massey equipped with blower and self-feeder and it seemed to put to shame Sheridan's older, smaller outfit.

But alas, the shippers forgot to include a separator belt. So when the master of the Ranch was going out on holiday in September of 1904, he instructed his brothers to be good enough, when they had finished the season's threshing, to lend his belt to the "Bay."

In a land rife with labor problems, the company as well as Sheridan suffered from the shortage of trained man-power and they had difficulty in finding an experienced crew to operate their machine. Now in 1905 because their work had proved unsatisfactory, several of his Métis neighbors again invited him to do their threshing. Again he constructed an enormous raft and ferried his machine across the Peace. When he had made the rounds on that side of the river, he ferried it back and threshed for all the small farms in the Paddle river and North Vermilion districts.

To have Sheridan's imposing outfit, the monster wood-burning "boiler" with its bulky separator—all a marvellous product from the far-away world of the white man—invade their tiny holdings cut from the bush brought a touching display of pride to swart-skinned faces. Among these were a number of Beaver Indians, with whom the Rev. Malcolm had toiled; when Sheridan recounted his experiences to Malcolm's daughter, she thought how the changes would gratify her father.

Most sensitive to the new order was the Beaver tribes-man Bulldog. Sheridan's booming laugh echoed in her kitchen when he told her how Bulldog had greeted him.

"Well, this is the first time white man come threshing for me. So I'm Frenchman now."

Bulldog's grin on his lean face widened as he went on, "Next year, I hope I have more grain. Then I'll be Scotch-man."

"Yes, you sure will," encouraged Sheridan.

"And next year after that, maybe I have more still. Then I'll be big white man. Like Sheridan Lawrence."

Prices for grain continued to be a bone of contention between the "big white man" and the Hudson's Bay Company. The latter, he felt, still charged prices that were too high.

"I could afford to grind grain and mill flour, selling it at wholesale prices," he calculated in his wife's listening

202

ear. The "Bay" was shortly planning to put into operation the steamboat for which he had supplied the lumber. Already the company was distributing northward by boat the flour and feed freighted to Little Red River.

"Also I figure I could grind wheat and sell it to the 'Bay' at a price they'd still make a profit on, provided they delivered it by steamboat."

He decided to try to work out a compromise, even though he was still ready to fight on an instant's notice.

"If they will cut the price of wheat to seventy-five cents per bushel in trade, they could still make a profit. Then maybe eventually I'll move out."

Again Juey seconded his plan with enthusiasm. She felt that for the sake of the children's education to move would eventually be for the best. Nevertheless she could not but endorse his next pronouncement.

"But I will not run out. Nor will I be run out."

He was unable to make a compromise agreement with the company. But again they paid him handsomely, an average during the winter of 1906-07 of one dollar and sixty-five cents per bushel for a total of two thousand, two hundred seventy-two bushels of wheat.

In spite of such satisfying success, the total ranching expenses were still exceeding income. Freighting in of equipment and paying out wages made the heaviest demands on the budget. Sometimes there were as many as fifteen men on the payroll; their presence now, along with Sheridan's expanding program, increased in turn his wife's responsibilities and made it more difficult for her to obtain help.

On one occasion after Grace returned to Manitoba she tried to engage a native girl who gave promise of being willing, even eager, to learn.

"Too many men about your ranch," objected the father. "My daughter stay home."

With the "green" girls whom from time to time she hired she tried her best to be patient and good-humored, a lesson she had learned from long association with their people. "In fact," she said, "we had lots of fun and laughter over the odd things the girls would do."

When her daughter Edith was born in December of 1906, she was again fortunate in having in attendance the wise native midwife, Mrs. Flett. That winter with its records for deep snow and low temperatures was also memorable in other respects for the young mistress of the Ranch; while she kept mainly to the upper storey of the ranch-house with the new baby and little Osborne, her husband and his men undertook to replace part of the foundation beneath it and to re-lay the floors.

When spring came at last, Juey looked forward to a new kind of outdoor chore and to attempting fresh triumphs in her garden. By this time her successes with Sutton seeds were assured; that English company, learning of her intense interest in and deep love for all growing things, wrote to invite her to collect for them the seeds of the wild flowers that grew in this northern and little-known territory.

Presently to Sheridan also came an opportunity to pioneer under official blessing in the realm of horticulture and agriculture. Down river at the Irene Training School and beyond on his own holding, his uncle E. J. Lawrence had been, like Anna Scott and her daughter Juey, fond of testing a wide variety of plants and shrubs in this untried area of Canada. Sharing this taste, E. J.'s son Fred obtained from the department of agriculture at Ottawa a large assortment of greenery and he was able at last to interest the federal government in setting up an experimental farm. When he moved out to operate a saw-mill in the Lesser Slave lake area, Sheridan and Fred Brick took over his farm on shares and officials wrote to invite Sheridan to take over also the project of a government-supported experimental farm. He declined, recommending in his place a neighbor, Robert Jones, who too had come to the area from the Lawrence's old home at South Stukely and Lawrencetown in Quebec's Eastern Townships.

As this federal venture became established, its succcesses put Juey on her mettle and visitors began to tease her about her efforts to outdo the government plots.

"So you're trying to rival the experimental farm," they smiled.

She had to acknowledge that competition added a fillip even to horticulture.

In season and out of season there was butter to churn and to wash and pack. Often during one week she would press, saltless, as much as one hundred and fifty pounds into three and five-pound lard pails, for saltless butter was a commodity dear to the heart of the Indians and for it eagerly they traded their furs. Then, in addition to cleaning and washing and caring for the children, there was a continually fluctuating number of men to cook for.

"A constant aversion to becoming stake-bound," was the reason, according to "Big Boss," why the number of ranch-hands varied even from day to day.

These men were mostly Indian or Métis, men who would earn enough to tide them over for a time and then, wearying of regular employment, would hit for the woods again. This meant a never-ending procession of changes at the ranch.

"One coming, one working, one going," as Sheridan expressed it, became the accepted pattern of life among the man-power which he hired.

With unwearied patience he re-employed a former worker or he staked a trapper to his winter's grub. More than once the Rev. Mr. White at the mission remarked to Juey,

"Sheridan Lawrence is 'mitootam ooche eyinew,' the Indian's friend."

She smiled in agreement. She was well aware that her husband's philanthropic streak sometimes exceeded even hers, which had been nurtured in her years of childhood training at the mission.

Sheridan found that his faith in the men was justified. Sometimes, in bad years, the debt of a man who spent his winters on the trap-line extended over several seasons.

"Sooner or later, we got it all back. The native people were amazingly honest."

During the winter of 1908 mail-man Louis Bourassa brought word that a group of white men in the near-by bush were ill with scurvy and that he feared for their lives. In exchange for a little wood-cutting for the summer use of the new "Bay" steamer, they had been able to obtain a meagre ration of flour and bacon and jam which they supplanted with what few animals they could find.

Following a two-days' tramp through the forest, one of Sheridan's men now reached their camp with an invitation to work at the Ranch for the remainder of the winter. At once also he began a corrective treatment for their ailment, with his native wisdom brewing a tea made from spruce needles which he persuaded them to drink.

The party arrived, and the master and the mistress of the Ranch delighted in watching them devour the anti-scurvy dishes set before them, quantities of Juey's home-made sauer kraut and boiled cabbage and canned peas and green beans, all the product of her garden. Most of the group accepted Sheridan's offer of jobs, several remaining until the following autumn; among them was a skilled carpenter whom he put to work building a multitude of cupboards for the home.

Oldest of the party was one Tom Cleary, who, sensing that he was not employable at the Ranch, made his way on toward the fort. Upon learning that Tom had frozen feet, Sheridan pursued him personally and soothed his spirit of independence by telling him that he could feed the pigs and do odd chores in return for his keep.

Fighting nausea, Juey treated the poor purple-spotted feet. She coaxed their owner to soak them in a solution of bluestone or copper sulphate and each day, as more "proud flesh" fell away, she applied fresh dressings.

So grateful was old Tom that he helped her lovingly with each of the children and with almost equal affection he cared for all of Sheridan's pigs. Every porker he petted and christened with what he considered to be an appropriate human name. By veiled questioning Juey discovered the town in the United States from which their elderly wanderer had come. She wrote to the post-master there, asking him to inform his family of the father's whereabouts. Presently a son replied, making a date to meet him in Edmonton, during the following summer.

When July came and the old man had to leave this Shangri-la on the Peace, with tears in his eyes he bade the children good-bye and he still protested to Sheridan.

"If I could go on working, you couldn't drive me away."

An obsessive love for horses marked Jack Sullivan, another lonely wayfarer and a conscientious worker who drifted to the Ranch seeking employment. The animal who most repaid his affection was the friendly mare Ponie, a dark-brown part-Arabian which Sheridan had acquired out of a herd that Twelve-Foot Davis had brought in from British Columbia.

One evening when Juey went to check a series of unusual sounds in the vicinity of the horse-barn, she came upon Jack conducting a one-way conversation with Ponie. That is, it was not quite one-way. The young man had his arms about her graceful head and she was nuzzling her nose tight against his neck. And, as every one said, Poine could almost answer you. Juey stole away without interrupting the dialogue.

Next spring, when Ponie met with tragedy, it was Jack who volunteered to end her suffering. A pinto stallion belonging to the "Bay" was racing about the countryside causing ructions among the various herds of horses. Several neighbors suggested to Sheridan that he shoot it. He refused; his killing of the stallion would only add fuel to his feud with the "Bay." When the beast kicked Ponie so badly that it killed her unborn foal and it was she who had to be shot, Sheridan's ranch-hands decided to take measures of their own.

With covered face, Jack fired the fatal gun-blast. Then the men lassoed the stallion and tied him short to a tree. While the small Lawrence children watched from the safety of the corral rails, two of the hands armed themselves with wide boards and prepared to spank the animal. As some one signalled to begin, the wily creature ducked and the men spanked each other. The youngsters roared with laughter and immediately the furious men improved their spanking technique.

When they had finished with their whipping, they drove the marauder into the Peace. Leaping into canoes, they tailed after him and forced him to swim all the way to the opposite shore.

Presently Juey was able to persuade Jack, who had been out of touch with his home near Toronto for several years, to write to his mother. When that lady replied to her son, she extended a special blessing to the mistress of the Ranch for having helped to re-establish contact between them.

Already the Ranch was attracting visitors not seeking employment but seeking, perhaps, information and inspiration. One of these looked challengingly at Juey.

"Well, you have quite a feudal place here."

At first she was startled, and a little annoyed.

The visitor elaborated on his point. "I notice that you and your husband always say, 'We do this,' and 'We do that'."

Smilingly, she relaxed. They had both been much too busy to think of such a thing. In a way, perhaps it was true. She and Sheridan had grown into the habit of using the royal "we." She supposed it must be because the men of the area saw her Sheridan as their unacknowledged leader.

For a moment, they paused to take stock. They realized that they both loved the life. The second five-year term was ending and the Ranch had become an octopus-like enterprise with arms crooking out in all directions. Each year now Sheridan was adding more buildings and more equipment, including by this time a separate trading store with shelves so well stocked that they elicited many a covetous gleam from smouldering native eyes.

At first, feeling that the Indians should confine their trading to the necessities of which they were often in dire want, he had stocked on his shelves only basic lines of food and clothing. But he came to be aware that some of his potential customers were taking their best furs to the "Bay" to trade for "frills," at the same time sending their women-folk to him with their poorer catches and with hard-luck stories to obtain necessities. Only too well he knew that through the long winter months the harsh existence in the bush involved surroundings that were everlastingly drab and that were relieved only by the white monotony of the snow and the sombre green of the spruces, and he came to realize that the cravings of his customers for bright-colored trifles was a kind of instinctive need. Accordingly he too widened the range of his trade supplies.

While he was thus attempting to offer the "Bay" substantial competition, he was at the same time still doing business with the company. In 1908 he sold them eight hundred and twenty-five bushels of wheat at a dollar and a half per bushel as well as large quantities of bacon and butter. Juey helped to prepare the bacon and to render enormous quantities of lard which they sold by the pail to the Indians. This lard, a product of the annual butchering of one hundred and fifty hogs, was a delicacy prized by the natives as highly as her butter, of which she still made sometimes as much as one hundred and fifty pounds per week.

Within the home her family responsibilities continued also to increase. In May of 1908 she gave birth to Velma and in August of the following year to another daughter Alice. Each new infant became a precious blessing in the heart of their doting father; Juey was equally proud of them but she was becoming increasingly concerned about the problem of education for the older children. Each day she tried to adhere to a short period of schooling for them, yet she realized that this was inadequate. Was it not, for the sake of the little ones, time to quit, to go outside where they could enjoy a full-time school routine?

Should she not attempt to deflect Sheridan from the path along which he was beginning to tread more and more confidently? Should she not try to turn him from the role that destiny seemed to be offering to him—in a small way of course—the role of empire-builder in this land of the northern Peace?

CHAPTER 4

With a sympathetic ear Sheridan listened to his wife's query about the children's schooling. Then he waved a letter before her face.

"Just listen to this first," he scowled. "It's from the district manager of the 'Bay'."

Everyone knew that the letters H.B.C., which stood for the name of the imperious company, were also frequently interpreted as "Here Before Christ."

" 'The Hudson's Bay Company'," Sheridan read, " 'was here long before you were thought of. It will be here long after you are forgotten.' You see, Juey, we just can't quit now. We'll have to figure out some other way about schooling."

The tone of the letter was so much in keeping with the autocratic reputation of the great company that she had to agree. They just couldn't leave after receiving such an epistle. It had been prompted by a letter Sheridan had written to District Manager Levick protesting that "the local representative of the company was apparently responsible for a rumor that the price of wheat was down" and that he was spreading this report "probably with the hope of depressing the price."

The reply of the company's spokesman continued its autocratic tone. "He said," so Sheridan recorded, "that their Mr. Wilson was buying wheat at Fort Vermilion, and what he said, went."

"I threw his letter into the fire. Afterwards, I thought I should have framed it to show to my friends. After duly considering it, I made plans accordingly."

Meantime the problem of schooling was unresolved. It was the year 1910 and the Rev. Malcolm, now Archdeacon of the diocese of Athabasca, was still in charge of St. Peter's mission on Lesser Slave lake. He suggested that a school under church auspices might be set up at the Ranch if Sheridan were to meet all the expenses.

At the same time, much as Juey dreaded the thought of the children's going outside, she consented to having appilcation made to St. John's college in Winnipeg to enter the two oldest, Hester and Malcolm. Remembering her own deficiencies of years before, with a will she set to work in the daily afternoon classes which she maintained for her little ones to try to bring the pair up to the schooling level of others of their age. The teaching discipline she had acquired at the Irene Training mission stood her now in good stead; in place of shy brown-eyed children awesomely studying her wishes, her own blue-eyed brood bent zealously but with much less awe to the tasks which she set.

In the following spring, in spite of the continuing friction, Sheridan continued to transact business with the "Bay." That company's enormous spread of posts entailed enormous requirements and sometimes because of the hazards of transportation desperate shortages occurred. Thus, Factor Wilson of the Fort Vermilion post received an urgent request from Chipewyan for one thousand sacks of flour. Having on hand an efficient mill but neither wheat nor flour to supply the order, again he came to terms with Sheridan, and the latter delivered to him over four thousand bushels of wheat at a dollar and a half per bushel, "in tip-top shape," he noted. Presently also he received and filled orders from the company for both oats and barley.

Then, after the break-up of the Peace in this spring of 1911, as a passenger he boarded that big "Bay" boat, the "Peace River," for which he had supplied the lumber. He was taking his two oldest children outside to school. For their watching mother it was as if twenty years had slipped away. and she saw her mother Anna eyeing the tiny dug-out with the "yaw" that was transporting her young ones to the faraway school. By comparison with her mother she was rich; during what must be a long separation she had all her other children about her to assuage her anguish and the health and the strength to tend to the thousand duties that compelled her attention on the ever-expanding Ranch.

When Bishop Robins, who had now succeeded their old friend Bishop Young as diocesan head, took steps to provide a teacher on the Ranch premises, she shared with her husband in the joy of preparations. Near the main ranch-house stood a small building in which Jim and Florence had lived before they moved on across the river; this Sheridan now converted into a combined school-room and teacherage, and both parents smiled over the delight of their young ones as they "tried out" all the tables and benches which he fashioned for their use.

When, in the summer of 1913, Juey welcomed her two oldest back from Winnipeg and the new teacher Miss Waghorn fresh from England, it was difficult to decide who was the more surprised. The lady was a tall genial soul of some sixty years with curly hair that still shone a vivid red. The big brown eyes of this easy-going spinster that now surveyed the harsh realities of life on a large isolated ranch had been fortified only by a childhood spent with maiden aunts and by the limited experience of a teaching post in an English all-girls' school.

In her uninitiated presence some one mentioned that Mrs. Dewhurst, whose husband taught at the Irene mission, was about to produce a baby.

"But how can she?" worried the newcomer. "I mean, with no doctor here."

To Juey, who now at thirty-four felt very old in comparison with such naiveté, but to whom supervising the birth of her own or others' babies was almost routine, the gentle teacher's inexperience with life was unbelievable.

For the sake of air and heat circulation, in the schoolhouse the partitions did not reach right to the ceiling. Speaking pleasantly in the softest tone, Miss Waghorn set her pupils to work upon a series of sums. Then, repairing to her kitchen, near the warmth of the big stove there she proceeded to take a bath. To embarrass her, mischievous Lawrence boys knocked against the partition and, exclaiming aloud, they pretended to peek over it.

In her most lady-like voice Miss Waghorn reproved the young imps, and Juey added supplementary punishment with the razor strap. When Sheridan heard of misdeeds in the schoolroom, being afraid of his great strength he applied rolled-up newspaper to the flesh of the small transgressors.

In later years the young ladies of the family laughed about the contrast between the punitive abilities of their five-foot-two mother and their six-foot-two father.

"Your loudest shout, Mother, wasn't as loud as Daddy's softest whisper." Thus for Juey they summed up the difference.

At last from Edmonton came word of a possible solution to the school problem. There the deputy minister of education in the Alberta government, D. S. MacKenzie, agreed to do what he could to help if Sheridan would submit a petition for the establishment of a school district that was signed by at least three ratepayers and if he would guarantee a minimum of six pupils and be willing to pay a teacher's travelling expenses.

When Sheridan consented to take care of their share of the school taxes, his Métis neighbors across the river added their names to the petition. Because of the mile-wide Peace, they would be unable to send their children to the school. Papers were duly drawn up and signed and the Lawrence Point school, in district number 3175, was entered on the rolls of the department of education and became eligible for an annual provincial grant of nearly four hundred dollars.

With overflowing hearts the two parents prepared for the opening of the novel establishment. In Edmonton Sheridan stocked up with fresh equipment for it and hired a Miss Patterson as its first teacher; she possessed sufficient pioneering spirit to be undaunted by the hazards and discomforts of the trip in, arriving by boat at the Ranch in the autumn of 1914. Soon even the reluctant boys admitted that they enjoyed the enlarged quarters—school classes were still conducted in the same building—with the glistening new desks which their father provided as well as the strict discipline of their pleasant-spoken but determined new teacher.

There were, they found, both advantages and disadvantages to this attending school on one's own premises. Sometimes a certain flexibility in programming could make it more bearable; if the afternoon were unusually fine and warm occasionally their teacher permitted them to work

213

right through until noon, after which she adjourned classes for a picnic at the river's edge. As their mother accompanied them on these outings, there was small chance to escape to the woods before the afternoon session began.

There were more of the same kind of problems after school was dismissed for the day. Since the building was only feet distant from the ranch-house, there could be none of the delightful after-scool loitering that other children enjoyed. And under their daddy's dread eye, skylarking had to be reduced to a minimum; as well, each of the older members of the family had chores to do which he insisted must be completed by six o'clock.

Word of a model school being operated at Lawrence Point, whose total enrolment usually comprised members of one family only, became presently another feature attracting visitors to the Ranch. As the basic number of six promised to be more than maintained, with Daisy born in 1911, Stanley in 1912 and Kathleen in 1914 all in turn added to the "cradle roll," the children learned to accept this being put on exhibition with more than the stoicism of monkeys in a cage.

Gradually the unique features of the Ranch spread its fame into wider channels. When in Winnipeg that city's pioneer hardware merchant, J. H. Ashdown, passed away, Juey wrote a note of sympathy to his relations, who were old-time friends of her family. She mentioned that she still used the baby's bath which Mr. Ashdown had presented to her mother when she had been born. For sentimental reasons his family asked now to make an exchange. She received a gleaming white-enamelled tub and she shipped out the veteran heaped high with a gift of enormous vegetables, including corn, melon, squash and pumpkin all grown in the Ranch garden. Presently the young Lawrences saw newspaper pictures of their bath-tub and its contents being prominently displayed in the windows of the Ashdown company in Edmonton and then in Winnipeg.

Exhibitions of this sort did not disturb the pupils of the Lawrence Point school. After all, they were being shown far away and they concerned only such dull things as vegetables. But when pictures and stories of themselves and their home and their school began to appear in newspapers and

214

magazines, their disgust became great. Why would any one want to make a fuss over such matter-of-fact things as their way of life?

Finally a picture of themselves grouped round about a stack of their mother's vegetables, cucumbers, tomatoes, melon, squash, pumpkin and the like, was displayed in an Alberta text-book and included in those shipped to their own school. "Products of the North," it was entitled. Now their disgust knew no bounds.

"We're not products of the north," they stormed.

For the most, however, such irritations did not ruffle for very long. Round about them the village-size spread of ranch buildings and corrals and fences offered delights galore to growing children. Beyond unfolded the enchantment of the wilderness and the eternal fascination of the great river. In both of these lay dangers at which they tended to scoff; in both lay dangers of which their parents constantly tried to teach them to beware. In spite of their mother's watchfulness lest a little one wander into the bush, on different occasions both Hester and Margaret had been briefly lost.

"Any fool can be brave," said Sheridan as he taught respect for the wilderness and common sense and caution.

When the children went berry-picking or on errands, their parents sent them in pairs. Only as far as the cow-pasture could a boy or girl go alone and if he or she did not return promptly some one was dispatched to check his or her whereabouts.

"In the woods only a true bush-man can survive if it comes to the worst. But," their father urged, "you can all use common sense."

He was a non-smoker, but he always carried matches. "Those who take chances are simply tempting Providence." Usually the Indians, he believed, possessed the know-how to survive the worst of wilderness conditions; if necessary they would eat even their moccasins. and some Métis and white men, such as the mail-carrier Louis Bourassa, for all their years of coping with the uncharted woods, never learned to be true bush-men.

"But Clement Paul, there's an experienced bush-man." Clement and his two brothers had made their way from Quebec into the Peace River country and for years this small red-headed Frenchman wandered through the woods, dependent on his rifle.

One afternoon Clement was sitting, rifle at knee, resting himself on the edge of a beaver dam. Suddenly he became aware that something was wrong, that danger lurked near.

"I feel my hair stand on end," he told Sheridan after.

He jumped and whirled about. There was a large she-wolf about to spring on him. His rifle put an end to that particular threat.

For a good many years bears and wolves continued to menace the Ranch animals. The same Clement Paul, recorded Sheridan, "killed more wolves than any of the rest of us." When the Frenchman was trading at Keg river prairie, a band of a dozen or more wolves attacked his horses, killing the stallion. Clement put poison on the remains and in the morning he had a record kill, nine dead marauders. Propping their frozen bodies up in the snow in life-like poses, he snapped a picture for proof; this was afterward printed on a post-card and sold as a kind of advertisement of the Peace River country!

At his Prairie Point out-ranch one autumn Sheridan discovered a steer walking on three legs, the fourth having been eaten off. "How it escaped the wolf or wolves that had attacked it remained a puzzle." He shot the steer and sold the meat at half price for dog food.

Winter often brought the wolves close to the Ranch buildings. But the mounted police had now entered the country and imposed strict regulations on the use of poison—a first mountie, Sgt. McLeod, was now quartered at Fort Vermilion. Himself aware of the need of extreme caution, Sheridan put out poisoned bait late at night and lifted it early next morning.

"Like to go for a walk?" With twinkling eyes one winter's evening he extended the invitation to his wife. She stepped outside and he handed her one end of a length of heavy string. The other end was secured, she saw, round about a large chunk of raw liver.

"Would you mind dragging this?"

He walked ahead, pulling a hand-sleigh on which he had loaded traps and chunks of poison-filled meat. When they reached the low bank of the Peace, they clambered down and headed toward the water hole that was kept chopped open for watering the cattle in the winter. The night was brisk and frosty and as they made their way along the snye, the ice beneath them crackled and growled. From the shadowed bank and from the dark woods on the long island that sheltered the snye, Juey could almost swear, sharp eyes were peering furtively and she remembered with what fascination she and Osborne years before had watched the wolves in winter taking short cuts past the windows of the mission.

Here and there for about a half mile along the snye Sheridan deposited traps and bait. Dutifully his helper trudged behind him, still dragging the liver to cover the human "smell."

At last they climbed the bank again and with profound relief she feasted her eyes on the golden lights shining from the windows of her home.

"Not that wolves had too much respect for buildings," she recalled. In fact, to bring their enemies closer, sometimes the ranch hands draped fresh hides over the fence railings quite close to the buildings. Then wolves would be lured to chew at the hides and the next evening Sheridan or his men would drop poisoned bait. Always they picked up the deadly chunks before the next morning's sunrise.

This warfare with wolves was by no means new to Sheridan. "It was after the flood of 1888," he wrote, "that we had our first trouble with wolves. They would follow the herd and sneak up on calves and younger cattle. One wolf in particular would bite a calf on the hip. If it bellowed, the main cattle herd would come and the wolf would sneak away. Invariably, though, the young animal was done for."

To guard the cattle against this daring beast, Henry Lawrence sent out his young son Harry, armed with an old Snider rifle. This rifle had been issued to Henry by American Confederate men, who had pressed him into their army back on the Vermont border in Civil War days. The lad's new chore was to ride round and round the herd keeping watch. Finally one day he spotted the wolf among the cattle.

"He jumped off the horse and took a shot at the beast, frightening it so badly that it ran straight toward him. He was so frightened too that he did not load his rifle again until the wolf saw him and turned and ran. Then he got brave."

Usually, continued Sheridan, "bears will stay around more persistently than wolves." Then it was the pigs who suffered the most from the invaders; after a bear's visit on one occasion they found that out of a total of fifty-eight young piglets eight had been snatched away. Bears too prowled at night. When Sheridan once was roused from his sleep by the squeals of an unlucky baby pig, he leapt from his bed and clad only in his nightshirt he grabbed his rifle and ran round the buildings in pursuit of the thieving bear. Juey laughed at the sight in the moonlight of his long white legs leaping fences; as the prowler returned for another porker for her cubs, he dropped her with a single shot. Then his wife's mirth turned to commiseration, for when he ventured close to the mother sow to check how many of her litter were gone, the enraged animal bit him severely on the bare leg.

As his sons grew to maturity, they too took their turn at helping to keep marauders at bay. One evening the frantic bawling of a calf in the edge of a tongue of brush near the river's bank alerted the family. Accompanied by young Malcolm, Sheridan ran with his rifle to the rescue. He was too late; a wolf had already pulled the calf down. He sent the lad into the brush toward the calf to flush the killer into the open so that he could pick it off with a rifle shot. As the boy drew near, he was horrified to see the wolf devouring the still-bawling calf.

For the young lads the prospect of the sale of a hide or the price of a bounty for wolf or coyote added to their hunting zeal. One morning in late winter when the snow was piled deep, twelve-year-old Osborne, armed with rifle, crept up on a carcass planted with poison bait in a small valley between the hills back of the ranch-house.. He was electrified to see a huge black timber wolf staring straight at him from out of the white drift. With racing heart he fired, aiming dead for the animal's nose so as to damage the pelt as little as possible. The animal jerked its head but it did not fall.

At that the terrified youngster turned and plunged at full speed toward the ranch buildings.

"You better go get him," he shouted to his Uncle Will, at that moment the only man about the place.

"A real live wolf!" scoffed his uncle. "I'll bet he is!" Even though, obviously, he didn't believe the boy's story, he hitched a horse to the carry-all and with his rifle headed toward the small valley.

Presently he was back and planting the big wolf carcass, as Clement Paul had done, upright in a snow-drift.

"Yes, he sure is alive!" Will's blue eyes were alive too with mirth as he roared with laughter. He had remained a bachelor and he loved nothing better than an opportunity to tease his oldest brother's lively children. "He sure is alive, boy!"

The wolf had died very quickly from poison and had happened to remain upright because of the deep snow. With the vibration from the lad's rifle shot, its frozen body had quivered as if it really were alive.

Sometimes the wild animal had the last laugh on the boisterous family growing up about the Ranch. There was for instance the coyote which they had trapped and which they were bringing home with enormous pride. In the carry-all or carriole, a genuine Indian-type vehicle with shaft-runners of birch and moose-hide body, they were chattering together noisily as they whipped along over the glistening snow. Some one thought to look back for a glance at the carcass.

The glance was indeed timely. The "dead" coyote had bounded from the sleigh and was heading for the distant bush!

Sometimes the domestic animals on the Ranch provided the occasion for hilarity among the young people, especially if Father Sheridan were absent. Throwing horse blankets over rebellious calves, the boys attempted to ride them about yard or corral, or they tormented the maddened yearlings, trying to provoke them to a stirring bullfight. Sometimes they and their sisters secured the end of a length of twine tight about the tail of a pig, fastening the other end to a nail hammered in the wall. Once when a suffering pig finally left its tail tied to the wall, their father, who was, so they

219

thought, far away, appeared on the scene, attracted by the squeals of the beast. Within minutes they felt that their anguish matched that of the tail-less pig.

For involvement in mischief and misadventure the young ladies of the Ranch claimed their share of credit. One autumn no coal oil arrived on the last boat and Juey set her girls to helping in the making of tallow "dips." These consisted of lengths of string dipped over and over again in beef fat.

"How we hated the job," they groaned in remembrance. "They made such a poor light. And they smelled so horrible."

One evening Edith and Velma set a lighted dip on the curtained shelf right beside their bed. They became absorbed in the blurred pages of the books they were trying to read, concentration being all the more necessary because of the meagre glow of light, and it wasn't until they at last smelled smoke that they discovered that their curtains were all ablaze.

Candles also played a part in a homespun prank the memory of which they cherished for many a year. It was Hallowe'en and the girls planned to become involved in a little seasonable witchery. Inside the pump-house they prepared an evil one, the tall pump whose body they swathed with an amply-folded sheet and whose head they fashioned of a human-head-sized pumpkin. In both head and body they concealed lighted candles; then they retreated into the autumn dusk, leaving the pump-house door wide open.

Presently past it came the ranch-hands on their nightly route from bunk-house to barns, where they bedded the horses down before retiring. They were a mixed lot, including several Indians out of the bush. Guessing that a Hallowe'en prank was being enacted, one of the "white" men among them played it up in earnest. He hollered "Weentigo!" and leapt over the fence as if in sheer terror.

Sure enough, a couple of Indians believed that indeed the evil spirit had come amongst them and they bounded away in genuine fright.

The hidden girls could not let the triumphant moment pass singly. While the men were choring in the barns, they rushed boldly into territory that was strictly out of bounds, the men's bunk-house. They slipped their ghostly pumpkin under one of the beds and again they hid until they heard the fearful cry of "Weentigo!"

This time one young Indian was so genuinely upset that the girls too began to quake. They trembled lest he tell their father of the evil spirit haunting the Ranch!

One afternoon when the warm March sun began to weight with water an extra-heavy fall of new snow, Juey sent the girls to clear the broad roof of the big machine-shed. With them onto the roof clambered their small brother Stanley. Soon they grew bored with the dull job of snow-sweeping and shovelling and for sport they began leaping from the roof into the six-foot snow-drift round about them below. The little boy followed them; his heedless sisters turned at last when they heard his frightened cry. He had landed out of his depth in the sopping snow and he was unable to move. They too became frantic in their efforts to extricate him, for there was danger of his feet and legs freezing. Fortunately a passing ranch-hand heard their cries and rushed to the boy's rescue.

When the burning rays of the spring-time sun finally swept all the ice from the broad-shouldered Peace, then it became almost impossible for the Ranch's vital youngsters to resist the challenge of the waters. On a balmy evening Juey noticed that little Stanley was missing and being well aware of the dread fascination for them all of the great river, she guessed where he might have gone. Velma raced over the quarter-mile trail that led to its bank. Sure enough, there was the small boy with his clothing already removed, about to plunge into the foaming high water of early spring.

On another occasion his big brothers used him as a kind of water plaything. They waded into the edge of the Peace, seating him astride a bobbing log. Eventually the swirling water turned the restless log right over; then the boys enjoyed the sport of seeing him tumbled into the water and of grabbing him and placing him back into position on the log.

At last the heaving water tossed the log farther out and the child dropped into water beyond their depth. By the time they had jumped into the boat and poled it out so as to reach the little one, he was coming up for the third time. That was the last time they played the game of "roll-the-log" with their small "game" brother.

In spite of repeated warnings from their parents, one spring when their father was absent up-stream, the big boys could no longer resist temptation. In time snatched away from chores, they shaped themselves a sturdy raft. After all, their dad had himself fashioned and journeyed upon many and many a raft. They put hours of careful work upon it and tied it securely to the pier at the Lawrence Point landing.

Presently Sheridan steered for the landing and as he began to unload part of his freight from his scow, he noticed the raft. Without a word to any one, he cut it free. Then he proceeded down river to the fort with the balance of his freight.

"By the way, boys," he remarked when he returned, "I cut your raft free." By now it would have been swept down stream and far away. "I didn't want to find a pair of drowned boys when I got back."

For some time there had been promise of tremendous change involving the whole Peace River country. Great things were being planned because of new developments particularly in transportation. With the outbreak of the First World War, Sheridan's mighty rival the Hudson's Bay Company stopped giving credit and, he wrote, "Their fur trade dropped to almost nothing."

Now he saw his chance. Now was the time to venture.

Everybody was hard up. "And every one said I was crazy. I bought fur and anything they had to sell, hired more help, and gave out a lot of my farm produce on credit."

Thus in 1914 did Sheridan gamble. Snatching at opportunity through a cloud of bleak predictions of the disaster that was going to overtake him, he began to expand his trading. From as far as a hundred miles or more, the Indians began to come to him with their furs.

"This trade gave me a chance to get acquainted with the Indians and the trappers. Though they told me I was crazy, I helped them out whenever I could and I got most of it back the following winter."

In spite of the war, changes in transportation continued to develop and presently he planned a new way to meet the competition of the "Bay." For some time settlers had been pouring by boat and river and overland trail into the upper Peace country. By 1912 a rail line had been completed between Edmonton and Athabasca Landing and slowly another line was being pushed between the former point and Peace River Crossing.

Part of the fascination of the land of the Peace, so report said, lay in the challenge of attempting to reach it. Separated from the more accessible areas of western Canada by a two-hundred-mile-wide band of dense wood and swamp and muskeg that was veined also with a network of creeks and lakes and rivers, it was an isolated Shangri-la that attracted attention partly because of its remoteness.

"God put the Peace River country so far away, you had to be good to get into it." Thus went the comment on its inaccessibility.

By 1916, when the plaintive whistle of the rail engine finally sounded over the ancient hills above Peace River Crossing, a Welsh coal baron, Lord Rhondda, had enacted plans which were going to affect the lives not only of the newcomers streaming into the country but of those pioneers who lived as far away as the Ranch and Fort Vermilion. For some years the Hudson's Bay company had maintained a steamer service on the Peace between Hudson's Hope and the Chutes, the first of these being that "Peace River" built at Fort Vermilion in the winter of 1904-05 for which Sheridan had supplied the timber. Ten years later she was replaced by the larger "Athabasca River," which could carry one hundred tons as compared with the earlier boat's forty-ton capacity, and which had be constructed at Athabasca Landing and hauled over the ice at the Chutes.

Meantime Lord Rhondda had shaped plans which included the developing of the coal deposits near Hudson's Hope and the building of a magnificent steamer right at Peace River Crossing. Sheridan inspected the great frame during 1915 as it lay on the stocks and he too planned accordingly. Instead of selling his wheat to the "Bay" at their prices, he would store it and ship it outside by way of the new boat and the new railway.

His policy of expansion became of course a two-way street. In proportion as his ranching and trading operations grew, so did his expenses and his desperate need to find still more markets for his produce. For butcherings he erected an abattoir and in it he rigged up not only hanging pegs for quarters of beef and for carcasses of hogs but a kind of windlass for hoisting up the animal to be gutted. This consisted of a wooden wheel ten feet in diameter with eight spokes that turned on an axle also of wood.

Here in his abattoir butcherings sometimes increased to as many as a dozen fattened steers or one hundred and fifty hogs all at the one time; frequently Juey still assisted in the preserving of meat or in the preparation of it in saleable lots. In one instance alone she took charge of the home canning in cans and tubs of eighteen hind quarters of beef. Over each lot in its container she poured the rich gravy and the fat or tallow, the "weenee" that the Indians sought so eagerly. Native catches of wild animals were "skinny" and usually their customers depended for the fat they craved upon the butter and the lard and the home-preserved meat with its tallow all sold by the Ranch.

Up-stream at Prairie Point Sheridan still operated the out-ranch which he had taken over from his brother Jim. Also on shares with Fred Brick he worked the land formerly held by his uncle E.J. and by his cousin Fred Lawrence. This meant that frequently he was absent from the main Ranch and that Juey had to learn to take his place at the trading counter. With not a quiver of the embarrassment she had suffered as a youngster in Calgary, in fact with the sharpest enjoyment, she now re-learned the game of counting by "skins."

Her husband prided himself on paying cash whenever he could; often this was impossible and of course the Indians sought goods and farm produce. But so greatly had times changed that once a year, when he might have to resort to barter, it was his darker-skinned neighbors who clutched in their lean fingers the cold currency of the realm. This was at the annual "treaty" time, when the federal government party toured the country, paying out "treaty" money to all the Indian peoples. This money was the heaven-sent answer to so many desperate needs that Sheridan came to find it essential to be right on the spot in order to capture a share of it. As a result he began trading in key areas remote from home as well as at the Ranch itself.

Following the old trails over which his wife's missionary father had tramped and chopping a clearance for his horses when necessity dictated, he began to freight equipment and trade supplies north-west one hundred and twenty-five miles to the point where the Hay lakes drained into the twisting channel of the Hay river. Here, in the homeland of Beaver and of Slavey and Chipewyan, he erected a modest store. Down-stream also, at the point known as Upper Hay River, he set up a trading shack, for here too was another strategic spot at which to intercept the flow of furs and to exchange goods for treaty money.

Presently the husky chief of the Crees dwelling to the south-east in the Tall Crees' prairie area brought a bulky load of furs to the Ranch. On the way, he told Sheridan, he had left more packets of moose and bear hides at the Hudson's Bay Company bunk-house. Nothing daunted, Sheridan accepted the whole lot from the chief, supplied him with what goods he had on hand, took him down stream to Revillon Frères where he had credit to outfit him with the balance of his needs, and then proceeded to the "Bay" bunk-house to claim the packs of furs and hides there.

"What are you doing here?" scowled the clerk on duty.

"Warming up and waiting for the chief to pack up my furs," he answered.

Afterward, Sheridan related, "I heard that he'd been offered twenty-five dollars to give me a thrashing."

The free trader's great bulk and reputed strength no doubt deterred the clerk.

At the same time the chief invited Sheridan to freight trading goods right into his country. They were to meet on a certain date at the chief's home on the Rat river.

"I'll be there," promised the trader.

The opening up of this new post, about one hundred miles southeast of the Ranch, proved another profitable venture. On the trail he met twenty-two dog-trains, with many of whom he traded, and his own brigade of horse-drawn sleighs brought back over two thousand dollars' worth of furs.

"The chief's like me, a great family man," he teased Juey on his return. "But he keeps three wives, all in separate teepees."

CHAPTER 5

Up-stream the building of Lord Rhondda's marvellous new ship was soon, he felt, going to put into his hand a new weapon which he could use against his mighty competitor the "Bay." So in 1915 he urged his neighbors to demand a dollar and ten cents per bushel for any wheat which they planned to sell to that company. The new factor, Gus Clark, consulted with his head office. They refused to allow him to offer that price. Sheridan ordered a thousand sacks, began paying that price himself and stock-piling wheat at the Ranch.

It was 1917 by the time the great boat, christened the "D. A. Thomas," Lord Rhondda's name before he received his title, chugged her queenly way down stream past the Lawrence Point landing. Already the children watching there could recite with pride something of her statistics. With her bow-to-stern length of one hundred and sixty-seven feet and her hold capable of loading two hundred tons of freight, she was the largest vessel between the Great Lakes and the Pacific ocean and in fact the largest ever to ply on the northern inland waters. Deep-toned as the whistle of an ocean liner her voice sounded as she announced the miracle of her presence on the tortuous Peace. While she continued her way down-stream to the post and on to the Rat river landing this side of the Chutes, Sheridan and his men hustled to have everything in readiness for the transfer of his huge stock-pile of sacked wheat into her enormous hold.

In some ways the experiment paid off well. That autumn of 1917 he shipped out by way of the beautiful new liner nearly four thousand sacks of wheat as well as four hundred sacks of potatoes. The wheat was transferred at Peace River

Crossing into seven railway cars and transported over the new line to Edmonton and the east. Sheridan was satisfied both with the grade, number two, and the price, a net of one dollar and eighty cents per bushel for a total of nearly eight thousand bushels.

But, in spite of the size of the shipment and the reasonable freight charge on the "D. A. Thomas" of only five dollars per ton, the experiment didn't really solve his marketing problems. There was far too much handling and too much risk involved. The cash returns from it, however, enabled him to obtain the means to offer fresh competition to the "Bay"; he proceeded outside to Winnipeg and there he bought a new Midget flour mill to replace the small mill he had set up in the spring of 1896; en route home he purchased a second-hand Case engine which had much more power than the one he had rafted in during 1899.

In his warfare with the "Bay" there were moments of almost friendly truce. Although the Fairbanks Morse company from whom he obtained the mill sent full instructions for operating it, at first he encountered difficulties. Then the m.ller employed by his great rival came to look over Sheridan's fine new machine and with his practised eye and expert knowledge he was able to adjust it so that it began to work with first-rate competence. Where the old-fashioned mill had been slow, producing only one hundred pounds of flour within an hour, this new model turned out during the next winter a total of ninety thousand pounds, all a better grade than that ground out formerly at the Ranch.

As well now Sheridan was able to offer his customers cracked wheat, cream of wheat and shorts, and a number of experimental mixtures that served both for porridge and dog-feed. The favorite proved to be a product he labelled "Cremo"; shoppers began to buy both for canine and human consumption. Especially for trappers, because of its small bulk, it was more practicable than coarser "chop" mixtures.

Generally the popular dog food was the residue known as "shorts", which came to take the place of the traditional corn-meal.

"With my mill I was able to make about thirty-five

227

pounds of flour per bushel of wheat, leaving the shorts, which I put up in fifty-pound bags, for dog-feed. The Indian trappers prepared it as porridge in big kettles with bits of meat and fish, and perhaps grease or tallow. It was so much in demand that the market for corn-meal for dog-feed entirely disappeared. I delivered this to customers by the sack or by the ton."

One phase of marketing which he entrusted entirely to Juey's supervision was the filling of orders for Ranch produce made by the captains of the river steamers, the "Peace River," the "Athabasca River," the motor-boat "The Weenusk," all carriers of the Hudson's Bay Company, and the great queen, the "D. A. Thomas," which that company eventually took over. Also faithfully she saw to it that the men had ready the fine butchered meat and other supplies on which the captains counted to round out their menus for passengers and staff. When the signalling ship's whistle echoed out as far as the lonely forest edging the cultivated river flats, then ranch-hands packed the orders by team across to the landing-pier and by small boat to the steamer's side.

One summer the mistress of the Ranch noted that the weights of the meat which she recorded and those for which Captain Haight sent her payment did not agree. Next time the whistle signalled, with weights in hand she herself accompanied the order.

"All right, Mrs. Lawrence," agreed Captain Haight. "We'll go down to the salesman and check."

Tests revealed that the steamer's weights were short. Juey spoke up promptly. "Very well, may I have payment in cash, please. To make up for the discrepancies."

"Gad!" grinned the captain. "I knew Sheridan Lawrence was a hard man to deal with." His grin widened as he bowed slightly. "But his wife's worse."

In these years of expanding production on the now thousand-acre Ranch as well as of expanding trade, Sheridan looked back to that early debate between his father and his uncle as to whether wheat could be grown successfully in this northern latitude. True, the most successful was Garnet, which produced a flour of a slightly yellowish cast; sometimes, too, there were complete crop failures, for a climate the record of which showed over a period of years only three days between the latest spring frost, on July the fifteenth, and the earliest autumn frost, on July the eighteenth, could not always be counted upon to bring even barley to first-grade maturity.

But the successes far outweighed the failures and the contrast between the magnitude of their production now and the first tiny beginnings made by his family nearly forty years before was almost unbelievable. Sheridan remembered that agreement drawn up in 1880 between his Uncle E. J. and Mr. Garrioch in which it was set down that if the total wheat crop amounted to fifty bushels, the latter was to receive twenty bushels and his uncle the balance; now in winter for himself and his customers his mill produced a ton of flour in a single day. Time had more than justified, too, those seemingly impossible dreams of his father Henry and his mother Maggie and their steadfast faith in this land.

Beside them on the great river, itself unchanged and changeless, itself still friend and still foe, transportation changes were thus making a difference to the lives of those dwelling on the Ranch. In springtime the whistle marking the first steamer voyage of the new season sounded a glad note across the lonely valley and the children scrambled to the roof-top to watch for the boat's approach. Then they pelted over the quarter-mile trail to the near landing-pier by the snye through which during the high water of June the ships could pass. Captain, crew and children hailed each other with mutual delight; the crew tossed oranges and apples down to the little ones and Captain Haight wrote his favorite's name on some he threw to young Margaret.

When the majestic "D. A. Thomas" began her long career of shuffling between mishaps and gravel bars on the often-thwarting Peace, new vistas of delight opened up for the children of the Ranch.

"She was like something straight from paradise," they recalled in after-years. "Especially at night, when she was all glowing with golden light, she was almost too gorgeous to be real."

In the spring they were sometimes saddened when a favorite teacher disappeared on the boat. And in the autumn when the last sailing before freeze-up was due, they watched with even more concern, for the last boat in might have aboard a new teacher for their school. Or it might not; then how delightful to contemplate long days without any tedious school-work to do!

There continued to be pupils aplenty, for now to the family were added Janet, born in 1915, and Isaac, who was born in 1917 and named after Isaac, Sheridan's brother who had for some time served as foreman on the Ranch and who had quitted it to go overseas where he was killed on active service.

"You look pretty pleased too," the delighted father beamed at Juey. She smiled again. In loyalty to her sex she must not express it in words. But she was happy, after having given birth to several girls, to present him with a new son.

The matter of finding competent help continued always to plague Sheridan; sometimes he sent out as far as Winnipeg for men who were supposed to possess the skills needed for all the varied phases of activity on the Ranch. So he was overjoyed with his wife's further co-operation when she presented him with three more sons, Elmer, born in 1919, Oswald born in 1921, and Walter, her last and fifteenth baby, who arrived in June of 1923.

While there were thus students sufficient to fill the rows of desks in the Lawrence Point school, great was the rejoicing if the Department of Education in Edmonton had failed to find a teacher for them and there was no teacher to step ashore from the last boat in. The rejoicing did not last too long, for in these emergencies their mother stepped in to fill the gap. At length, in September of 1923, young Edith, who had been out at Edmonton attending high school, received a permit to teach at her home school.

This arrangement proved hard on the children and harder still on Big Sister. Their father's trading store was only a few feet removed from the school building. To have one's own sister in charge was a definite challenge on the path of mischief, but a mischievous or rebellious child could not guess at which moment a heavy footstep might shake the threshold and the possible nearness of their father's presence was a wondrous aid to discipline.

When Edith left to be married, her sister Velma and next Juey again carried on successively. Then, in 1927, the department arranged for a Mr. Stitt to take charge. This gentleman confronted the rigors of his new northern post with a double handicap; he hobbled about as best he could with the help of an artificial leg and, because he had failed to meet the requirements in algebra, he taught school by permit only.

"Try to get your algebra from our encyclopaedia," advised practical Juey. "It will give you something to do during the long evenings." It was her father's voice, all over again, directing his children's program during the dark winter nights.

At this time the two sons of the Keg River trader Frank Jackson boarded with the family in order to take advantage of the school. Much to the chagrin of all the lively young people, Mr. Stitt took Juey's advice. As he wrestled with the values of x and y and z, at the same time he insisted that the whole school range themselves round the dining-room table so that he could supervise their home-work.

By an ingenious variety of tricks, Juey learned later from her girls, the boys tried to retaliate. The most obvious answer of course, and the most embarrassing to the luckless teacher, was the hiding away of his artificial leg whenever he took a bath.

In the intimacy of such a teaching arrangement among so many high-spirited children, and with a lonely outsider who enjoyed participating in family chores, it was difficult sometimes for Juey to maintain a proper discipline and decorum. Both she and Mr. Stitt suffered mortification when one Saturday morning he attempted hair-cutting among the girls. A scuffle ensued which ended with the unlucky man being given a shove, posterior first, into the crashing glass of a kitchen window.

Such shindigs always took place when Sheridan was absent from the Ranch.

When he was present, it was exceedingly difficult for the young people "to get away" with anything without his

231

knowledge. There was, for instance, that rare Sunday afternoon in early winter when there was no snow on the frozen snye. Protected as it was by three islands, whereas the ice on the wide main channel was always rough, here it was comparatively smooth and inviting to skate blades. Its only drawback were air-holes formed by bubbles rising from the quicksands below, but these in reality made skating much more interesting and challenging.

Gathered on the snye, all the young of the family were enjoying themselves on skates when Janet and Stanley began racing round and round the largest of these air-holes. They wanted to discover just how close they could venture to it without the ice breaking beneath them. Soon they were circling so fast through a slush of surface water that they failed to heed that the ice was weakening. It gave way and down they plunged into a hole that had opened up some six feet wide.

With the "expertise" of veterans, their brothers and sisters dropped to the ice to form a human chain that dragged them clear. Wrapped in borrowed jackets, they rushed to the back wash-room of the ranch-house to change into dry clothing. Though every one was as quiet as possible not to alert their father, who was relaxing in the living-room, somehow he got word of the mishap.

"There will be no more skating this winter," he announced at the supper-table.

Velma tried to object. After all, there were so few Sundays when the snye provided good skating.

"Very well," thundered her father. "You're now earning your own living. You can go if you wish to."

Tears of disappointment filled her eyes. "I can't skate by myself," she sobbed.

Years of intimacy with the untamed might of the Peace taught Sheridan to be very cautious in its presence and adamant in his rules. His sons remembered how in a small boat on one occasion he rebuked a fellow-passenger for recklessly moving about.

"What's the matter? Can't you swim?" the man retorted.

"When I want to swim, I'll get undressed. Right now, I choose to ride."

In spite of all his precautions, there were accidents. There was the occasion when he was in a boat with his older sons. The vessel hit a submerged log, gave a sudden jolt and toppled him head-first into the river. Near to panic with fear for him, the boys almost swamped the boat in trying to manoeuvre it into a position to help him. Meantime, half swimming, half wading, he scrambled to the shore and safety.

"He wasn't nearly as excited as we were," they admitted ruefully.

Once in mid-winter, when the Peace seemed safely imprisoned under a foot-thick wall of ice, the crossing of it developed into a fearful melee of horror. The matter of planning for and providing of sufficient feed ahead for each winter sometimes became ill-starred. The business of marketing also depended in part on seasonal vagaries. If trapping were poor, the demand for beef slackened both at the trading posts and among the Indians and stacks of frozen quarters on the Ranch waited in vain for customers. In such emergencies the mistress and her helpers rose to the occasion with gigantic canning bees that preserved the meat for future use.

But if a combination of a wet summer when it was impossible to harvest sufficient hay and a generally poor crop-growing season coupled with an early and long winter, then the problem of what to do with cattle not yet fattened for marketing could become acute. The long winter of 1919-20, for instance, found the Ranch tragically short of feed and more than once Sheridan was obliged to knock on the head cattle so weakened that they could not struggle to their feet.

Again, three winters later, he saw that feed was growing alarmingly scarce. At Tall Crees Prairie, some thirty miles south across the river, there was plenty of hay available. He decided to organize a drive of some sixty-five of the bigger animals to the source of supply.

Strung out against the winter whiteness, the trekking party of teams, cattle and saddle ponies made an imposing sight. In the lead was the hired man Bill, driving a team hauling a sleigh and rack heaped with hay to entice the cattle along the trail that led to the river bank and forward over the ice to the distant shore. Strung out behind was the herd of bawling Shorthorns pushed on their way by young Malcolm and two more ranch-hands, all on horseback. Sheridan himself, in a second sleigh carrying camping equipment and supplies, followed up the rear.

It was a bitter cold morning, twenty below zero, and no suggestion at all of any chinook that might weaken the foot-thick ice-pan on the Peace. The surface was rough and hummocked and here and there swept bare of snow. Urged on by the shouts and the whips of the riders, obediently the cattle began to follow the lead sleigh onto the river. A few kept close behind it and their weight combined with that of the sleigh caused the ice to crackle and rumble. Within minutes the main herd, alarmed by the ominous sounds, began to attempt to turn back, and soon in spite of the lashings of the whips and the brave efforts of the ponies they were milling round and round in a distraught circle.

By now Sheridan saw the peril they were in. "Break 'em up!" he boomed from the rear. "Break 'em up!"

Twisting and turning, the valiant ponies did their best. Bawling their protest, the terrified cattle still milled in a tight circle.

"Break 'em up!" roared Sheridan again.

The riders leapt from their horses and on foot with shouts and threats and flaying whips they tried to force the animals forward.

Suddenly in the middle of the fearful jam the ice gave way. Sharp cracklings and reports of splitting ice mingled with the frightening bawling as the cattle began to find themselves plunging into the water.

Within moments the gap widened to a diameter of near fifty feet. Dozens of cattle, some layered one above the other in their frantic efforts to escape, and the three saddle ponies were in the water. Light and nimble-footed, the riders scrambled to firm ice and to safety along the backs of the helpless cattle.

"You get home and change," Sheridan commanded. "Bill will help me here."

A few cattle followed the men out, clambering over the bodies of those floundering beneath them. But most of the attempts to escape only broke more ice chunks round about them.

Alerted by the shouts of the men and the fearful bawlings of the cattle, Bill in the head sleigh had turned about and began to assist Sheridan in rescue operations. They unhitched their teams and with chains and lariats hurried the horses as near as they dared venture to the scene of the disaster.

"First," wrote Sheridan, "we pulled out the saddle horses. That was a ticklish business."

With one end of a lariat he lassoed each pony in turn, securing the other end to a chain looped about a clevis on the evener. Then he urged the team to tug on their traces with all their power. Fortunately, being shod, the straining animals were able to hold their footing on the ice, and one by one the trapped ponies were dragged up and out of the water. Working with terrified creatures in sub-zero cold, with dripping water turning to ice on animals and rope, was in itself an ordeal.

"I had to grab hold of the rope round the horse's neck, force the animal down and hold it there until I worked the rope free."

Speed was of the utmost. As some of the helpless swimming cattle saw the horses at last walking away, they too made their way to that end of the opening and this facilitated rescue operations.

"We're in the water," shouted young Malcolm as he reached the ranch-house and a change of dry clothing.

As he told in a few excited sentences of the tragedy that had befallen, Juey and the girls hurried to do what they could to help. They filled a jug with hot tea, collected matches, kindling and fire-wood, hitched another team to a sleigh and hurried the horses along the trail to the river. They began to pass a pitiful procession bound for the warmth and shelter of the barns, ponies and cattle with bodies sheathed with white frost, eyes almost frozen shut and icicles some a foot long dripping from their bodies. On the river bank the girls got a bright fire blazing where the rescuers who had collected could warm themselves and they passed out hot tea to any who would take time to drink.

Sheridan himself would not budge from the edge of the water while there was any hope of saving more animals.

"We worked fast, but the cattle got tired out trying to keep afloat in the icy water. We did our best. But we knew that some were carried under the ice."

As they checked on the number of bawling icicle-hung animals that straggled mournfully back to the barns, they realized that about a third of the herd had been swept under the ice by the current and drowned.

"Well," said Sheridan sadly, "now we'll have feed enough for what are left."

He employed his cross-river neighbor, William Flett, to recover the carcasses of the victims. That astute river man searched along the surface of the ice where he guessed the current had carried the bodies. Tapping with a stick to sound for them, one by one he located them. He chopped each one out, hauled them to the Ranch and stacked them in a shed.

The children came to watch how the heaps of carcasses grew. They were dread reminders of the menace of their river, even under its broad blanket of snow and ice. A winter-white weasel came to make its home in the shed. The youngsters whistled at the slim little creature and tried to tease it.

"Sk-sk-sk!" it hissed angrily at them from among the grisly stacks of carcasses.

Gradually their father sold the meat to his Indian customers for dog food.

Again the great queen of the Peace, the "D. A. Thomas," became a factor in helping to balance loss and gain. The next summer he shipped out in her hold the balance of the herd that had attempted the tragic crossing. By now the prices had advanced so much that the difference nearly made up for the financial losses by drowning.

With the assistance of his older sons, Sheridan continued to expand his interests. On the business letter-head which his wife used as she kept all the accounts and attended to all the necessary correspondence was summarized something of the varied phases of the enterprises of the Ranch. Sometimes pausing to remember its struggling beginnings, the pair glanced with justifiable pride at this heading:

SHERIDAN LAWRENCE
"The Ranch"
Horses and Cattle, Hides and Furs
Milling, Sawmill, Lumber
General Merchandise

Though simply entitled "The Ranch," the spread of buildings on the river flat above the Peace resembled a thriving village. In winter smoke rose from thirty-five wood-burning fires in as many stoves that had to be kept lighted to maintain the necessary heat; to the adolescent members of the family returning home on holiday from sojourn outside at high school or college, the sight of all the twinkling lights of home was "simply beautiful." Sometimes as many as fifteen "hands" as well as all of the family and the teacher sat down to the enormous meals served three times daily in both kitchen and dining-room.

In spite of the magnitude of the "home" operations, now in their middle years both Sheridan and Juey contrived to spend more and more time in the fascinating and challenging business of "trading." This brought Juey especially into closer contact again with the shy proud people of her childhood and youth. To read their secretive minds and to outwit shrewd business rivals brought more excitement and fresh zest to the lives of both husband and wife.

CHAPTER 6

Statuesque and taciturn, the plank-nosed Beaver Indian stood across the counter from Juey in the small trading shack. Behind her, rainbow-streaked shelves displayed packages of temptation, an assortment of staple human foods and simple household articles.

"Well?" she smiled her brightest. "What can I get for you today?"

The tall man spoke one word only, and in his native tongue. "Bayulay." His leathered face remained impassive but his brown eyes glowered a challenge down at the small white woman.

The almost wordless exchange was a sample of the battle of wits that whetted the appetite of both husband and wife for "trading." Both of them were fairly proficient in the Beaver tongue, though not as proficient as they were in the long-familiar Cree. This customer now, Juey was sure, could speak some English. Stubbornly, he continued to refuse to try.

"Bayulay," he repeated.

For another moment her mind raced over the possibilities. Then she reached for a vividly red can of baking powder.

"Oh yes," she smiled again. "Bayulay. For a minute I forgot."

"You should know," the man reproached her, still speaking in the Beaver tongue. "You've been here long enough."

She felt herself being reproved, deservedly perhaps. Even after so many years of living and working among the Indians, there was still much, more than even a mere matter of mastering all the dialects, that she could learn of them and from them. In her life as in Sheridan's, their contacts

238

with the native peoples were constantly being shaped from new angles.

As the areas nearer to the Peace became trapped out, competition among the traders for furs and for "treaty" dollars grew intense. It now became the practice at treaty time to drive loaded sleighs or wagons of goods right to the reserve on the very day that the government agent arrived with his bonanza. By moccasin telegraph on one occasion word reached the Ranch that the treaty party was to arrive at the nearby Aliska Beaver reserve on the following Saturday, several days before it had been expected.

The news struck a sorry blow to the family. Sheridan, absent somewhere far up-stream, was engaged in piloting a scow-load of freight from Peace River Crossing. He was going to miss the all-important annual trading day at this reserve.

Together his family consulted and pondered. Right now the older sons who shouldered many of their father's former duties could not spare the time from necessary operations at home to go "trading." They looked at Juey.

"Why don't you go, Mother?"

The idea of a middle-aged woman undertaking such a chore was so novel. Yet, thought Juey, why not? Her girls would see to everything in the ranch-house during her absence. She was accustomed to confronting inscrutable faces across a counter. Trading from a wagon would not be more difficult.

She agreed to try. On the Friday evening the girls stacked the wagon box high with supplies from the store. Next morning at four, with ten-year-old Isaac for company. she set forth.

"May I drive?" the lad begged.

Under her watchful eye he guided the horses over the rough trail that twisted northwestward through swamp and bush. Fording the stream with equine know-how, the team dragged the heavy wagon through the Paddle river; fifteen miles from their starting point they rattled up to the clutter of shacks and tents and teepees that were the core of the Aliska reserve.

Already three other "trading" wagons, representing the "Bay," Revillon Brothers and the independent trader, Mr. Edgecombe, were lined up in waiting.

From under an awning the agent began paying out "treaty," five dollars apiece for every man, woman and child. With this marvellous "open sesame" in hand, the impatient customers then crowded about the wagons. Soon Juey could not keep up with demand, and young Ikey fell to helping, making change and handing out goods like a veteran store-keeper.

Speaking in the Beaver tongue, several potential customers shook their heads. "I come tomorrow." Juey knew that they had a gambling game planned.

"No," she objected. "Tomorrow's Sunday. I don't trade on Sunday. What about Monday?"

Sadly they shook their heads. "No money then."

"You had better trade now," she urged. A good many were persuaded to take her advice and she kept her "shop" open until midnight, when she had exhausted all her supplies.

As a precaution, she had brought blankets and food for herself and the lad. Now, since the weather was fine and the northern summer night was dusky dark only and not black, she decided to head for home at once.

She tucked a blanket about the boy. Swathed in its warmth, he stood manfully peering in the gloom and guiding the team. Presently the monotonous bumpety-clang of the empty wagon overcame desire and he slid to the wagon floor, sound asleep. Juey grabbed the reins and stared into the shadows, trying to direct the plodding horses.

An army of poker-straight black dwarfs loomed into view, menacing their path. They were, she knew, the eerie charred stumps of burned-off trees, but she could no longer select a way among them. She gave the horses their heads and prayed a little prayer.

With dread she recognized at last the silvered gleam of the Paddle river. Again she realized that the team, and not she, must choose the crossing. Water began to splash all round about her, showering cool refreshing drops upon her face. In their wisdom the horses found their way safely through the stream and up onto the opposite bank.

They arrived at the Ranch and she roused the sleeping boy, sending him at once stumbling upstairs to bed. In the soft grey of early morning, she unharnessed the team and turned them into the pasture. At last she crawled up the stairs herself.

There a surprise awaited. Sheridan, safely home from Peace River Crossing, stretched sound asleep in bed.

"Weren't you even worried about me?" she queried next morning.

"Of course not," he smiled. "The children said you wouldn't be home till Monday."

Proudly she turned over her returns from the day's trading, three hundred dollars in cash.

Although it was Sunday, the family had again to scramble about to prepare for more trading. The treaty party was proceeding on farther northwestward to Upper Hay River; hustling so as to be on time for these next "treaty" days, Sheridan directed the unloading of his scow straight into five wagons.

As the quintuplet train set forth into the forest, Juey regretted the new spirit of commercialism that made such work necessary even on Sunday. Fifty miles out, at High Level, the cortege divided, with Sheridan sending one wagon on to Upper Hay and himself guiding the others forward to his key post at Hay Lakes.

In his diary he recorded figures revealing the scope of his trading in some peak years. "In 1920-21, I sold thirteen thousand dollars' worth of furs. In 1924, we took in from Tall Trees, Bear Creek and Hay Lakes ten silver, fifty cross and seventy-five red fox, one hundred and fifty mink, one hundred skunk, one hundred and twenty ermine, eighty coyotes, eighty-five lynx, fifteen marten, nine hundred rats, two fishers, and eighty-seven horse and cow hides.

"The next year we took in, from various sources in parts where I was freighting, seventy-three fox, one hundred and sixteen beaver, four hundred and thirty-six ermine, three hundred and twenty-six mink, two wolves, three otter, one hundred and twenty-five lynx and two thousand and twenty-eight muskrats. During those years I sometimes paid out more in cash than I took in fur. I also sold a lot of flour, shorts, lard, butter and bacon, some of which I got from neighbours.

Since the Hay Lakes post lay by zigzagging trail nearly one hundred and thirty miles to the northwest, the nearer and

241

more northerly Upper Hay post perhaps a hundred miles distant, and Tall Trees prairie nearly as far on the right hand region of the Peace, his trading area was now reaching out tentacles over some ten thousand square miles of wilderness. Merely to arrive at the key points inevitably involved a variety of challenges, for the trails led through bush and swamp and over muskeg that could be deep in snow or glassy with ice in winter and in summer miry and almost bottomless after heavy rain, or up and down steep hills and precipitous banks where again varying weather meant varying travel conditions.

In spite of these, he noted with satisfaction, "by 1921 I cut the freight rates from Fort Vermilion to Hay Lakes to fifty dollars per ton. In 1925 we cut a road from the Hay River road on high land southwest of Watt mountain right to Hay Lakes. I spent nearly two thousand dollars making this road but I liked it better because it didn't drift so badly and supplied feed for stock in summer," though, he added, "there were a few more hills to get over and mud holes to get through or around." Eventually this became the main road between High Level and Hay Lakes.

Each mile along the trading trails came to have its special associations; the stopping points were generally selected according to their availability in providing water for the horses. At the Graveyards on the Aliska reserve a creek sang a lullaby to the sleeping buried beneath the tiny roofed-over houses that protected their graves. Buffalo lake took its name from Buffalo Head prairie where an escarpment resembled the massive head of the wild bison. At Sauer Kraut creek the hungry teamsters, craving the anti-scorbutic refreshment of Juey's home-made cabbage favorite, had broken open a tub of sauer kraut and feasted upon it alone; Chicken Pox creek derived its name from the misfortune of the Métis driver, "Manny" Charles, who had to be left behind there with a male nursing volunteer when he suddenly broke out with that infection; at Alexie's creek the wagon of another Métis driver, Alexie Cardinal, became stuck fast in the treacherous creek bottom. Groping under water as Sheridan himself had first done at the age of sixteen at that crossing of the Red Deer river, Alexie somehow got his thumb cut off in his struggle with draw pin and chain.

Competition to catch up the precious "treaty" money became even more acrimonious and in 1926 it was rumored that a regulation was going to be passed which would prohibit altogether any trading on reserve land. Again Sheridan was absent and again Juey undertook to drive to the Aliska reserve at treaty time.

Under a lowering sky, she paid a visit to the Indian Maurees. Rain was imminent, he assured her.

"The birds say so," he explained.

Juey was worried. Somehow she must find shelter for her goods and for her daughter Kathleen and herself. According to time-honored custom, the tribesman Maurees and his family had vacated their cabin for the summer months to live in their teepee of poles and skins.

"May I rent your cabin?" she asked him in his own tongue. Laughingly he agreed.

The pair of female "traders" scrubbed out the cabin and set up their wares.

That same day Juey's son Stanley was down-river at the post when the federal commissioner, Mr. Christianson, arrived on the steamer.

"So you're the son of Sheridan Lawrence," he said when he learned of the boy's identity. In a lowered tone he added, "Let me give you a message for your mother."

This Mr. Christianson was an old family friend who had been present at Juey's wedding. On one occasion when treaty money had been paid out in advance of the advertised date, as a result of which Sheridan missed most of the resulting trading, he complained of the trick and the commissioner had assured him that it would not happen again.

Now he stooped to plant a warning in the lad's ear. "Tell your mother that it's illegal this year to trade on a reserve."

The message loaded the boy's shoulders with a weight of worry. Was his mother, all unsuspecting, going to be guilty of violating this new law? That evening he rode thirty miles along the bush trail to carry the commissioner's message to her.

Juey was pleased with her conscientious son. But she couldn't help chuckling a little.

"I suspected this was coming. That's why I rented this cabin."

The cabin had been built, so she reminded the lad, before the reservation had been set up. "You know your Dad's keen sense of direction. Well, I'd heard him tell Maurees that his cabin was just outside of reserve land."

Still concerned about the warning, young Stanley himself proceeded to hunt in the brush for the survey post. At last he was satisfied; his father had been right.

Next day another trader paid Juey a visit. "You'll be in for trouble," he forecast.

Feeling secure, she smiled at him. "I just don't care," she answered blithely.

Using an interpreter, the trader turned to repeat to Maurees that Mrs. Lawrence was going to be involved with the law. Her familiarity with the Beaver tongue made it easy for her to follow the conversation.

"Don't you worry," she soothed the perplexed Indian. She reminded him then that Sheridan had told him that his house was beyond the boundaries of the reserve.

Next morning with Kathleen's help she gave the cabin a second cleansing. Then she invited the treaty party to come and have dinner with them.

"You are quite a fox," grinned the Indian agent.

She smiled. "It takes a fox to outsmart a fox," she countered amiably.

For her this kind of incident gave added sparkle to the infinite variety of the trading game. For her son Stanley there unfolded later on another aspect of the conflict arising sometimes out of "treaty time."

Because there had been early reports of money having been paid out to those long dead or to those not yet born, now all the members of each Indian family were required to be present for the all-important day. Between the Hay Lakes area where Stanley was trading for his father and Upper Hay where "treaty" was usually counted, regions of the Hay river, because of the many rapids, were almost impassable except in June's high water. At the same time long stretches of muskeg made the overland trail difficult for the native families to traverse. Yet the rules insisted that they make the journey.

Young Stanley encouraged them to take a stand to have the "treaty" paid to them in their home area of Hay Lakes. Finally, in spite of opposition, the representatives of the white man's government consented to the change.

His mother in turn reflected the teaching of her parents. Never could she forget the sense of responsibility and the spirit of kindly paternalism that had been instilled by her father. When the Rev. Malcolm passed away in 1919, Bishop Robins spoke of him as "one of the noblest and most heroic men that I have ever met . . . who had given so generously of his means that he died a poor man." She remembered his example when impoverished Indians appeared before her and both she and Sheridan tried to strike a happy balance between outright giving and offering credit that would foster their pride and their self-reliance.

It was in this same Hay Lakes region that there dwelled some of the northland's most primitive tribes. Sheridan felt that it was his special duty to help and to protect them and word of his generosity began to bring him in early spring the role of canoeing soup-kitchen. Light of foot and light of heart, the native men hurried off to hunt, leaving behind all the women and children. The only food of these unfortunates would be whatever fish they could catch. But husbands and fathers knew that the tall white trader would not permit any one to die of hunger.

For a few days the families fended off starvation by trapping muskrats and bringing the skins to him to trade for food. When this source failed, they came to him with tales of hardships being endured in their camps and they begged for extended credit.

"My harem is growing larger all the time," he jested as he loaded a canoe to take supplies to them. This jest he was forced to repeat a good many times.

"The natives are like children," agreed his wife, echoing the words of her parents. "You have to help them. And try to lead them. But at the same time try to nourish their spirit of independence."

Like Juey, Sheridan endeavored to avoid outright handouts. Though he was aware of the longing in native lives for color, he disliked having to stock tawdry trash and he persisted in trying to sell to his customers what was good for them. At the same time, he advanced food on credit and kept a record of all his transactions.

"Hand-outs by the government are all wrong," he stormed. "It should buy their fish or their furs so that they know they are earning what they get."

While he budgetted several hundred dollars each year for gifts, these extras he usually handed out with trade goods. To the ill or the elderly whom he knew could never repay him, in order to bolster their native pride these gifts were always recorded as credit advances. Thus did he earn the title of "the good friend," Meyootootam.

There were moments when his sense of fair play irritated the practical mind of the mistress of the Ranch.

"Send me as soon as possible two hundred pounds of sauer kraut," he wrote to her from his trading post at Hay Lakes.

Usually her garden grew an abundance of cabbages so big and so splendid that, hurled through the air, they could strike a person down. In fact one did just that, felling Juey herself one afternoon when with her son Malcolm she had turned the arduous cabbage-harvesting into a kind of game. The youth tossed the hard pumpkin-sized globes to her; she in turn caught each one and dropped it down a chute whence it slid into the root cellar.

For a moment her attention wavered and a football-like cabbage, aimed straight for her head, sent her sprawling unconscious to earth.

She recovered quickly enough and the thought of one of her own cabbages knocking her out, together with the sight of the lad's stricken face as he helped her to her feet, sent her into gales of laughter. With relief he joined in the merriment.

Now, when Sheridan's call came for sauer kraut, she had remaining on hand only sufficient whole and fermented cabbage for the needs of the Ranch. So with no time, unlike the walrus, to talk of else but cabbages, away she hustled to drive by buggy to all of her neighbors. Paying five cents per pound, she bought up all of their surplus crop. Soon her home-constructed chopper was biting through great quantities of ringed cabbage foliage and she had barrels of pressed cabbage fermenting into fragrant kraut.

Feeling highly pleased with herself, she forwarded the two hundred pounds as requested by the next freight sleigh carrying in supplies to Sheridan.

"How much did you charge for my sauer kraut?" she inquired of him presently. She expected a nice little profit to be deflected back to herself as recompense for all of her time and labor.

"Why, the usual," her husband informed her. "Four cents a pound."

"But I paid five cents a pound for the cabbages," she wailed.

"That doesn't matter," soothed the philanthropic master of the Ranch. "You know the men have to have it. You can't expect a profit on a necessity like that."

Among men in the bush camps or following trap-lines, and subsisting largely on meat and bannocks, sauer kraut was much prized as a precious anti-scorbutic.

"You know, Mother," added son Osborne shrewdly, "Dad will never be rich." The young man had been assisting with his father's trading and had watched his practices.

She thought it over. "No, maybe not in material things, anyway."

As members of the second generation of the tiny mission colony, she and Sheridan were constantly being sought out to solve all kinds of problems, questions of policy, family squabbles, illnesses, neighbors' quarrels. Finally Sheridan received official status in this role; he was named a justice of the peace.

A visitor remarked at their wholehearted concentration in attempting to resolve the difficulties of others.

"Well," she pondered. "I guess we do take a kind of pride in it."

Was this, perhaps, the real riches that they owned? This place that they seemed to have earned in the minds and the hearts of their neighbors?

247

CHAPTER 7

Into the woodsman's wiry fingers Juey thrust a number of pills.

"Take two per day," she directed through the medium of the interpreter Jean Bourassa.

"Those little things!" retorted her patient via Interpreter Jean. Whereupon he clapped the whole handful into his mouth.

"Oh!" exclaimed Juey aghast. "They might kill him."

As Jean reassured her, he shook with laughter. "Tough Indian like him, no kill easy."

So far as she could discover, Jean had been right. The man appeared not to suffer any ill effects.

Gradually the young woman who had wanted to be a doctor or a nurse acquired a training in the school of necessity that equipped her to meet all contingencies and eventually to face up to the direst emergencies. Sheridan too learned early to confront crises with cool common sense. But whenever his wife was present or near, in matters of injury or illness he looked to her to take over. Among the most frequent calls for her help were those requiring treatment of jagged cuts and wounds.

There was, for instance, the Indian who came to her with a fish-hook jabbed right through the thickest part of one hand. Already the flesh was inflamed and badly swollen and horrible to behold.

She took a quick look and had the man plunge the hand into a basin of near-boiling water.

"I'm going to hurt you," she warned him. At the same time she steeled herself for what must follow.

With a file she sawed off the projecting pronged end of the hook. Then, gripping the hand tightly with her left fingers, with her right she yanked the balance of the hook out of the inflamed flesh. Into the raw hole she poured turpentine. The perspiration stood out in beads on the man's forehead but he did not utter a word and his courage became hers.

In a few minutes she had him soaking the hand in hot water and salt. Then she dressed it with iodine. A week of this treatment completely cured the wound.

Sometimes the native people or those of mixed blood reciprocated with a knowledge that apparently stemmed from generations of self-helping. There was, for instance, the skill of Charlotte Flett in midwifery on which Juey so often depended. There were native remedies of which she learned, spruce needles steeped for scurvy, the gall of ox or other animal for chilbain or frostbite, the berries of the leatherbark and the dried stems of the blue-eyed grass simmered for a kind of tonic.

Female knack and know-how were demonstrated for the Ranch family by the Slavey squaw who dwelled just back of the ranch-house when her French husband worked for Sheridan. When this slight woman carried two five-gallon pails of water up the slope to her cabin, they noticed how she walked erect with head thrown back. When her "man" carried the water, he stooped far forward.

The Ranch family hid their smiles on one occasion when her husband, like other white men, put his foot down on a length of "squaw wood"—light poplar chunks of the size favored by Indian women for cutting up for fires—and then began to chop at it with his axe. Shyly his wife came forward, with a little laugh took the axe from his hand, held the length of wood almost upright, chopped at it, turned it, chopped again and turned again, and in a twinkling had severed the stick.

To his credit, when the young husband inherited a title and was obliged to return to France, he wanted to take his clever native wife with him, but friends finally persuaded him that she would be happier among her own people.

A near-tragic incident involving an Indian woman and an

axe occurred when Salootsie Lazotte was trapping muskrats in the open water of early spring. She was working alone on a creek; something caught the handle of her axe so that it slipped and almost severed her hand. She contrived to tourniquet her wrist, and with the hand dangling in a pail of water she struggled in her canoe to reach a spot by the bank where she stuck up a "trouble" signal—in this case a bit of bloody rag on a pole—and finally made it back to her cabin. A passer-by found her presently, near collapse, but still with the nearly-severed hand in the pail of water. In vain she still hoped to reach the doctor so that he could sew it back on again.

A happier outcome followed another misfortune which came to the attention of those dwelling on the Ranch. Sheridan brought to Juey word of the severe illness of John Judd, whose father had been a Methodist minister in eastern Canada and who camped at Prairie Point to cut hay for the Lawrence ranch.

"You'd better come with me in the canoe and take a look at him. His wife says he's so sick he can't move."

The man lay swathed in blankets arranged on a bed of stones by the side of a fire. In her native tongue, his Cree wife explained her treatment. She had thoroughly soused the blankets in hot water and spread them over heated stones. Then she had swaddled her husband tightly within them.

This treatment, she told her white visitor, she had learned from her mother, who had used it long ago when members of the tribe had been very ill.

"I hear my mother talk all about sickness like this," she explained. "Some died. And my uncle still very lame."

Juey concluded that the man Judd was in capable hands. Perhaps, she guessed, his illness was poliomyelitis. When she came to learn of the Kenny treatment, she decided that in her native wisdom this woman was following a somewhat similar method of cure.

A few days later, Sheridan reported that the ailing man was back at work.

Within the family, emergency and illness tested its busy mother sometimes to the very brink of endurance. During a period of bitter cold when Sheridan was absent, one by one his brother Will and each of the children fell ill with influenza. She spread mattresses on the floor of the master bedroom and there she tended the sick youngsters while at the same time she stoked three wood-consuming fires.

One night, feeling very ill herself, she picked up the baby Stanley who was fussing in his crib. Half delirious with "flu" and with lack of sleep, she swung open the top of the big heater. Then she stooped to pick up a hefty chunk of the wood to feed the fire. In the act of stoking, she caught herself. Almost she had dropped the baby, instead of the log, into the heater.

As she realized her near-mistake, her knees turned to water. Clutching the infant, she sank down to the floor. For a couple of minutes, until she recovered, the opened heater belched acrid smoke into the room. Next morning she sent for Ellen Charles, a young neighbor girl of mixed blood, to come to her assistance.

There were other crises by the score, both minor and major, crises that were often inevitable in bringing up a large lively family in Swiss-Family-Robinson-like circumstances of isolation and self-dependence.

There were the bloody minutes when she had to sew up little Edith's scalp after a piece of galvanized sheet iron had dropped from the roof upon her head and knocked her unconscious. As well as her medical and veterinarian texts and a well-stocked cupboard of supplies, she kept always on hand sterilized needle and basin, bandaging cloth and sewing gut; presently, upon the advice of a doctor, she added a catheter and this she used several times to relieve the suffering of dangerously-ill native men.

There were the emergencies when, in spite of all her precautions added to those of Sheridan's, fires broke out in their wood-burning "village." Within the large ranch-house, partly because of her program of precautions—which included twice-monthly cleansing of the stove-pipes that accumulated a thick inflammable coating of creosote from all the wood-burning, of regular fire-drills with the children, and of keeping water always at strategic spots—fire losses were kept to a minimum.

There were the broken bones when Daisy, racing her

pony, fractured a collar-bone, and Janet, also enjoying a forbidden gallop, was thrown under a work-horse to suffer a badly smashed leg.

"What will Daddy say?" were the first words Janet sobbed when she returned to consciousness and sharp pain.

Always beside them flowed that friend and foe, the Peace that brought danger and delight, that brought life and commerce and messages of inspiration from the outside world and that also brought death, death in new and virulent forms. From one of the boats that plied its waters stemmed the greatest multiple crisis that was to overshadow the Ranch and to tax to the utmost the skill and experience and powers of endurance of its mistress.

By the year 1920 there was a government-operated ferry on the Peace near the Fort Vermilion trading centre and no longer did residents of the Ranch have to paddle themselves across the milewide stream. On a September day of that year Juey drove her buggy over the twelve-mile-trail to the ferry. When she had clattered onto the sluggish wooden monster the operator, Eli Minault, came forward to speak to her.

"Will you please look at my little girl?" he asked. "She very sick." Eli's wife was dead and he and his four children occupied a tiny shack a few yards along the river bank.

"Seeing her won't tell me much," Juey replied. "Describe her symptoms."

"Please," the father begged. "You see her."

Arrived at the south bank, Juey tied her horse to a tree and made her way through the bush to the motherless cabin. At the open door the frightful stench of smallpox hit her nostrils. From where she stood in the doorway of the one-roomed dwelling, she could see the child lying sprawled on a rough cot. Her small face was blotched with hideous scabs.

Smallpox was not new to Juey. At school in Winnipeg, where she had first been vaccinated, she had been among girls of St. John's college who were permitted, during a fearful epidemic of the pestilence in Winnipeg, to go out and assist with the nursing.

She returned now to the frightened ferry-man. "Why don't you ask the Superior at the Roman Catholic mission to see to her?" This was a Roman Catholic family. "I'm told she's as good as a doctor."

The man protested that he could not leave his ferry.

"Then I'll go and see her."

At the mission the sister was not co-operative. "Perhaps the child has chicken pox," suggested Juey. She wanted the sister to take the responsibility of diagnosis.

The latter was shrewd too. "What do you really think it is?"

Still Juey would not say.

"It's worse than chicken pox," the sister persisted. "You know that." There had already been, she admitted, several other cases. But she refused to go to the child.

"What medicine do you want for her?" she asked now as if the little one were Juey's own.

Juey accepted what the woman gave and went on her way to get her mail. The presence of obvious smallpox in the little cabin substantiated several rumors that she had already heard, that there had already been several cases among the Indians in the area and that the first case had been that of a woman passenger who had disembarked from one of the boats and had lain in the Indian camp at the post.

She drove along the old trail that hugged the river bank that she had followed so often as a child. She hailed every one whom she met, told them that a serious epidemic was beginning, and advised them to keep their children at home. To Gus Clark, the post manager, she described what she had seen of the smallpox plague in Winnipeg and she suggested that all places of business should close.

"You are simply trying to get up a scare," he retorted.

She was furious. "Never in my life have I done such a thing."

"There's always a first time."

She knew, she told him, about the woman who had lain ill in the "Bay" yard where the Indians camped sometimes. "That is where this plague started," she charged angrily. "Your yard should have been in quarantine long ago."

"Prove it," stormed the factor. "Just prove it."

She had no proof but hearsay.

At that moment the mounted police constable arrived.

She reported to him that the ferryman's child was ill with smallpox.

He too was reluctant to take positive measures. "I have no authority to do anything," he told her. "I don't know where I'd get the authority."

"It's your responsibility to make a report to Dr. Grimshaw at Peace River," she retorted. Dr. Grimshaw was in charge of Indian health. Every one was obviously reluctant to take steps that might interfere with the regular routine.

On her way back, she left the medicine with the ferryman. At home she hustled to write a blistering letter to the Department of Indian Affairs in distant Ottawa. To her it was shocking that there should be such complacency in the face of a threat from this hideous menace. It was a full month before her letter could be mailed.

Eventually, she heard later, Dr. Grimshaw received word from Ottawa. By this time the river that had brought the scourge was locked in its winter prison; navigation being closed no restrictions were imposed and no help arrived. Here and there smallpox continued to raise its ghastly head, chiefly among the Indians, and ten or more succumbed to the disease.

Meantime, the married couple Mr. and Mrs. George O'Connor returned to the Ranch, he to help with the outside work and she to teach in the Lawrence Point school. Sheridan would not permit classes to resume. Customers still came to the store and he tended to their needs. The children were not allowed near, nor were visitors permitted inside the usually hospitable walls of the big ranch-house. Even the littlest ones knew that the enemy lurked near.

"You can't come in," three-year-old Isaac announced to a neighbor at the door. "Mummy's got some smallpox cooking."

It was a jug of pine tar that his mother kept simmering on the back of the large kitchen range in the hope that its disinfecting qualities might be helpful against the fearful contagion of the disease.

Presently she received a note from a Métis neighbor, Sara Charles. Billy, her husband, was very ill and would Mrs. Lawrence come to see him? She was afraid he was going to die.

Here was indeed a quandary. Smallpox was frightfully contagious and among the native people now nearly every home was infected. Should she go to Billy? If she went, she might expose not only all her own children but the two youngsters boarding with them.

"What shall I do?" she asked Sheridan.

"You must make the decision," he answered. He himself was still trading and therefore running a constant risk.

Juey thought of the time some years before when this same Billy Charles had been hit on the temple by a tooth from the threshing machine. Carefully the men had carried him, unconscious and with blood streaming from his head, into her living room.

She stanched the flow of blood and issued a directive. "Take him to the Mother Superior down at the Mission." Quickly Sheridan agreed.

At this point Billy recovered consciousness. "No, no," he protested vehemently. "Not go."

Juey proceeded then to cleanse and dress the nasty gash.

"You my doctor," he grinned feebly and his luminous dark eyes beaming upon her lightened her spirit. Once or twice before, she had treated him for minor cuts. She worried over the deep head wound, changing the dressings faithfully. To her amazement, it healed quickly.

Now maybe at last Billy was dying and the family looked to her. There seemed to be no alternative.

"I'll go," she decided.

"I knew you would," agreed Sheridan.

Following the recipe set forth in her fat Mrs. Beeton's "Book of Household Management," she prepared a generous quantity of "Imperial Drink." This was a refreshing mixture comprised of cream of tartar, sugar and lemon essence and water. She gathered together medicines and swathed herself in her coat of muskrat fur; one of the men brought up a horse-drawn sleigh and off she drove.

At the opened door of the Charles' cabin, a blast of hot stale air assailed her nostrils. From the inner room she could hear the delirious patient threshing about and retching horribly. She set down the remedies she had brought and began to issue instructions. In her fur coat she felt as if she herself were about to expire in the warm fetid air.

"Won't you go in?" begged Sara. "Won't you go and look at him?"

"You can tell me more than I can see." Still by the doorway, she added, "Give him bits of ice to hold in his mouth, a teaspoon of cascara three times a day and plenty of this Imperial drink diluted with water. Nothing else."

As she turned to go, she smiled encouragingly. "Keep fresh air circulating, but keep him out of the draught. And let me know how he is."

Outside, she passed by the small window near the sick man's bed and she heard him utter her name as if it were a charm of healing.

"I get better now," he was muttering.

Such faith in her was a possible liability that long ago she had learned to accept.

At her own door she shed the protecting fur coat and hung it in the outside porch where the cold would isolate any germs.

At noon on New Year's day, the sharp tone of Sheridan's voice made her look up at him. "You must be getting ill," she joked, inwardly sick with fear. "It's so unlike you to be cranky."

"I have a back-ache," he confessed. With secret alarm she saw that his face was flushed under its coat of ruddy "weathering." He went out, planning to run the mill to grind some flour.

Fate had caught up with them. With a sinking heart, Juey called the children to help her remove all the curtains.

"Why are we doing this?" they wanted to know.

"To keep down the germs. Daddy's ill."

About four o'clock Sheridan stumbled back into the house. She saw that his flush had heightened. "I just can't go on," he muttered.

Neither uttered the dread word. They both knew. In spite of precautions which Sheridan had taken as he continued to trade at the store, smallpox, the scourge of the pioneer land, of Indian and Métis and white man, had overtaken them. Always before, their very isolation had made them almost immune to the continued ills of civilization and they had not worried because no vaccination was available. Now

256

the boats brought help and harm as they invaded the fringe of their Eden.

Upstairs, Juey coaxed the sick man into a hot bath and clipped closely his badger crop of grey-brown hair. Within hours his temperature soared to over one hundred and five degrees. He became delirious and she sponged his burning body and poured Imperial drink into him.

At one end of their room, she made up a cot for herself. In his delirium he wanted her to sleep near him. Then he protested, "I could sleep if you'd take the sacks of potatoes out of the bed." She crept out again and stayed out.

After three days of high fever, the blisters of smallpox came to cover his skin so thickly that there was not even room for a pinhead between them. "My teepees," he called them.

To soothe their fearful burning, she soaked his skin with glycerine. "Do wash my head," he begged in the midst of delirium. With one hand she washed off the glycerine and with the other she re-applied it.

As each of the children in turn became ill, she placed them in another upstairs sick-room. She took every precaution, changing her shoes and putting on a gown to go into the sick-rooms and keeping steam going upstairs and down. Presently she had eight patients in bed at the same time.

Over at the school-house, Mrs. O'Connor had a baby girl to protect. In spite of this, her husband was a hero of helpfulness to Juey. He fetched and carried for her; he hung out laundry to freeze and brought it in to thaw; he saw to it that she had on hand a plentiful supply of fuel from the woodshed and frozen meat from the abattoir. She continued to do the cooking for the ill and for the well, including the ranch-hands.

Fortunately her eldest son, Malcolm, had been vaccinated when he had been out at school in Winnipeg and he escaped the pestilence. Such was his capability with things mechanical that for some years Sheridan had entrusted him with the operation of engines round about the ranch, particularly the "threshing" engine, and the family had bestowed on him the enduring nickname of "Chief." Now during his father's long illness, he rose manfully to the occasion, supervising all the work of the ranch-hands and running the engine to set in motion the wheels of the grist and flour mill.

Presently, weak and swathed in blankets but smiling in spite of weakness, a helper arrived. It was Ellen Charles, a sister of Billy, who had by this time, like Ellen, recovered from the plague. When Juey saw how she still staggered about from the effects of her illness, she wanted to send her home.

"No, no," the girl protested. "I can keep fires going for you."

For two weeks, Juey did not remove her own clothing. When her daughter Velma in her delirium sang out, "Mother, don't you hear the angels singing?" in her weariness Juey was almost ready to believe that she too could hear them. At some time during each long night, she remembered her father, the Rev. Malcolm, and his faith in the strengthening power of prayer.

"Please God, spare us," she whispered.

Finally she had no more soothing glycerine to ease the maddening itch of the fever-ridden bodies. In desperation, she tried a new concoction. She crushed lime tablets and dissolved them in whipped linseed oil. This mixture she applied liberally to the burning "tepees."

Last to contract the disease were the two little ones, Janet, nearly five, and three-year-old Isaac. The baby, Elmer, escaped. She put the pair in a double bed and to soothe their fussing she crawled in between them with an arm about each. She had reached the point of exhaustion; no more could she crawl up and down to wait upon them.

Spring came and they had all survived. For days Sheridan hovered near death and he needed months to regain his former herculean strength. One day when at last he had left his bed, he tapped on the window pane to attract the attention of Mr. O'Connor.

The man turned and took a step back. "Oh my God!" Juey heard his exclaim as he gaped in horror at Sheridan's gaunt and yet still half-swollen face.

That next summer a medical team arrived with vaccination equipment.

* * *

258

The big boats on the great river brought near tragedy and they also brought blessings. For several years the Hudson's Bay Company operated the motor-boat "Weenusk," and then in 1924 it undertook to put the big wood-burning "D. A. Thomas" into service again. Once more, after two years' silence, the deep-throated whistle of the giant river queen echoed to the lonely woods and hills back of the Ranch and once more the startling boom evoked shrieks of delight from the children. Like Maggie's little ones before them who ran to intercept any passing "Klondikers," they pelted to the landing stage to chat with captain or crew or passengers.

"What a fine lot of children," the nurse of a visiting medical party remarked to Juey. The latter had come to speak on business with Capt. McLeod. "They aren't all yours?"

"Yes, they are." Their mother smiled fondly. "And I'm proud of every one of them."

"They look remarkably well," added the woman, who was, thought the mistress of the Ranch, perhaps a little startled at finding such obvious signs of good health in such isolation. "All except the little one." She pointed to five-year-old Elmer.

Juey took a look. For some time the youngster had been ailing and she had been experimenting with various remedies. Now she realized with a little shock how really ill he appeared.

At home she began a routine of more special care. Still the boy did not improve. She got down her "Doctor" book and, beginning with the A's, she began to read systematically through the alphabetic list of diseases. She came to Diabetes and stopped. This, she was sure now, was the cause of the child's ill health.

By this time the government of Alberta had arranged for a Dr. Hamman to establish a practice at Fort Vermilion. Juey hurried the lad to him; independently he too arrived at the same diagnosis, diabetes. This was 1925 and he told her of the wonder drug insulin that was now beginning to be used to correct hitherto fatal cases of the disease.

"If you want to try insulin, you'll have to take him to Edmonton."

Though the railway now shunted trains with fair regularity between that city and the town of Peace River, the old Sagitawa or Peace River Crossing, the prospect of getting help there to a desperately ill boy seemed faint and far distant. Besides, the D. A. Thomas was not due for another week. Of course, Juey agreed at once with the doctor, the child must go to Edmonton.

While she waited for the boat, she tried the medicines and the diets which the doctor prescribed. The child grew worse and she appealed to him again. Meantime there came word that the great ship, which already had, apparently due to her enormous bulk, a checkered record of performance on the Peace, was marooned up-stream on a gravel bar. With news of this delay, the boy's mother grew quite frantic.

"Keep him very quiet," warned Dr. Hamman. "Don't even let a door slam near him. That might put him over."

Stealthily the children stole about the ranch-house. It was so quiet that their mother could have heard a mouse squeak. At last came the welcome whistle of the big boat. Away the youngsters raced to talk to the captain while the usual order of meat was being taken aboard.

"Our brother's very ill. Maybe he's going to die," they confided to Capt. McLeod. "He's got to go out to Edmonton. Mother wishes you didn't have to go all the way to the Chutes."

"In that case," said the great-hearted captain of the queen of the Peace, "tell your mother I won't go to the Chutes. I'll turn around at the Fort and come back right away for your brother."

In Edmonton a specialist, Dr. Heber Jamieson, was already prescribing to patients the life-saving insulin that was being produced by the University of Toronto laboratory; with it he saved small Elmer's life and Juey began to learn something of the long journey involved in caring for and teaching patience to a child suffering from diabetes.

The boy had been named for Caroline Elmer, Sheridan's grandmother and a Vermont school teacher who had a special place in the family annals. By letter she had accepted, sight unseen, the offer of marriage from the pioneer widower Isaac Lawrence and when he rode across the border from the

Eastern Townships to claim her, she sat his horse postilion fashion as she journeyed into Canada to face her new duties. Thus she became distinguished as "the mail-order bride, personally delivered." She assumed the care of Isaac's three motherless little ones, bore him eight more children and lived to see three of her sons, Henry, Isaac and Erastus, venture beyond the frontiers of civilization into the remote northwest.

Sometimes it seemed now to young Elmer's parents as if something of her spirit and durability persisted in the ailing lad.

"Shove the insulin into him," Dr. Jamieson had directed.

These words rang often in Juey's mind to guide her through many perplexing and critical moments in the years that followed.

Meantime the extensive reach of the Ranch enterprises meant for its master and mistress always the seeing and accepting of needs quite remote from those of the family. Sometimes this need lay in rough tent or in crude cabin buried deep in the choking bush; sometimes it beckoned from the central channel of the wide river.

Bound on an errand for Sheridan in Peace River town, one sunny summer day his wife embarked with their daughter Daisy on the scow of a Capt. Kepler. This scow was nearly as primitive as the rafts with which she had become so well acquainted in earlier days; it was a bulky rectangular affair built of coarse planks and pushed by a small boat propelled by a "kicker" or outboard motor. Sheridan set up a canvas tent on the scow to shelter the pair and he also produced a tiny heater.

"You don't need that," objected the captain.

Juey was presently to bless her husband for insisting that they take the heater along. They had crawled up-stream nearly one hundred miles when she caught sight of a lone Indian pursuing them in a canoe. As he neared the scow, he signalled frantically and he called out in the Cree tongue. The captain ignored the canoe and the calls and continued on his way.

Sensing urgent need, Juey insisted that he halt the scow.

Perhaps he did not heed the man because of unfamiliarity with the Cree tongue.

"I'll interpret," she offered.

In Cree the stranger told her that the children of the McLean family at Carcajou lay deathly ill and were in urgent need of the doctor's help.

"You go back for Dr. Hamman," she coaxed the captain. "Daisy and I will wait and watch over the scow."

The captain pushed it to the river's edge and tied it up. With the protection of the tent and the warmth from the heater, Juey and her daughter sheltered in comfort from the bitter wind while the kicker sped the captain back to Fort Vermilion.

When Dr. Hamman arrived in the small boat, Juey saw that he himself was in bad shape. He hadn't been able to sleep, he told, because of the pain of a stubborn infection in one hand. She persuaded him to take some food and to allow her to soak his swollen hand in a hot saline solution. When they got under way again, bound up-stream for Carcajou and the home of the sick children, she succeeded in coaxing him to swallow a sleeping pill and to stretch out on the scow for a nap.

At last they pushed to the river's bank below the lonely little trading post at Carcajou that was operated by the McLean family.

Dr. Hamman turned to Juey. "You come with me," he begged.

Having met face to face so often with northland tragedy, he was apprehensive, she saw, about what he was going to find. "You can help the mother," he urged.

The distraught face at the door of the shack in the tiny clearing told that his fears had already come true. On one cot lay the dead body of a tiny girl. A second had now reached the point of death and he could do nothing to save her. They had been struck down by summer complaint, through which Juey had once nursed her own critically ill baby Alice; this, the doctor told her, was a particularly virulent form which could be fought only with the strictest sanitation methods.

Presently Capt. Kepler resumed the journey up-stream.

A storm blew up, with more icy winds, and again the little heater proved a godsend. Dr. Hamman had agreed to continue on to Peace River town to receive professional treatment there for his hand. Once more Juey coaxed him to lie down and to sleep while she tended to the inflammation. As she changed the hot compresses, he did not stir.

To make up time, the captain decided to travel through the night. Juey was terrified lest he fall asleep, when further tragedy might surround them. From time to time she brewed fresh coffee and young Daisy stepped over to the shadowed stern of the swaying scow to reach it out to him in the small boat.

In the midst of the gloom and the grating and creaking noises of the bulky scow, Juey heard the splash of water.

"Are you all right, Daisy?" she screamed in terror as she peered into the shadows.

The girl stepped calmly back into the dim circle of lantern light. "Sure, Mother. Here I am."

Dr. Hamman wakened and mumblingly consented to take some nourishment. Delighted to be of more assistance, the youngster stepped forward to spoon-feed him.

Upon the river on a later occasion, another daughter of the Ranch found herself pressed into life-bringing nursing service. On that boat which the children had christened, because of its varied personnel, "The League of Nations," a native woman was about to give birth.

In turn the worried captain begged each of the other female passengers to come to her assistance. Finally he turned to seventeen-year-old Kathleen Lawrence. She, too, protested that she knew nothing at all about child-birth.

With firm assurance he looked full in the face of the young girl. "If you are Mrs. Lawrence's daughter, you'll be able to help her."

Kathleen went forward with the nervous captain to lend a hand with the birth.

Their river, the family on the Ranch knew full well, was always capable of hurling upon them scourge and sorrow. They could not guess what destruction and what tragedy it might yet have in store for them.

In propitiation, it proffered to them many kinds of assistance as well as comedy and joy and even a kind of fame.

Like the celebrated mouse-trap, the idyll which Sheridan and Juey had contrived to create in the wilderness brought the world beating to their door, down the tortuous Peace.

Among the visitors who made their way to the Ranch were the merely curious and the restless who sought escape; there were the notables on semi-official or official tours of the north; there were too the reporters and the magazine writers who spread the fame of the Ranch and began to hail Sheridan as "Emperor of the Peace." There was the charming Countess Rhondda whose deceased husband, born D. A. Thomas, had initiated the building of the splendid Queen of the Peace.

Accompanied by her son-in-law and daughter, Sir John and Lady Mackworth, in 1919 Lady Rhondda paid a visit to to the Ranch and won the hearts of all by her warm delight in everything she saw. As she admired Juey's magnificent garden she engaged in forthright discussion of the merits of different varieties and she demonstrated a Mrs. Beeton's knowledge of excellent ways in which to serve the bulging marrows there displayed.

There were also the governor-general Baron Byng and his party; their visit also in 1919, concluded with a scene of high comedy that overjoyed Sheridan. At the Ranch, so it had all been carefully arranged, one half of the entourage was to remain to be served as his wife's guests at luncheon. Part way through the meal the sonorous whistle of the steamer, the D. A. Thomas, that had brought the party thus far, caused a rustle of uneasiness among the guests. Sure enough, when the group reached the landing pier, the queenly vessel, now being operated by the Hudson's Bay Company, was puffing down the river without them, bound for the next point of interest, the Vermilion Chutes.

In a fury an Edmonton judge in the group squatted himself down upon the shore. He refused to budge, he swore, until the steamer turned back for him .

This delighted Sheridan. Rocking with laughter, he warned, "You'll wait a long long time before the lordly 'Bay' will come back for you."

With high good humor he proceeded to arrange for transportation for all his guests so that they could overtake the boat down-stream at the trading post. The ladies he collected in his long freight canoe and himself ferried them over the fifteen down-stream miles; as he waved farewell to all, across the water they chorused together, "For he's a jolly good fellow, for he's a jolly good fellow."

Mirth and frustration of a different flavor mixed with a visit to the Ranch of a Mennonite priest from Manitoba. Near the wide garden he came upon its mistress engrossed with several of the children in pulling stinkweed up by the roots. As the youngsters heaped the pernicious stuff into a pile, their mother poured kerosene over it and set it ablaze.

The dark-bearded priest duly marvelled at the garden. Then he turned toward the stinkweed.

"Wherever did you get this? Away up here?"

"It came in registered seed," Juey answered in disgust. "But I'm getting rid of it, every last root."

The visitor laughed. "Why, back in Manitoba where I come from, we've been trying for a hundred years to kill it all out. If you burn it, and five years later turn the soil over, up it shoots again."

"I'll get rid of it," she repeated stubbornly. "No matter how long it takes."

With merry eyes the priest handed her a slip of paper. "Here's my name and address. If you really succeed, let me know. I'll see to it that you make yourself a fortune in the years to come."

Another day, from the Cree Julian Showan, she accepted an exquisite token of nature's more pleasing aspects.

"You like growing things," smiled Julian. He opened

brown cupped hands to reveal to her wondering eyes a delicately beautiful wildflower.

She studied its all-pink sepals and petals, its enchanting tuft of yellow contained in its purple-streaked pink sac, and its one ovate parallel-veined leaf growing from the base of the single flower stem, and she guessed at once that it was a species of orchid.

"Flower have feet in ice," explained Julian. To the eager white woman he described the location of the cold, wet marsh where he had found his prize.

She hunted in her flower guide and she discovered that it was named for the bewitching nymph Calypso who for so long had held Ulysses in her spell. It also suggested a second mythological female of incredible loveliness, for its alternate designation was "Venus slipper."

She longed to feast her eyes upon the sight of the blossoms growing in their natural habitat but she feared to enter the deep and treacherous bog that was buried behind woods some distance back from the Ranch. The next summer, bolstered by the presence of two of her limber young daughters, she made her way to the marsh. There they ventured into it over a precarious footing of dead trees which they laid before them as they advanced.

In a setting as wild and haggard as a Shelleyan landscape but where a poet's eye would never behold them, they found the flowers. Again Juey marvelled to see them in all their enchanting loveliness, blushing here rosy and unseen and fragile as a Shelleyan vision.

Then there were all the visitors to the Ranch bearing practicality in their minds, the reporters and the scientists, the inspectors and the professors. Long before, the dedicated horticulturist the Rev. J. Gough Brick and father of Sheridan's part-time partner Fred Brick, had pivoted attention on the agricultural possibilities of the Peace River country. Lydia Lawrence's brother Albert Kneeland had carried outside with him a sample of the wheat which the missionary had grown on a plot in the Shaftesbury area and in 1893 this sample won special mention at the Chicago World's Fair.

Presently there came to the Ranch all the way from

California's Stanford university a team of professors intent on studying growth conditions in this northern latitude and on taking samples of Sheridan's Bishop wheat. As well as himself testing a number of varieties, red fife and marquis and garnet and others, he was also still experimenting with the market outlets so essential to the enterprises of the Ranch.

"The Grand Mogul of Alberta's Far North," the reporter J. S. Cram labelled Sheridan when he told in the Family Herald of his interview with him.

"I had been anxious to meet this almost legendary figure of the northland about whom I had heard so many vague enchanting tales."

Over a full-page spread in the Montreal-published weekly, Mr. Cram described the Ranch with its lawn-edged home and its garden sheltered by a grove of Manitoba maples, a garden that yielded pumpkin and potatoes, citron and squash, tomatoes and bush fruit, and all the vegetables normally grown elsewhere in Canada.

He told of Sheridan's mill that produced one hundred and seventy thousand pounds of flour annually, of his hog slaughter house with its capacity of twenty-five porkers per day, of his cattle abattoir that could handle ten head daily, of the cannery that manufactured six hundred pounds of sausage and rendered twenty-seven hundred pounds of lard all in the one season and of all the bacon and the hams that were cured there.

"No by-products are wasted," added Mr. Cram. "Shorts, middlings and slaughter-house waste are used in the manufacture of feed for trappers' huskies, to afford a little change from the dime-novel ration of dried hide."

All of the products of these industries, beyond the actual needs of the family, "are used as media of exchange at the Lawrence trading posts. In order to keep these supplied and to bring out the furs received in trade, it is necessary to maintain a regular freighting schedule.

"Therein lies the real ordeal in Mr. Lawrence's life. He does not shirk the task; he does not deputize his men to this task while he warms his heels by a roaring fire. No, sir; not Sheridan Lawrence. He goes out and defies the elements on their own hunting grounds."

And still, concluded Mr. Cram after he had described Sheridan's trading empire, his wife Juey had arrived in that land a month before her husband and she can still tease him about her longer experience in it.

Another delighted visitor who wrote eloquently of the Ranch and its inhabitants was the dainty Englishwoman, Doris Leedham Hobbs. For three years her husband had served as secretary at the Experimental Farm across the Peace; he had been sent there by the distant government offices at Ottawa and presently a severe clash of temperament began to develop. Finally, in mid-winter of 1925 he tendered his resignation but at this season it was impossible for the family to move outside.

Having heard by the grape-vine of their dilemma, Juey paid them a visit.

"Come to us," she invited.

Next morning men from the Ranch arrived in a caravan of five sleighs; in a sixth, driving her own team, followed the mistress herself. The men stripped the pleasant log cabin, loading all of the Hobbs' possessions into the sleighs; then the cavalcade wound back across the Peace and up to the Ranch buildings. Juey's sleigh brought up the rear, with Mrs. Hobbs beside her clutching two precious possessions, her small daughter Jennifer and her violin in its case.

Like the Klondikers, the family brought with them riches which repaid in full measure the hospitality. Juey saw them established in a large upstairs bedroom and their furniture stored in an unused building. Then she turned to her musical guest.

"Now, will you tune the piano for me? It's very badly in need of it."

A little dazed but bolstered by her hostess' confidence in her, Doris set to work. With the piano, which Sheridan had had shipped in six years previously, had come a key and rubber wedges and instructions for tuning but no middle C tuning fork. He had previously replaced Anna's flood-damaged organ with a new one, converting the water-scarred veteran into a shelf-lined bookcase for the Lawrence Point school. Fortunately, Doris discovered, the organ was in tune.

With it she attuned the A-string of her violin, and she used it then for the basis of her operations.

With concentrated effort, all day she worked at her novel assignment. "There," she exclaimed with pride to her husband when she had concluded her task, "Isn't that an accomplishment!"

Their hostess, she told him in wonderment, had inspired her with confidence, and she described how Juey had picked up a clock that had ceased to tick.

"Needs cleaning, I expect," Juey had remarked. Whereupon she had proceeded to plunge its works into a basin of kerosene.

"She's daunted by nothing," Doris concluded.

"Mrs. Hobbs, you taught school in England. Will you undertake to teach on my permit until the boats can travel on the river?" So the mistress of the Ranch proposed next. During this season a teacher had failed to arrive on the last boat in and Juey had been obliged herself to operate the school.

Infected now by her hostess's contagion of self-sufficiency, Doris undertook the teaching. The children loved her and even the boys proved co-operative pupils. From out of a fund of experience, for the lighter hours she introduced new songs and new games; with wonderment the children watched the fairy-like movement of their teacher's dainty fingers and arms floating above her violin strings to the accompaniment of piano or organ.

On her part, Doris Hobbs was astounded at the clock-like rhythm of the activities round about the ranch-house.

"Our hostess is a born organizer," she marvelled to her husband. She described for him how, in this big self-contained establishment, each one knew his or her duties.

"Two small boys fill wood-boxes; then they are free to play. Two girls do the beds one week and the next another chore; at noon two little girls must be excused a few minutes early to lay the long trestle tables for the meal." Doris sighed with pleasure. "What a lovely life!"

On a spring Saturday of sapphire sky and champagne air the mistress invited her guest to share a clean-up bee at the out-ranch at Prairie Point.

269

"The horse loves it as much as I," smiled the English-woman as Juey's buggy careened along the woodsy trail and bumped over the lengths of corduroy.

In capacious overalls, the two women scrubbed out the log dwellings where those men who cared for the herd had made their winter quarters. They washed all the bedding and the blankets and the sox and hung them on the fences in the sun; they scoured down the walls and cleaned out the bunks; for the men's midday meal they prepared masses of bacon and beans and eggs.

In the mid-afternoon Doris picked up the lunch to carry out to the hands working in the fields. "Now I feel that I'm really a part of the great essential life of the soil," she bubbled.

There were awkward moments too. One day young Jennifer Hobbs persisted in peppering two-year-old Walter Lawrence's head with sand. Each infusion meant a head-washing that was most distressing to the small boy.

"If you do that once more, Jennifer," threatened Juey, "I'll duck *your* head in the rain barrel."

Of course the experiment-minded child tried it again. Whereupon Juey seized her and inside the rain barrel soused the thick mass of dark hair.

"Justice is served," agreed Doris as she noted the efficacy of the punishment meted to her daughter. The child threw no more sand.

Describing in detail the marvellous self-sufficiency of the Ranch which so impressed Doris Hobbs, one newspaper report mentioned that the place even possessed "its own tourist camp." While no such adjunct actually existed, such an addition would have been helpful to the hospitable couple who always contrived to accommodate the most unexpected of wayfarers and visitors.

A year after the Peace carried away the delightful Hobbs trio, it brought to the door of the Ranch another unusual threesome. It was a summer's day in 1926 when Sheridan, on board the D. A. Thomas, made the acquaintance of "Daddy" Rose, a small white-bearded man of seventy-three, who with his tiny wife of forty-six and his little boy of nine, was plan-

270

ning to file on a homestead somewhere in the vicinity of Fort Vermilion.

Their scheme, Sheridan tried tactfully to tell them, was an absolutely mad one. They had disposed of what meagre means they possessed to finance the journey from their former home in the western United States; obviously they lacked even the funds to turn about and trek back to their homeland or to hire the essential help that a man of seventy-three would require to develop a homestead.

"Daddy wants to die in Canada," sighed Hilda Rose, the little wisp of a wife. "It's the land of his birth."

The man had suffered injury in a train wreck between Edmonton and Peace River town. He had been accompanying his settlers' effects—which included three work-horses—when a number of the rail cars, including that in which he was riding, turned turtle and piled up along the tracks. Obviously he was not going to be long in achieving his dearest wish if some one did not lend the family a hand.

Sheridan undertook to do what he could. He called the purser and asked him to give the ailing old man a good stateroom and the best of care.

"I'm so glad Mr. L. has taken charge," wrote his wife Hilda. Her letters describing her experiences were published the following year in the Atlantic Monthly. That one dated July 10th, 1926, began, "I am now on the steamer going north . . . We will land at Lawrence Point . . . There is only one white settler there and he is on the boat. He has fifteen children, is a very large fine-looking jovial man . . . He has taken a great fancy to Daddy and as he is a very rich man his word is law on the river."

Hilda went on to tell that "Daddy" had been in a dreadful state when he arrived at Peace River town after his eight gruelling days on the freight train. "I took him to a hotel and gave a woman a dollar to carry me four pails of water from the creek and heat two cans of it. Then I bathed the poor dear and put him to bed. He couldn't even eat for exhaustion. He was just a helpless baby."

This was the unfortunate who was going to challenge the rigors of the north Peace country in setting himself up on a homestead.

When Sheridan took charge, continued Hilda, she quit worrying. "Now everything will be all right."

He could not shake their determination to go forward with their plans, so he described available land to them and they chose an area near Prairie Point. He helped them to get their "effects" ashore, noting at the same time the utter impracticability of much that they had spent nearly eight hundred dollars to transport, items such as logging tools, a monster brick-lined heater, a grand piano and the worn-out horseflesh. They set up a temporary camp at the Lawrence Point landing where they insisted on sleeping after they had taken their meals in Juey's dining-room.

Presently they made their way to the site of their proposed home near Prairie Point. Then, while the frail father journeyed back to Peace River town to file on their homestead claim, like Alexander Selkirk his wife began to understand better something of the awful predicament of such isolation.

"What about a house?" queried the master of the Ranch.

With profound misgivings he watched as Hilda and nine-year "Boy" collected fire-wood outside the new home. This was a fragile tent erected in a lonely clearing and surrounded by the clutter of freight that had made the journey with them.

The small American woman was adamant. She would accept no more aid from him or his family; they would get out logs and build their own cabin. Already she saw her son as another Abraham Lincoln, growing to manhood in the great wilderness.

"I have reached the garden of Eden," she wrote in one of the letters published afterward in the widely-circulated Atlantic Monthly. "The land is green, lovely and lonesome. There is wood aplenty but it is work to get it ready, and there is plenty of water in the majestic river."

When "Daddy" returned, Sheridan gave him several days' work on the mower in exchange for which the Ranch hands raked and stacked wild hay for the winter needs of the American's three work-horses. Acting on the "Big Boss's" instructions, from time to time the men living at Prairie Point checked on the well-being of the tenting newcomers.

The plucky little woman's next letters were still optimistic. "We're going to cover the tent with poplar poles and put hay and dirt over them . . . I expect to make a living catching rats and a few foxes . . . By salting one place against the prevailing wind, deer and moose can be got easily and there's big fish in the river."

But another sentence suggested the ominous fate that might be in store for these innocent "babes in the woods." "It was twenty above zero in the tent last night," wrote Hilda.

Presently it was October and fifteen miles away in the big ranch-house Sheridan heard that, as he had foreseen, the cabin was still unbuilt and that the tent, partially walled up with logs, was his neighbors' only shelter against the now-bitter north winds.

"They'll freeze to death," worried Juey.

"Oh no, they won't," announced Sheridan. "Not if I know it." Again he visited them and suggested that his men build them a home. Still the determined couple insisted that they would erect their own dwelling.

Finally came, near the end of October, a heavy fall of snow followed by temperatures dipping to twenty below zero. A messenger arrived with word that the "crazy" Americans had got only eight logs ready for their cabin and that their boy was ill with pneumonia.

Sheridan had his men heap a sleigh with fire-wood; his wife contributed nourishing soup and home-baking treats. Away in haste with a couple of helpers he drove over the fifteen miles to the new homestead.

There he found the fragile little man down on his knees, exhaustedly still pushing away at the tool that had kept alight the spark of life in his almost-helpless family, the bucksaw.

"Mr. Rose," Sheridan spoke kindly but sternly to his likeable neighbor, "I've come to lend you a hand. I hear your boy is ill."

The small man grunted belligerently.

"If anything were to happen to him, the authorities would be here to investigate."

"What authorities?" bridled the proud old man.

Sheridan of course meant the mounted policeman. "It isn't going to be necessary for him to come," he added. "I'm going to build you a house. Right now."

As the sawyer straightened a little, Sheridan softened his words with a friendly grin. "I'm just protecting myself, Mr. Rose. You see, I can't have your deaths on my conscience. Let's choose a site, right this minute."

The white-bearded man tottered about beside his Samson of a neighbor, agreeing to the site which Sheridan deemed most suitable. Then they called Hilda out. Like her husband she was bundled in a multitude of wraps and appeared to be wearing all the clothing she possessed against the below-zero cold.

"We're going to build you a house," Sheridan announced. "Your husband thinks this is the best spot."

Already he and his men were shovelling snow from the rectangle they had tramped. Then they dumped the load of wood that they had brought and proceeded to build a roaring blaze over the site.

"I want you to keep this fire going all night," Sheridan directed. "We'll be back first thing in the morning and we we must have the ground thawed to dig you a cellar."

Meekly the Americans agreed to his request.

Next morning he arrived with four teams and four helpers and with sleighs piled high with lumber and logs and building tools and food and a large flat-topped heater. The temperature still hovered near twenty-five below zero but the little lad was no worse. Obviously the haggard parents had spent most of the night feeding their heater and cookstove and the fire that still smouldered on the building site.

It was grim going but the men set to with a will. Scooping out the thawed earth, first they hollowed out a cellar and deep in the centre of it they set up the heater which they had brought. On its level surface they warmed tools and nails and as the walls began to rise they kept a second fire going outside to help limber up their numbed fingers. At mid-day Hilda Rose heated and served to them the food which Juey had sent and at night they sought shelter in the out ranch buildings at Prairie Point.

274

Within a week, the imaginative Hilda might almost have believed that a good fairy waved a wand. Sharply defined in the below-zero mist stood a brand-new cabin; above its roof a broad band of smoke belched upward into the biting atmosphere; the men had installed both heater and cook-stove and then transferred the sick boy to the hospitable warmth of the new home. Even the grand piano, which had stood out all those weeks with only its shell of a packing-case to protect it from the frigid temperatures, they now set up in proud dignity in the resin-spiced dwelling.

"It's queer," commented Hilda in one of her letters. "They arrived just in the nick of time." It was forty below zero, she wrote, when Mr. L. and his men came to build. "Icicles hung from their eyelashes as they worked. They danced and whooped round about the fires to get warm."

Her published accounts indicated that by the following May she was sensitively aware of the charm and magnitude of the country and better aware of the difficulties confronting the novice. At first, she wrote, "I had felt like Robinson Crusoe as I stood on the shore of this mighty river and looked at the swamp that edged it, so dense and so luxuriant that I'd never seen anything like it."

Now in the sudden onrush of spring she delighted in the presence everywhere of frogs and ducks and geese. "It's so lovely it hurts." But she had had no luck trapping musk-rats, she had learned that deer were scarce and that moose might be found in the muskeg, which was impassable except in winter.

Then, again "in the nick of time," for starvation was facing the little family, a kind-hearted correspondent had forwarded her letters to the Atlantic Monthly and a cheque arrived from that magazine.

"I've been reading about you and yours," some one told Sheridan and Juey presently. "In the Atlantic Monthly."

Finally, when the lead story of the Atlantic issue of September, 1927, appeared under the heading "The New Homestead," and was dated from Fort Vermilion, it loosed a tempest of emotions round about the heads of the family on the Ranch. Gratefully Hilda acknowledged the help of the "white settler, Mr. L." but the errors and exaggerations in her letters outweighed her facts. Sheridan was, she told, "the son of a missionary and the first white man here," whereas white fur traders had been up and down the river and had established Fort Vermilion a century and a quarter earlier. Among the present list of residents of the post she included "a Governor," a creature of her fertile imagination, and she pointed out that her location was "just this side of the Great Slave lake region," she having overshot the mark by a couple of hundred miles.

"The white settler's wife," she wrote of Juey, "is a college woman and she teaches the children and conducts a real school in a log cabin." Graphically she pictured the mistress of the Ranch "gathering her children around the organ for a few hymns . . . it gave me hope and strength to carry on when I looked at this wonderful family singing so earnestly alone here in this vastness."

Side by side with this glowing tribute were errors and exaggerations that roused rages of indignation and gales of laughter. "Only dogs are used here in winter," Hilda affirmed. The mounted policeman, that fair game of the sensation-seeking writer, received his share of the attention.

"The mounties," she wrote on, "lead a very strenuous life here," and the family at the Ranch and all the neighbors were uproariously delighted with her next words, "protecting the white settler" (Sheridan) and "keeping the Indians peaceful."

Her description of the big Christmas party at the Ranch caused further dismay and mirth.

After the program of music and recitations by the children, the spacious dining-room and the immense kitchen were cleared for dancing. As the square dances and the Scottish reels proceeded, the men called out with the enthusiastic "Hooghh!" that is a tradition imported from the Highland glens. Wrote Hilda in the Atlantic Monthly, "dancing the breakdown, they grew so excited that Cree and Beaver war whoops made my back hair rise up in horror. I thought they'd start scalping next, but a glance across the room at the gleaming pistols and full cartridge belt of the mounted police reassured me."

"As a matter of fact," smiled Juey, the gentle hostess

who permitted neither rowdyism nor liquor in her home, "the mountie never wore his one and only pistol nor his cartridges in my house. He always brought them to me to put safely away in an upstairs drawer."

Far way in old New Hampshire, the presses of the Atlantic Monthly roared on and its American editors were doubtless completely unaware of the furore that had been raised along the Peace. Presently the letters swelled into a book called "The Stump Farm," and in it there was more blending of fact and imagination. Above the Ranch piano hung a reproduction of Custer's last stand; Hilda told how on one occasion a fierce dark Indian with long hair hanging down leaned near the piano during a sing-song and when she saw him glance at the picture she knew by the wild gleam in his eye where his heart was.

This man, scoffed the family as they exploded in laughter, wasn't a wild Indian at all, but the Métis Pete Lazotte, who was really quite a well educated young man. Moreover, none of their Indian or Métis neighbors, they were quite sure, had ever heard of General Custer and his exploits against the Sioux.

As a matter of fact the teasing young folk were in part responsible for feeding Hilda's creative flare. When they discovered her apparent gullibility, they spun for her more and more "cock and bull" yarns. To kill a wolf, they advised her, you put pepper all round the foot of a tree-trunk or you place a mirror close against it. When the wolf sneezes, he will knock his brains out against the tree, or if he tries to kill the enemy wolf in the mirror, he will eventually cut his own throat.

Even such stories as these, they laughed, "she half believed."

Up-stream at Peace River town the editor of the Peace River Record, Charlie Fredericks, took up cudgels in behalf of "Mr. L." "You should sue her and her publishers," he advised Sheridan.

The "Big Boss" answered with the hearty laugh for which he was famous.

"It's best to ignore that kind of thing," soothed his wife

to any suggested legal action. "After all, Hilda Rose lives in a world of her own imagining."

There was as well the humanitarian point to be considered. The stories brought the helpless family desperately-needed funds. As well, a generous quantity of gifts from well-wishing readers in various areas of the United States began to trickle down the Peace and the celebrated New Homestead at Prairie Point began to be showered with packages of books, bags of flour, drums of coal oil and a variety of furnishings for the cabin that had risen out of the sub-zero mist at the decree of the man whose "word was law upon the river."

"Lots of the stuff shipped in was useless to them," summed up the oldest son of the Ranch. "But I traded a nice big rug that they got for a milk-cow."

"It's a big wild country," wrote Hilda in her last letter published in the Atlantic Monthly. "Big lakes, rivers, muskegs, no trails, no people. Less than two human beings to each one thousand square miles and that means Indians too.

"It's a Robinson Crusoe existence. Like being alive, yet buried."

For the first two years, it's said by some newcomers to the Peace, you don't want to get out. After that you can't. And it's a case of "Root, hog, or die." Perhaps this was true of the Ranch's American neighbors. The storm subsided and the two families continued to see each other from time to time, sharing harmoniously their splendid isolation by the river whose name was Unchaga.

Quick to answer some of Hilda's stories was the former guest of the Ranch, Doris Hobbs. "Wolf and bear stories," she wrote in a half-page lay-out in The Edmonton Journal, "belong to the past."

Sheridan agreed that the increase of settlement along the Peace resulted in diminishing numbers of these marauders. But dwellers in the backwoods were sometimes still hard pressed to outwit them. He described to his family a novel cabin he had attempted to visit on the bank of Bear creek. It had no apparent entrance.

"Wherever is your doorway?" he asked when eventually he came upon its owners, a couple of youths who had moved

278

in from British Columbia to try to make a living trapping in the vicinity of the Peace.

"We put it in the roof," they answered with pride. "To outwit the bears."

This delighted the pioneer son of the Peace. "That'll never stop our bears," he laughed. "They're much too smart for that. They'll soon find that door of yours."

In response to Hilda Rose's comments about the "hundreds of Indians," Doris Hobbs in her article added, "The few Indians I ever met were garbed in strict European clothing. In winter they were slightly more picturesque, the men wearing red strand cloth chaps and embroidered moccasins and gauntlets, the women the colored assumption belts and brilliant sweaters."

Of her former hostess she wrote that "what she has accomplished is in itself an epic. What woman among us in these days could bring up a family of fifteen and train and clothe and educate them so far from city conveniences; teach them to play the piano and the organ; teach them to love and care for the garden, to know the birds and the wild flowers; and to inculcate in each of their minds the rule, 'Nothing is too difficult'."

Sheridan's achievements she rated "an inspiration and an incentive." After seeing what he has accomplished "in that wonderful northern part of Alberta," many, she added, adopt for themselves the motto, "What man has done, man can do."

A venerable volume in the family's possession traces the genealogy of that Isaac Lawrence who in 1794 removed from Vermont "to Canada East" away back to a Sir Robert Lawrence of Aston Hall in Lancashire, England. "Surely there is something significant and symbolic," added Doris, "in the fact that the coat of arms of the Lawrence family, won seven centuries ago, was a silver shield bearing a cross of rough-hewn trunks of trees with the branches lopped.

"The hewing of wood still has a large place in the work of the Ranch, but the buzz of the saw-mill has taken the place of the ring of the pioneer's axe."

CHAPTER 9

The face of the male visitor was bleak as the Peace in a dark squall.

"You come to the meeting," he begged of the Big White Chief. He explained to him and his wife about the dilemma that he faced.

The visitor was "Chee Chum" Lambert, the chairman of the new board that had assumed the management of the soon-to-be-built school in the North Vermilion area. A meeting of ratepayers was about to take place and among them was sure to be present the ringleader of a certain group who disputed the building's proposed central location. Chee Chum knew himself to be inadequate to handle the situation.

"Please, you come," he repeated.

Sheridan turned to Juey. "You go. I just can't take the time. Besides, you know the ropes as well as I."

Now it was Juey's turn to ponder. For many years illiteracy had been widespread. But in this new era many of the parents who were themselves unable to read and to write began to understand their children's need for schooling.

Sheridan, said the reports, is a man who will not spare the pennies if he can help his children to further their education. Because he owned land in several of the newly-forming school districts that were being organized in the 1920's, the residents turned to him as an eligible ratepayer to help iron out all the problems that arose. He in turn delegated some of the chores involved to the person who took care of all the accounts and the correspondence on the Ranch, his wife Juey. As a result, she was appointed secretary of the North Vermilion board.

For a moment as she looked now at Chee Chum, she hesitated. Her zeal to bring education to her children and to the many growing up about them in dark illiteracy was as great as that of her husband. But she was apprehensive about facing the meeting alone. "Couldn't you come?" she coaxed him.

"No, no," he insisted. "There's no need at all for me to take the time. You're the secretary and you know the procedure as well as I."

Chee Chum could neither read nor write. So she set him now to the painful business of practising the inscription of his signature. She also instructed him to tell the meeting, if he were asked to read anything, that this was the duty of the secretary.

During the meeting, sure enough, the ringleader who wanted the location of the school to be changed handed Chee Chum a paper to read. He passed it on to Juey, who saw at once that there was nothing printed on it having to do with the North Vermilion school. She pretended to confer with Chairman Chee Chum and then she spoke.

"Mr. Lambert wants me to announce that this paper does not apply to this district; it is the ordinance for consolidated school districts." She paused.

"He would also like me to remind you that at this meeting only ratepayers can vote."

At this point two sleigh-loads of men who had been brought in to sway the vote stamped out and drove away.

Shaken but triumphant, she returned home to report victory to Sheridan. In the face of cunning, illiteracy was enabled to take a step forward toward the curing of its own blight.

When a quarrel also arose over the location of a new school across the river in the Stoney Point area, several of the ratepayers there turned to the master of the Ranch for help. At his request his wife wrote to the chief inspector of schools, Mr. Yule, who saw to it that the building was established in the centre of the district where the greatest number could benefit from it.

Similarly, down river at Lambert Point, Mrs. Bill Ware pleaded with the Lawrences to assist with the setting up of another school. Again Juey attended the meeting of rate-payers in place of her husband, who owned land in this area. Regulations which had been submitted to Mrs. Ware stipulated that the chairman of the new school board should be a Canadian citizen able to read and write. But within the district there was but one settler, the American Ed Utz, who was competent to fill the post. To resolve this dilemma Juey wrote to the Department of Education requesting that an exception be made in this case.

Even more difficult was the problem posed with the formation of the Boyer River school district north-west of the Ranch. Here there was no adult at all within its confines who could read and write. Finally some one proposed that Sheridan, who had also taken land in the area in payment of a debt, be appointed senior trustee.

This still did not supply the right answer. Sheridan had undertaken to supply the lumber and to erect the school building. Therefore it was unethical for him to accept a position on the board. Mr. Yule, the chief inspector in Edmonton, finally reached a solution. He decreed that he himself would be senior trustee, and, since communication with his headquarters sometimes still involved a matter of months, he appointed Sheridan as his representative and Juey as his proxy. She also undertook to be secretary here as well.

When efforts of the district priest, who had undertaken to find a teacher, proved unavailing, the sympathetic parents at the Ranch produced a surprise for this district deep in the "bush." In answer to the continued pleadings of the fathers and mothers who saw their children growing up in the helplessness of their own illiteracy, Sheridan hastened to put the finishing touches to the school. Then in her buggy Juey drove through the woods from settler to settler, telling each family the day on which the school was going to open.

"My daughter Velma will teach your children," she announced to the delighted parents.

Velma had both a teaching permit and experience that

would be of great help among pupils who knew little English; while she had been a resident of Alberta College in Edmonton she had devoted part of her evenings to work among new Canadians.

Presently, for her pains, Juey received official status. The Department of Education appointed her audtior of five school districts, all located within a fifty-mile radius of the Ranch. Her duties involved the checking of all the books and of the financial arrangements of each, and her salary was set at ten dollars per year. As her father's daughter, this money she would not accept.

For twenty-two years the Lawrence Point school beamed its pilot light over the region of the Northern Peace and flashed its unique example into the face of snail-paced schoolboys in less remote areas of Canada. In all this period no more than two boarders were required at any one time in order to maintain the required register of pupils, for in the last years of its operation several grandchildren of the Ranch were added to the roster of students. In this period too her maturing family made it possible for the Ranch mistress to deflect an increasing portion of her energy into helping others toward an education and to doing her extra bit in the way her parents had instilled "to help keep the world turning."

The assistance of capable sons also made it possible for Sheridan to lend a hand, particularly in the role of justice of the peace, toward solving the problems of neighbors near and far. As a practical-minded sort of Solomon, he sometimes suggested remedies that were of the simplest. For instance, when one woe-begone petitioner came to him with the sorry tale that his own brother had stolen his wife away, his answer was brief:

"Give him the toe of that size eleven boot of yours."

Long ago he and his wife had learned that laughter is the salve for many sores and also that laughter helped to counteract the isolation and the loneliness that Hilda Rose found so appalling—laughter and the knack of finding fun. When the office of marriage counsellor was added to his duties, the family sometimes enjoyed together the small human comedies that evolved from this attempt of the white man's law to regulate and sanction native practices that were millennia-old.

In the dispatch of this chore for the Alberta government's bureau of vital statistics both Sheridan and Juey, who acted for him during his frequent absences from the Ranch, tried to be most conscientious. If a pair came seeking a license who were of mixed religious faiths, they always inquired if the couple had first approached the Roman Catholic priest. If the applicants were of Indian blood, the fee charged by the provincial government was only two dollars instead of the usual six. Sometimes a lengthy debate arose between the couple as to whether to spend the precious hoard of money on a license or on trade goods from Sheridan's store.

To the great delight of the young people on the Ranch, one solemn-faced customer who had been for some time sharing a teepee with her "husband" requested a marriage license. Painstakingly Juey wrote it all out and the woman carefully counted silver change in the amount of two dollars as payment. Then she tucked the slip of paper deep in her dress and with her man departed toward their waiting horses.

Within five minutes she was back in the store. She had changed her mind, she explained. Could she have instead two dollars' worth of butter?

With grave face Juey tore up the license and gave her customer the equivalent in butter.

Another change of mind in an applicant came a whole day after the mistress of the Ranch had issued the license; already she had forwarded the two dollars and the record of the license by the boat to Donald Mackie, the registrar of vital statistics at Edmonton. Pleadingly the woman fixed her beautiful dark eyes upon Juey as she begged for her money back. She needed it badly today for trading goods, she insisted. Relenting from her first refusal, Juey made the refund. Then she composed a little note to Mr. Mackie, telling him of the change of mind of the applicant and would he please refund the two dollars now owing to herself.

The registrar replied, tongue in cheek also, to the effect that he was sorry but the government of Alberta could not revoke the license issued and that she would have to bear the loss out of her own pocket.

The knack of finding fun and the philosophy of lending a hand continued to bring enrichment that belittled isolation. The casting of bread upon the waters as it were of the Peace itself that had been practised by their families before them was returned in many ways beyond the simple joy of having shared.

Sometimes there was payment of an especially heart-refreshing kind. In Edmonton Juey asked a taxi-driver to wait while she hurried to the front office of a local hospital to secure the release of her son Isaac, who had undergone a tonsillectomy. Repeatedly she rang the bell but she could get no answer. In frustration, she returned to dismiss the driver.

"I'll go get the boy," he offered with a wide grin.

In a few minutes he was back with the lad in tow. Being familiar with the ways of city hospitals, he had proceeded straight to the floor where the boy waited. Juey was quite overcome with such helpfulness on the part of a stranger. He smiled down at her.

"You don't remember, Mrs. Lawrence, a lonely survey party camped back of the Peace one Christmas-time."

She did remember the campers. She had extended an invitation to the men, who were buried some thirty miles back in the bush at Child's lake, and they had exchanged a cheerless Christmas dinner of canned goods for the bountiful hospitality and the lively cheer of the big family at the ranch-house.

The man looked at her now with a wide grin. "I was one of those campers."

Again there was the ambulance driver who hurried Janet to the Edmonton hospital for treatment for her badly smashed leg. For his services he refused payment of any kind.

"You forget, Mrs. Lawrence, a canoeist on the Peace." For a moment his words seemed almost a rebuke. "Dead beat and half starved," he added as his eyes lit with memory. "But I'll never forget your cooking and your hospitality."

While the Ranch became a kind of fountainhead of hospitality and of helpfulness and even perhaps of wisdom, still the temperamental river beside it continued to mete out both good and ill. For the most part Sheridan made use of the steamers to ship out his annual accumulation of furs, sometimes himself accompanying them on the rail trip outside to the Edmonton market. Then, on the return, he accumulated his freight needs at Peace River Crossing and there constructed a boat or a scow to take himself and his "stuff" down stream to his home.

"Sometimes there was ice at the river's edge, but I was never caught in it. I always figured to return down river by October 20th."

On one occasion he sent a trial shipment of big steers down the Peace from beyond the Chutes. They were bound for the Hudson's Bay Company post and the mounted police at Fort Smith on that extension of the Peace, the Slave river. The experiment proved a failure.

"The freighters didn't understand handling cattle and some of the animals were in bad shape when they arrived. So I shipped no more cattle down-river but tried up-river instead."

The largest of these shipments also ended in partial disaster. Into the wide hold of the D. A. Thomas, in September of 1928, his "boys" drove seventy-three head of fattened steers. Alas, though the big stern-wheeler was piloted by Mail-carrier Johnny Bourassa's son Louis, a knowing riverman, up-stream some two hundred and twenty miles from the Crossing she ran into grief. Apparently hugging too close to shore, she scraped a submerged limestone ridge, tearing away several planks low on her side. She started taking water. In haste her captain steered for a gravel bar near the head of Green island.

"The water finally rose in the boat and covered the engine. When the docks settled to water level, we drove the cattle off into the river. All but nine swam ashore and came out on the south bank. We could likely have saved them also had we been supplied with a boat.

"Frank Lambert and my son Stanley rounded up about half of the survivors on shore at the time. Next morning with daylight, they gathered up the remainder."

The alternative now was to attempt to drive the steers overland along what was termed the "infamous" trail that by this time straggled through bush and muskeg and across creek and tributary stream all the way to Peace River Crossing.

"Using pack-ponies and fording streams where necessary, we made Peace River town in four days. From there we shipped the cattle to Edmonton."

Again the price netted from the survivors, nearly thirty-five hundred dollars, helped to make up for the loss of those that the river had taken.

In 1934 the lurking giant waged its second major battle with the Ranch that had, since the flood of 1888, so greatly swelled its operations in defiance of its might. Sheridan's stock of practical wisdom had been nourished by its continuous involvement in his life and in the late autumn of 1933 he began to foresee that a second great flood was imminent.

"The signs all point to it," he told his delighted family.

After forty-six years, their river was again preparing for an onslaught that might drive them from its shore. After a summer of heavy rainfall, in the autumn the water level was unusually high. Then came prolonged spells of severe cold that froze the ice in some reaches right to the bottom. Convinced of what was going to be in store for them in the coming spring, all through the winter of 1933-34 Sheridan had his men in their spare hours make preparations to do battle. Bit by bit they moved supplies and equipment to higher ground; as spring approached they emptied all the low-lying buildings and snubbed them down with ropes.

Finally came abnormally high spring-time temperatures. Up-stream, tons of melting snows cascaded torrents of water into the channel of the Peace and now the master of the Ranch directed the moving of all the animals to the plateaus above the village of buildings.

Unable to sleep, Juey kept watch. Vividly the sights and sounds of the stupendous wash of water that had terrified her as a child assailed her senses now. Suddenly, in the grey light that gives a soft web-like bewitchment to the northern spring night, actuality took the place of memory. Once again she heard the roar of advancing water and the crashing of trees that were beginning to be snapped off by the tank-like charges of the huge bergs of ice.

She ran to rouse Sheridan. "It's come," she called. With difficulty she wakened him.

"How can you sleep at such a time?" she chided. "Aren't you worried?"

His answer was perhaps comforting in retrospect. "I didn't need to worry. My watch dog was on duty."

She was furious. Never again would she act as guard. He had, of course, already done all in preparation that it was possible to do. Now, as in those days and nights of long before, to a constant accompaniment of grinding, crashing sounds monster leviathans of bobbing ice swept landward with the wide sea of water that invaded the flatlands of their valley. They bombarded fields and meadows and carried away fences and strawstacks.

Soon water rose several feet above the floors of all the lower buildings. It washed over the counter in the store and lapped near the footings of the sprawling ranch-house that had been, in anticipation of this recurrence, built on a slight rise of ground.

Again, hundreds of squawking ducks and honking geese and snowy swans settled on the mighty breast of waters flooding all the lowland below the ranch-house. To the young people the sight afforded the thrill of a life-time. They clambered into boats or canoes and paddled about to enjoy the spectacle. Young "Joker," the family's pet name for the boy Elmer, scrambled into a floating pig-trough and with stick for paddle converted it into his own special sight-seeing canoe.

Along the banks in neighboring settlements the torrent ripped buildings loose and snatched away animals of those who had been unprepared; as the ice jams gave way, buildings, bodies and debris were swept onward to the further death-dealing menace of the Chutes.

After a day, the waters began to recede. Again, monster marauders of ice, some as high as twenty feet, stood guard over acres of debris and smashed fences and shattered trees. With grim faces, Sheridan and his men began the enormous chore of cleaning up. Presently they planted the field and harvested a fairly good crop; the following year, with the sand and other alluvial deposit better blended with the soil, again the yield was excellent.

In her big garden Juey found to her delight that most of her perennials and shrubs were still intact. This second flood had, as before, performed a small gesture of atonement. For years she had been trying to bring her antirrhinums or snapdragons, a perennial in such climates as that of England, through the winter successfully. But all her attempts so far had failed.

"My antirrhinums are growing, sending up new shoots from the roots!" she told Sheridan with delight. "Imagine! The first time in all these years. The flood has done the trick."

To the young people the sight of their river in flood was awesome and magnificent. In summers they agreed that there was no more beautiful spot than their valley, framed in its plateaus and its hills of spreading green, centred by the humming village of the Ranch, and adorned at times on a dusky midsummer night by the twinkle of lights from a passing steamer.

In mid-winter, it was an even more cherished picture. From the beating heart of the valley, the sprawling ranch-buildings, pulsed the smoke of thirty-five stoves to infuse with life the immense panorama of whiteness; hoar frost added a tinsel of exquisite loveliness, and on crisp clear nights the aurora danced a welcome that added mystery and enchantment.

But the spectacle of their river and their valley in flood was the show-piece of a lifetime. "We wouldn't have missed it," they told their parents, "for a little farm."

More and more in these years their river was carrying them away from their cherished valley, to high school and to college, to nursing school and to agricultural college, and to interests and to employment in other areas. Their father was reaching that period of life when some men contemplate retirement. With reluctance he and their mother began to see the wisdom of making changes.

At this time, too, Sheridan wrote, "The school problem

has become acute. Finally, as our youngest boys are still of school age, we decided to move to Peace River town."

By 1937, when the move had been completed, Juey and her youngest sons were established at the old Sagitawa in a house not far from the spot where she had first camped as a child. Sheridan and the older boys continued freighting and trading, both along the Hay river and along the Peace, their means of communication still with the outside. While for him the transition was gradual—with members of the family assuming part responsibility for the Ranch operations—to the energetic woman who had furnished so much of the nourishment, both literal and spiritual, to the many-tentacled spread by the Peace, it was much too abrupt. Accordingly, for her, it was sheer torture.

"I feel so lost, so cut off from everything," she wrote to him. "It's so lonely here without you. I'd like to come and join you if I could." She knew that her teen-age sons could manage for a while on their own, especially since there were near-by sisters and brothers to whom they could turn in case of need.

Sheridan's reply, dated in early December from Hay Lakes where he was spending the winter trading, sent her into a flurry of joyful preparation. "Take the plane to Fort Vermilion," he directed. "Then get a lift in one of my freight sleighs. I'll arrange for the driver to rig up a caboose for you."

One of the thrills awaiting her, she thought as she stepped aboard the small aircraft operated by a "Bush Pilot" would be to survey from above the broad river whose twists and turns held so many associations for her. Alas, an overcast shrouded it and before she had been able to distinguish a single landmark the pilot was putting down at her destination.

The journey by caboose, a loaded freight-sleigh rigged over with tarpaulin and fitted with a small heater, was much more physically and mentally satisfying. Because of the load the horses travelled at a walk; where once before she had gone afoot for fear of the jolting of the wagon, now for the sheer joy of the exercise in the snow-covered woods she tramped much of the one hundred and thirty miles ahead of the sleigh.

Arriving at her husband's Hay Lakes trading post after five days and nights on the trail, first of all she flung herself into the housewifely chore of making the log cabin dwelling into an attractive little home. For final touches she spread skin rugs on the floor, framed the small windows with bright red and green cotton curtains and centred them with pots of tulips and hyacinths and daffodils that she had tucked into the heated "caboose."

Soon she was caught up in a kind of idyll, a pocket edition of their lives that was a balm to her spirit. Sheridan traded and meted out decisions; she cooked and cleaned and helped sometimes with the trading and began to care for the ill and the ailing. With the first freight-sleigh returning to Fort Vermilion she sent a request to Dr. Hamman for drugs to treat her patients and for specific instructions as to method of treatment of certain cases; she also wrote to the Department of Indian Affairs for a supply of much-needed medical supplies, for in this remote area were bands of Slaveys whose condition seemed to plead for special assistance.

Her pots of flowering bulbs throve like her spirits and proved a never-failing source of delight to her visitors. Particularly poignant was the joy of one elderly Slavey as he gazed at the bright flowers framed by the gay curtains.

"Un chula!" he exclaimed with a wide grin of pleasure.

The man was weathered and wrinkled and broken-toothed, a product of a rugged and bitter struggle for life. These were the first flowering bulbs that he had ever seen and he could scarcely contain his joy.

"Un chula"' Good, good. His gap-toothed grin widened to hearty laughter. "Un chula!" he roared again and again.

There were other things besides her blossoms and indeed her own person that had the charm of novelty for these hardy children of the forested wilderness. Especially the illustrated magazines gripped their imagination and their sense of wonderment. Sheridan told her how he had spent many long evenings before she arrived; ringed round about him in the cabin his Indian guests sat night after night pointing to the pictures and putting questions to him about them. With a thirst for knowledge that was both pathetic and wearying, sometimes they lingered until the clock hands signified at last that it was three in the morning.

Already Juey found herself, with the assistance and co-operation of Dr. Hamman and the Department of Indian Affairs, treating colds, chest complications and accident cases—as well as scrofula or Beaver disease, and tuberculosis. Her enquiries which travelled by sleigh to the doctor he answered over his radio transmission set; sometimes she wanted to shout back, over the one hundred and thirty miles, words of further explanation that would facilitate his long-distance diagnosis. This was especially true in the case of one critically ill woman. At first he diagnosed her illness as typhoid.

The next day she turned on her set to hear, "Mrs. Lawrence at Hay Lakes. Mrs. Lawrence, are you listening? I have re-read your letter. I believe your patient has pneumonia, and I am sending the plane in for her."

The nurse's relief was great. This second diagnosis was assuredly right.

At this point Sheridan was undecided about the future. If he were going to stay on at Hay Lakes, she could employ herself usefully conducting a school for the Indians. So again she wrote to the Department of Indian Affairs, proposing that they assist her with a grant of two hundred dollars and a modest supply of books to enable her to open a school.

Meantime both husband and wife did what they could to assist and to instruct. A spring-time phase of Sheridan's teaching involved simple rudiments of gardening, and particularly that favored chore of his father's, the planting of potatoes. In this slow uphill work on one occasion his patience failed and he turned to his helpmeet to give the guidance.

With a tale as woebegone as his naturally woebegone cast of features, the Slavey Digenee stood before them. Yes, he insisted, speaking in his own tongue, he had followed carefully the directions of the Big White Chief. But there was no sign at all of growth from his tubers.

Sheridan looked to his wife. "Perhaps you'd better go see what's the matter."

In Digenee's canoe, Juey permitted herself to be paddled ten miles up the Negus stream, a tributary to the Hay river. In a minute clearing in the forest, the man pointed out to her his potato patch. It was a small strip of dank clay and on it there curled not a single wisp of green leaf.

"Show me," she directed in the Slavey dialect.

With a spade Digenee dug, and dug, and dug.

Nearly two feet down, in the cold hard clay, he laid bare a shrivelled tuber, one of the "seed" potatoes that Sheridan had given him to plant.

"No good," she shook her head. At the same time she tried to explain how potatoes needed light soil and warmth as well as moisture. "Dig a trench," she instructed. "Fill it with light soil mixed with moss and let it get warm and dry. Sprout your potatoes indoors and plant them no more than six inches deep."

With the spade she scooped up leaf mould and top soil and in the mixture she planted the tuber to serve as a model to Digenee.

After the better part of a life-time of employing and working with Indians and Métis, Sheridan had some very definite ideas about methods of trying to help them. "It's a mistake to give them handouts of any kind that become mere charity."

When government officials sought advice from him and his friend the Keg River trader Frank Jackson, both men agreed that the reserve or colony was wrong.

"An Indian is smarter than you think," they commented. "He knows what you're going to say before you open your mouth. And he may agree to what you propose, not because he intends to carry out your proposal, but because he wants to make you happy.

"He has very different values. For one thing he's not acquisitive. To him a white man is stupid in many ways, for instance because he can't catch a weasel."

Repeatedly both men had attempted to assist, or to set up on their own, natives who had worked diligently while they were employed by them. Always attempts ended in dismal failure.

"If they have no one to chase them, they won't get a

thing done. I even gave one man a milk-cow to help him make a start," added Frank Jackson. "She ended up in the cook-pot. No need to go hunt moose if you've got a cow to eat."

A drowning accident demonstrated to the Big White Chief and his wife something of the superstition prevalent among their Slavey neighbors in the Hay Lakes region. It was now June, spring trading was over, and Sheridan decided to pull out of the area. Assisted by his son Stanley, he had built a large scow which he used round about the lake and on which he proposed to load goods and furs for the trip down river to Upper Hay River post. Journeying between the two points was difficult, since the choice of route lay between the river with some thirty miles of swift water and rapids, and the overland trail through much almost impassable swamp and muskeg. So a number of natives had "hired" a ride in the big scow.

Just as the party was about ready to depart, an Indian youth drowned near by in the river. In their boat Sheridan and Stanley searched up and down the bank until they found the body. They would take it with them, they decided, down stream to Upper Hay for interment in the burial ground there.

At this, their passengers demurred. They would not ride in the scow with the corpse of their tribesman. Nor would they, nor any of their people, trade for goods being transported therein.

Sheridan resolved the dilemma by building a small second scow to serve as a resting-place for the body. He loaded the larger with pelts and passengers, tying the second along side. In the high water of June his boat with its kicker could push both crafts down the sixty-mile run to Upper Hay.

His wife Juey added a bit of picturesqueness to the strangely assorted loads on the two scows. Having arrived in December with no definite plans as to how long she was going to stay, she had brought no hat. Now to protect herself from the burning sun of June, from pieces of carboard she shaped a sunbonnet which she covered with bright "trade" cotton print.

With the skill attained from years of coping with the

vagaries of the Peace, the Big White Chief manoeuvred his way through swift water and rapids. At Upper Hay as in former days he made a satisfactory deal with his long-time adversary; the Hudson's Bay Company factor agreed to purchase both scows.

Leaving the body in a grave at the post, they proceeded forward, still in picturesque fashion progressing next over the portage to the Peace.

"After removing our cargo and leaving the scows, we took the passengers and the pelts across the portage to Fort Vermilion. On the way we picked up forty head of cattle and thirty hogs, and continued on to Fort Vermilion. From there in company with Mr. O'Sullivan, we took our cattle, hogs and pelts to Peace River town."

Though he was done with Hay River trading, he had not yet settled final accounts with the Peace. For some time, sharing with his sons, he continued freighting and trading operations up and down the river. While the push of new settlement farther and farther into northern wilderness frontiers meant changing times, the hazards of life along the temperamental stream had not changed. Eternal watchfulness was the keyword to safety; yet sometimes there were accidents. For always, it seemed, the Peace waited for the unwary.

In fact, summed up Sheridan's sons, "the old river's got quite a few."

They had recalled a couple of youths who had attempted to swim out to overtake their runaway boat, a child of the Paul family who had crashed through the ice, a purser who had tumbled from the triple-decked D. A. Thomas.—That boat had fought her last battle with the Peace in 1930 when, in an attempt to transfer her to the Athabasca-Slave waterway, she was dropped down the Chutes under the piloting of Louis Bourassa. She smashed her wheel badly and ended her days of glory in ignominy, serving as a storage shed on the Slave.

In 1940, the Peace claimed a victim from among the family that had shared long intimacy with its caprices. Seventeen-year-old Oswald assumed charge of a shipment of his father's cattle that was being freighted up-river by scow.

From Carcajou Point Sheridan received a wire to notify him that his son was missing from the craft.

In the dead of night, apparently, he had disappeared. Sometimes, his parents knew, he had been in the habit of sleep-walking. They concluded that, perhaps hearing some restless movement among the animals, he had crawled from his bed-roll and stepped into the river. In the night, the captain recollected afterward, he had heard a splash; thinking it perhaps a swimming bear, he had not investigated.

For days his brother Isaac and the neighbor John Ward searched up and down shore by motor boat and his brother Stanley dragged areas of the river bottom. The mounties also joined in the hunt but no trace of him could they find.

"You have always loved the Peace," said a friend to his mother Juey. "Surely now you hate it."

"No," she answered. "I'm pretty sure Oswald was planning to go outside and join up. We might have lost him somewhere overseas."

Weeks of searching brought no clue as to the fate of the young man's body. The Peace, mighty and inscrutable, would not yield its secrets.

"A tombstone is, after all, only a symbol," his mother concluded, to assuage the family's sorrow. "What better tombstone could our boy have than the Peace?"

PART III

"Through the battle, through defeat,
  moving yet and never stopping,
Pioneers! O pioneers!"

Outside the cathedral the crowd was gathering.

In Canada's capital at Ottawa, men recognizing the achievements of Sheridan Lawrence had taken steps to honor his memory. He was duly declared a figure of national historic importance and here, at this Peace River Crossing where he had begun his long association with the tortuous and mighty stream, the Government of Canada on the advice of the Historic Sites and Monuments Board, erected a cairn to perpetuate his accomplishments.

To the memorial service at which the cairn was unveiled flocked family and friends and neighbors. To Juey this day bore resemblance to that sad day three and a half years before when they had held a burial service for her Sheridan here in this town of Peace River.

On that day too there had been respect and honor paid that had eased the grief of parting. There had also been for her the remembrance of the last tranquil years which she and Sheridan had shared together here in Peace River town. Gradually they both had learned to make the difficult adjustment from the management of a huge ranch and trading enterprise to living less actively. For a time, when he had at last terminated his trading, he had operated a mill at near-by High Prairie. But difficulties in finding skilled help during World War Two finally forced him to shut down and eventually he retired to a life of comparative ease in their home above the Peace.

In his eighty-second year, death had come to Sheridan Lawrence and the town made a generous gesture in tribute to its celebrated resident. In the manner of honoring royalty, for the man who had become a legend in his own life-time, the man known as the Emperor of the Peace, the town declared a half holiday on the day of his funeral. From all over the Peace country came pioneers and children of pioneers to overflow the site of the burial service, beautiful St. James Cathedral.

Now again, three and a half years later, the crowds were gathering to pay tribute to Sheridan at the unveiling of the impressive cairn. On this day, September the 25th of 1955, they collected on the grounds fronting the cathedral. For here, only a few yards from the shore of the Peace, the monument stood waiting for the moment when it would begin to tell the world of human achievement, made possible through the co-operation of the mighty stream. From up and down the river journeyed men and women to honor once more the man whose life outshone any Horatio Alger tale, whose true story was in part their story too, the story of a man who from meagre beginnings had surmounted impossible objects and who had achieved the heights of success.

Again the town of Peace River proudly and officially joined in marking Sheridan's accomplishments. His Worship Mayor Mann and the Council and the Chamber of Commerce together sponsored the memorial ceremony, and the town prepared a handsome souvenir program illustrated with a photograph of the master and the mistress of the Ranch.

In the deep northern woods beyond the Ranch dark-eyed denizens consulted together. "We should be present to honor Muchi Oukimow," they said. "To pay respect to Mitootam Ooche Eyinew, the friend of the Indian."

To the Rev. Jack Pitt at Fort Vermilion they brought money. "You take this and fly in the plane to Peace River town to speak in our place," they directed.

Glowing words of distinguished speakers paid many tributes.

"Sheridan Lawrence was the patriarch of the Peace," said his friend Bishop Sovereign. "In him the spirit of the adventurer and of the pioneer, were deeply blended.

"His was the philosophy that if a thing was difficult, he would do it at once. If it was impossible, well, it might take him a little longer."

"Strength and independence," added Bishop Pierce of the Diocese of Athabasca. "That was the spirit of Sheridan Lawrence throughout his life."

His widow Juey, waiting in readiness, at the appropriate moment unveiled the bronze tablet to reveal the words enscrolled thereon. Now the eyes of all, fixed upon the inscription, began to read,

SHERIDAN LAWRENCE
"Emperor of the Peace"

Born at South Stukely, Quebec, 8th April, 1870. Settled at Fort Vermilion, N.W.T. 1886. Farmer, miller, meat packer, merchant, friend of the Indian, road builder, freighter, magistrate, patron of education; he embodied the endurance, enterprise, versatility and vision of the pioneer. Together with his heroic wife, Julia Scott Lawrence, their seven sons and eight daughters, he helped to push hundreds of miles northward the frontier of agriculture and community life.

Died at Peace River, Alberta, 1st February, 1952.

At last, when the stirring words of praise and the moving music were concluded, and the heart-warming gathering of family and friends had left, humbly Juey returned to her garden above the Peace.

With every one of her thoughts about the great honour that had been done to them in this year of 1955, Sheridan would have agreed. He, too, would have understood that this was a tribute being paid to all of the pioneers of the Peace, to missionary and to priest, to fur trader and to factor and to settler; to men like her own father Teeny-Muttiga-Mutu-tully; and to men of the great fur-trading company, men like Gus Clark, of whom it was reputed, for his employers "would trade the very shirt from a customer's back, but who would then hurry to give his own to cover him." These were men whose efforts in behalf of the people of the north set a shining example of helpfulness.

With full heart and tranquil spirit, gradually Juey

learned to find solace in experimentation with growing things in house and garden. Like a token of life everlasting, the lilies descended from those bulbs which her mother Anna brought as an eager missionary from England, still bloomed in beauty in her home.

Looking back over the period following Sheridan's passing, Juey had but one regret.

"If I had known I was to enjoy good health all these years, I'd have looked for a spot in a mission where I could lend a hand."

Not far from the door of her home twinkles the Peace, wide-flowing and majestic in the valley under the towering hills.

A few yards from its shore, one of the ever-fresh-arriving bands of newcomers to the frontier regions of the north-west, spells out the words blazed on the memorial cairn in the quiet churchyard,

"Sheridan Lawrence, Emperor of the Peace . . . ."

The End.